THE BASE OF THE PYRAMID PROMISE

THE BASE OF THE

PYRAMID PROMISE

Building Businesses with Impact and Scale

TED LONDON

STANFORD BUSINESS BOOKS

An Imprint of Stanford University Press
Stanford, California

Stanford University Press
Stanford, California

Special discounts for bulk quantities of Stanford Business Books are available to
corporations, professional associations, and other organizations. For details and
discount information, contact the special sales department of Stanford University
Press. Tel: (650) 736–1782, Fax: (650) 736–1784

Printed in the United States of America on acid-free, archival-quality paper

Library of Congress Cataloging-in-Publication Data

Names: London, Ted, 1963– author.
Title: The base of the pyramid promise : building businesses with impact and scale
    / Ted London.
Description: Stanford, California : Stanford Business Books, an imprint of
    Stanford University Press, 2016. | Includes bibliographical references and
    index.
Identifiers: LCCN 2015014934 | ISBN 9780804791489 (cloth : alk. paper)
Subjects: LCSH: Social entrepreneurship—Developing countries. | Industrial
    management—Developing countries. | Success in business—Developing
    countries. | Business planning—Developing countries. | Markets—Developing
    countries. | Poverty—Developing countries. | Low-income consumers—
    Developing countries.
Classification: LCC HD60.5.D44 L66 2016 | DDC 658.4/08091724—dc23
LC record available at http://lccn.loc.gov/2015014934

ISBN 978-0-8047-9733-7 (electronic)

To Meghan, Zach, and Ariana; thanks for all the joy you bring to my life.

CONTENTS

FIGURES AND TABLES

ACKNOWLEDGMENTS

This book has been a fun and interesting journey. And that journey would not have been possible without the support and guidance of many people. While it is not possible to name them all, I want to recognize some key contributors.

First, I thank all of those great colleagues who read and commented on the many drafts of this book. Jim Koch, Colm Fay, Megan Levanduski, and Stu Hart: Your comments were always on point and helped push my thinking. The level of thought and detail was amazing. Vijay Sharma, Hennings Alt, Sebastian Fries, Chris Jochnick, Deborah Burand, and Sateen Sheth: You made sure the voice of practice was well represented in key parts of the book. Heather Esper, Yaquta Fatehi, Andy Grogan-Kaylor, Lisa Smith, Molly Christiansen, Garrett Kirk, Tim Polkowski, Aditya Rayala, Kwaku Sefa-Dedeh: Thanks for your research support on specific topics over the years. Thanks also go to all my students over the years who took my Business Strategies for the Base of the Pyramid course. You were often the first to hear some of these ideas, and as a test market, you provided wonderful comments, insights, and feedback.

I also thank all of my colleagues who have been leading or engaged in base-of-pyramid (BoP) impact enterprise development over the years. Your willingness to share with me what you had discovered and your eagerness to co-invent new approaches were welcome sources of learning and inspiration. I have quoted some of you in this book, and others I have cited as sources. Many, many others have made and continue to make contributions to my growth and to the growth of the field.

I have been lucky enough to spend a good deal of time working closely with welcoming colleagues who live and transact in BoP markets—first in

Malawi as a Peace Corps volunteer working with local entrepreneurs, then in Indonesia as a general manager of a spice factory sourcing from local producers, and from there across many more countries with many more colleagues. Our conversations and interactions were almost always enlightening, and sometimes tremendously so. You have always treated me with great respect. I hope you feel I have done the same with you.

I also thank my academic mentors and collaborators. First, at the Kenan-Flagler Business School at the University of North Carolina and subsequently at the William Davidson Institute and the Ross School of Business at the University of Michigan, they kindly chose to overlook my limitations as a scholar and researcher while at the same time helping me close those deficits. Over time, my circle of academic collaborators, sounding boards, and, yes, challengers has broadened; I have tried hard to acknowledge their enormous contributions throughout this book, but I have surely missed some good people and some good work.

I also acknowledge the support I received from the William Davidson Institute, especially Paul Clyde, Rosemary Harvey, Bob Kennedy, and Bill Lanen, in enabling me to write this book.

Here, I can't fail to draw a double line under two specific names. C. K. Prahalad was a leading light in this field and was always available when I needed him most. Stuart Hart, who along with C.K. was the first to articulate the ideas central to the development of this domain, welcomed me into his creative circles and supported me in my earliest journeys as a scholar. Our intellectual collaborations, including coauthoring an edited book and several articles, were a joy. Thanks, Stu.

Jeff Cruikshank was an important contributor to this book. He worked with me to find a voice that I hope speaks to my several target audiences and has supported me throughout the long process of summarizing decades of work between two covers.

I thank Margo Fleming and Geoffrey Burn, my editors at Stanford University Press. Margo supported me from the earliest stages, when I first put together the proposal for this book. Geoffrey gracefully stepped in when Margo went on maternity leave, and our team didn't miss a beat. Throughout the process, both have continued to offer advice and encouragement. Douglas Schuler and Madison Ayer provided important feedback on that initial book proposal; thanks for helping me get started in the right direction. Two anonymous reviewers provided valuable feedback on the full draft; thanks for helping me at this final stage. Also thanks to James Holt and Tim Roberts from Stanford University Press and Beverly Miller for all they did behind the scenes to get this book into production.

My mother, Elizabeth, helped shaped me in many positive ways, both large and small. Thank you for all that you have given me.

Finally, I thank my family for supporting me in my work, which so often takes me away for weeks at a time, and allowing this particular project to intrude on their lives when it monopolized my time. A low point was when we all got the flu and my next draft was coming due. Thanks, Danielle, Meghan, Zach, and Ariana for pulling me through and for putting things into perspective when I most needed that perspective.

INTRODUCTION

In 1989, a young man traveled to Malawi in hopes of making an impact.

More specifically, he wanted to use the power of business to help address social issues. An engineer and MBA by training, he had grown disillusioned with his professional activities—first as a design engineer and then as a senior consultant focused on business valuation. So he set off for Malawi as a Peace Corps volunteer, tasked with providing useful advice to micro-, small-, and medium-scale enterprises. These were businesses run by some of the poorest people in the world. Certainly, helping build those businesses would improve people's lives and make the impact he hoped for.

Two years into that experience—in late 1991—the young man was riding his motorcycle between the large towns of Mulanje and Blantyre in Malawi's southern region. Rolling through the lush countryside, with bright green tea plantations pushing up against the bases of the surrounding hills, he was thinking about both his greatest successes and his biggest disappointments. The Peace Corps had always stressed that its volunteers would learn more than they would teach. That was certainly true in his case: He had learned an enormous amount.

But that doesn't quite capture it, the young man thought. In his experience, the most productive outcomes seemed to arise when people moved beyond "sharing from the bottom up" or "teaching from the top down." The powerful, enduring successes in working with local entrepreneurs came when nobody was the teacher and everybody was the learner. In those cases, neither party assumed they were the main source of the answer. The emphasis shifted to co-creation, innovation, and integration—that is, collaboratively building something that didn't exist before.

Without even realizing it, he had adopted a new mind-set. During those two years in Malawi, he had found the local people extraordinarily friendly, caring, and generous—a fact that he and his non-Malawian colleagues often reflected on. This wasn't unexpected; after all, Malawi was known as the "warm heart of Africa." More unexpected, although in retrospect it really shouldn't have been, was that these Malawian entrepreneurs were very smart and very creative. He had never thought of the poor in that way. (He had noticed too that increasingly, he was having trouble using the word *poor* to describe his local colleagues.) He had come to give good advice—to use his business training to help them and tell them what they should do. But they didn't necessarily need him to tell them what to do. Sure, a little training in marketing, costing, or cash flow could help. But, he thought again to himself, the biggest impacts came through jointly innovating to create solutions that neither could have come up with or implemented on their own.

Why hadn't anyone told him *that*?

Focusing on the road in front of him, the young man saw what looked like a small cloud just ahead. His first thought was that it might be smoke from a small fire or perhaps a localized cloudburst—a minor obstacle on the road to Blantyre. In any case, there wasn't any way to avoid it. As he reached the edge of the cloud, things began thumping against his helmet and chest. Looking down, he suddenly realized what was going on. Crawling around on the seat and gas tank cover, right between his legs, was a fast-growing pile of stunned bees—presumably very *angry* bees. At 80 kilometers an hour, he had driven directly into a swarm.

Thinking fast, heart pounding, he tried something he had never done before. He stepped high up on the pegs, leaving only his toes and his hands on the bike, and gunned the engine as he yanked the handlebar to the right. The bike swerved, and he barely avoided running into the ditch on the side of the road, but the maneuver succeeded in getting the angry ball of bees to slide off the bike and onto the road. Heart still thumping away, he accelerated again, putting as much distance as possible between himself and the bees.

Once safely in Blantyre, he began to think more about the swarming African bees and how his experience on the road represented an analogy for his time in Malawi. Some of the obstacles he had faced in his efforts to create enterprises with greater impact were expected. Others, like the bees, were totally unanticipated. In dealing with both the expected and the unexpected, however, the most enduring solutions grew out of a collaborative model grounded in mutual respect and patience that valued co-creation, patience, and a deep understanding of impact. It occurred to him that these insights, and the details that lay behind them, might serve as a useful guide to those who came down this same road after him. The problem was that he hadn't written any of his observations down. They resided only in his head.

As you may have guessed, that young man was me. Over the next two decades and across some eighty countries, I lived through varying versions of that same story of jointly overcoming obstacles—without the bees, luckily—to achieve social impact. The same lessons for enterprise success cropped up again and again. And still there was no road map that captured the mindsets, capabilities, and tools required to use business to tackle some of the most daunting social issues facing our global society. Indeed, most of the prescriptions that I came across for doing business in low-income markets seemed to rely on the usual set of suspects, practices, and expectations that were primarily drawn from experiences in the developed world. To my mind, they were based on the wrong assumptions, lacked adequate respect for the poor, and failed to embrace what was right in the local context.

In 1999, after working in Africa, Asia, and the United States in both the business and nonprofit worlds, I returned to academia. I wanted to think harder about two things that continued to drive me. First, I needed to better understand how to use the power of business to address social challenges. And second, I wanted to create academically rigorous and practically useful tools and frameworks—a road map, if you will—that would help others who found themselves traveling on the same journey I had been on for the past decade.

It was at the University of North Carolina where I first met Stuart Hart, who became my friend, colleague, and advisor. He was one of the few academics in a business school context who was thinking about the important role that profitable, scalable enterprises could play in alleviating poverty. The first major article on the topic, by Stu and C. K. Prahalad, came out in 2002.[1] The idea of there being a "fortune at the base of the pyramid" (generally contracted as BoP) was just taking hold. At that stage, the objective was more motivational than operational: more on why managers should get involved with in BoP markets and less on how they should do it.

In 2005, I accepted a position at the University of Michigan. That is where I first had a chance to interact with Prahalad, a deeply stimulating and motivating experience. He was committed to developing approaches that either catalyzed or facilitated action. Both Stu and C.K. were instrumental in creating awareness of and knowledge about the base-of-pyramid (BoP) domain and in shaping how I chose to make my own contributions.[2]

This book grows directly out of that work. It is about creating enterprises that thrive in BoP markets; about creating sustainable, scalable ventures that generate substantial impact on the poor.

There's that word again. As you read this book, you'll find that I try to choose my words carefully. *Poor* is not necessarily inaccurate, insofar as it describes someone who doesn't have many assets. But in the context of the BoP in the developing world, it is generally loaded with all kinds of baggage and implies all sorts of other deficits that may or not pertain, so I try and avoid it. I similarly try to avoid talking about things happening "at" the base of the pyramid, as if it were a place that one could walk up to and knock on the door. There is no such place—and there's a real risk in objectifying people in this way. The base of the pyramid is an aggregation of many different kinds of individuals and groups who represent potential markets for goods or services. As I stress throughout this book, these markets are not found *at* the BoP; rather, they are created *with* the BoP.

Interest in creating impact enterprises for BoP markets has increased dramatically in the past decade. There's a growing portfolio of these enterprises, and a growing number of entrepreneurial leaders seeking to craft more of them. This interest transcends, and blends, industries: energy, sanitation, health care, agriculture, technology, and consumer goods, to name a few. Equally, this interest transcends institutions: Company leaders, entrepreneurs, nonprofit managers, development professionals, and government officials all see great promise in investing in impact enterprise development in BoP markets. The lessons and frameworks in this book apply across these industries and institutions. I have found strategies and models that can guide the development of these enterprises.[3] My goal in the chapters that follow is to create standardized frameworks that enterprise leaders can customize to respond to the specific contexts and circumstances they face.

The debate around BoP focus has also changed substantially over time.[4] The focus is no longer, *Should we be doing this?* Today that debate is over. Business is and will continue to serve the BoP. Furthermore, most business leaders don't need motivational stories encouraging them to consider BoP markets. Nor do development community professionals need to be convinced of the potential poverty alleviation benefits of BoP impact enterprises. Rather, the focus has moved on to, *How can we do this better?*

Yet despite this steady growth in interest and investment, enterprise performance to date has been mixed. We know that success is certainly possible, as the cell phone revolution in emerging markets has shown.[5] Yet many of these new BoP impact enterprises are not as good as we want them to be—or as good as they have been represented to the world—and few of them have yet achieved the necessary scale to which we aspire. We need more BoP impact enterprises that are sustainable at scale.

So what is to be done? How can we help the next generation of successful enterprises emerge? How can we build more sustainable, scalable enterprises with impact?

What's urgently needed now are managerially friendly tools, frameworks, and guidelines that can help move BoP impact enterprises forward: away from wishful thinking and hyperbole to practical, hands-on advice for for-profit, nonprofit, and development sector leaders who want to build enterprises that can generate sufficient profits while also having substantial poverty alleviation impacts.

Until now, no such integrated set of tools and strategies has existed. In its absence, all too many entrepreneurs and enterprise leaders are making the same mistakes as those who have gone before them—continually reinventing the wrong version of the wheel, if you will—thereby limiting their impact, scalability, and profitability and wasting precious time, money, and talent.

Since 1989, I have lived in, worked with, and studied BoP markets and impact enterprises, including engagements with dozens of leadership teams across the globe. Through this work, I have found that three key components must be correctly implemented and integrated to build enterprises with impact. I have translated that discovery into specific and actionable recommendations and frameworks for creating, sustaining, and scaling BoP impact enterprises.

My approach has three cornerstones:

- **Leveraging customizable tools, frameworks, and strategies to enhance enterprise development.** The unprecedented wave of interest in and flow of resources into BoP impact enterprises in recent years has generated a wealth of information to use to examine what works—and what doesn't—in this unique and challenging market environment.[6] We need a rich and detailed understanding of key enterprise activities as they move through the development process and a set of manager-friendly tools and frameworks based on that understanding.

  For example, what should enterprises do to set themselves up for success? How do we design with scale in mind from the beginning? Why do so many enterprises never move beyond the pilot stage, and what can be done about that? What constitutes competitive advantage, and what capabilities are needed to achieve scale in BoP markets? Based on the lessons learned, how can we build businesses that are likely to succeed and flourish in BoP markets?

- **Creating value with the BoP by truly understanding the poverty alleviation opportunity.** The number one lesson taught in business school is that businesses must create value for those they seek to serve. In other words, building viable enterprises that will have an impact requires a deep understanding of how to assess and enhance impact. Yet enterprise leaders operating in BoP markets frequently ignore or poorly execute this lesson, all too often with perilous consequences for the success of their venture. Without a clear appreciation of the value proposition the enterprise offers, enterprises struggle to build viable business models. Lacking a deep understanding of the value that the BoP actually wants and how this can change over time, enterprise leaders have no basis for improving their business model.

Enterprise leaders must be able to answer the following questions: What is our value proposition, and how much and what type of value are we creating for the BoP? How can we understand and enhance our poverty alleviation impacts, especially if (as we will see in subsequent chapters) poverty has multiple dimensions? How do we know if we have been successful in value creation, and how do we keep learning and delivering more value?

- **Understanding how to establish an ecosystem of partners to sustain those enterprises**. When operating in BoP markets, enterprise leaders must not only focus on building their ventures and creating through understanding their poverty alleviation opportunity. They must also actively engage in establishing a network of partners to support their efforts. That means finding partners willing to invest in the enterprise and creating the markets around them. In the developed world, we take the business environment for granted. We assume that we don't have to think much about the institutions, infrastructure, and shared resources that make the market environment flourish. But this simply isn't true in BoP markets. BoP impact enterprises primarily operate in a context where platforms, channels, and information flows are often lacking.

  The savvy BoP impact enterprise leader therefore must keep one eye on the business and the other on the surrounding environment. In addition to seeking support in building the enterprise, how can he or she create a robust set of cross-sector collaborations that can also fill the gaps in the market environment? Who makes up that ecosystem of partners? How does an enterprise build and maintain a targeted portfolio of partners? How should a partnership ecosystem evolve over time to maximize effectiveness?

I argue that for BoP impact enterprises to succeed, each of these cornerstones must be considered and effectively addressed. Indeed, these three cornerstones are mutually reinforcing—and, in fact, they are inseparable.

In the chapters that follow, I intersperse *description* and *prescription,* with an emphasis on the latter. In other words, what's the problem, and how can we solve it? What's the opportunity, and how can we pursue it?

This is the road map that I contemplated on that long-ago ride from Mulanje to Blantyre. It is my prescription for building enterprises with impact and scale for the benefit of all. I am grateful to the bees for helping me along on this journey.

1 IMPACT ENTERPRISE FOR THE BASE OF THE PYRAMID

The ideas are powerful: Creating enterprises with impact. Using the power of *market-based approaches to address social issues. Alleviating poverty through enterprise. Creating value with the base of the pyramid.* And the stories that grow out of those ideas are compelling: Entrepreneurs, company leaders, nonprofit managers, and development community professionals are talking and writing about how well their enterprises are doing and their profound impacts on the base of the pyramid (BoP), which I define as the 4 billion or so people who primarily live or transact in informal markets in the developing world and have an annual per capita income of less than $3,000.[1]

Not surprisingly, given this wealth of ideas and stories, the bookshelves are starting to fill with striking titles like *Fortune at the Bottom of the Pyramid, The Business Solution to Poverty, Business Solutions for the Global Poor,* and *Capitalism at the Crossroads.* Terrific books, all—replete with powerful ideas and filled with great stories of success.[2] They show us what is possible. They are motivational. They are about promise and potential. As C. K. Prahalad, arguably the intellectual pioneer in seeing the business opportunity in the base of the pyramid, wrote about the aspirations he had for his own book: "Does it change the conversation? Does it show opportunity? Does it lead to action?"[3]

These books have found a receptive audience. The past decade has seen a surge in the number of impact enterprises for the BoP, the provision by these enterprises of high-quality goods and services to the poor and vulnerable, and investors' growing willingness to support these efforts.

All in all, these are exciting times for those who believe that business can play a key role in addressing social issues, especially alleviating poverty, and who are interested in exploring and helping to realize the promise of impact enterprises for the BoP.

But something is missing. Hundreds of ventures aimed at serving the BoP have been launched, but comparatively few have achieved significant scale.[4] Either they have closed up shop and gone home, or they suffer from "pilot-itis"—in other words, they remain small and highly dependent on continued financial support to maintain the piloting activities. This collective failure to thrive underscores a key point: Developing sustainable, scalable enterprises is a challenge in any context, and it is especially difficult in BoP markets.

Individually, we have gained much experience. But collectively, in confronting the challenges of the BoP market, we still have yet to share and build from these experiences in a way that productively moves the entire domain forward. For example, a colleague who was visiting my office not long ago is an experienced and successful entrepreneur in the technology industry. He had become engaged in BoP impact enterprise development in India several years ago, and I hadn't heard from him in a while. The first thing I noticed on this visit was that he had become far more humble.

"We thought we knew what we were doing," he said, in a forlorn voice, "but we have made all the mistakes in the book." He had believed that his years as a successful top-of-the-pyramid entrepreneur would translate smoothly into the BoP context. It didn't work out that way. As he told me what had gone wrong, I found myself thinking: *Why did he have to go through the same pains that many others have already suffered?*

Too many entrepreneurs, enterprise leaders, and development community professionals fall into this trap—a trap of their own making. They assume that these are still uncharted waters and we don't know all that much about successfully developing impact enterprises for the BoP. Because they persist in starting from scratch, they continue to make the same mistakes.

It doesn't have to be this way. Our collective learnings can offer insight into what works and what doesn't. That's what was on my mind when I sat down to write this book: a road map—a set of tools, frameworks, and approaches— for contributing to success in this exciting and challenging domain.

I readily admit that this is an audacious goal. Setting out to create a tool kit that can help enhance the success of business in BoP markets, with the ultimate goal of addressing a major social issue that challenges the very fabric of today's society, is a bold undertaking. The relentless poverty that the BoP faces is a large and looming threat to any vision of a more equitable and peaceful world.

Building sustainable, scalable enterprises in BoP markets won't be easy. Perhaps more than anything else, embarking on this journey will require embracing new mind-sets, new strategies, and new approaches to collaboration. As much as we might like to, we can't donate our way out of poverty. Business has a role to play, but business also can't do it alone—and that means that incremental additions to what we know, and incremental adjustments to how we do things, are not likely to yield the transformational change required. We need a much deeper understanding of what works and what doesn't when it comes to building what I will call impact enterprises for the BoP.[5]

WHY BRING TOGETHER BUSINESS AND DEVELOPMENT?

New knowledge and new ways of collaborating are needed. Fortunately, enterprise leaders and development professionals alike are excited about pursuing market-based opportunities with the prospect of achieving positive social impact. It's worth exploring why they are so excited about this promise and this potential.

Let's start with the business perspective. The 4 billion people comprising the BoP constitute a huge socioeconomic sector that lacks access to a multitude of goods and services, and at the same time faces constraints when trying to bring its own production to market—things that well-designed businesses could provide. At the same time, as economic growth slows in the developed world, the BoP represents perhaps the world's last great untapped market, so when it comes to future growth opportunities, the BoP is increasingly seen as an exciting market worthy of deeper consideration.

The cell phone phenomenon hints at this opportunity. There has been astonishing growth in cell phone subscribers in the developing world, whose numbers increased from 370,000 to 16.8 million in only five years. One telecom company, Celtel, started as a shaky venture in 1998, operating in the Democratic Republic of Congo, with a population of 55 million and only 3,000 phones. Seven years later, when it was acquired by a U.S. company for $3.4 billion, Celtel was operating in fifteen African countries, with licenses covering more than 30 percent of the continent.[6] It is hard to travel anywhere in the developing world, urban or rural, and not see people across all socioeconomic segments carrying cell phones. First-time visitors to BoP markets are prone to marvel at how many people have one.

Total annual household income in BoP markets is estimated at something like $5 trillion, or about $1.3 trillion when adjusted for in purchasing power parity.[7] Yes, the average size of transactions is relatively small, but their aggregate number is extremely large. Furthermore, the BoP holds something like $9 trillion in unregistered (or hidden) assets, an amount approximately equivalent to the total value of all companies listed on the twenty most developed countries' main stock exchanges.[8]

In addition, the opportunity for learning and growth to flow upmarket should not be underestimated. General Electric, for one, has made the argument for the value of reverse innovation.[9] Although many top-of-the-pyramid models don't work well in BoP markets, it's increasingly apparent that BoP innovations may revolutionize aspects of top-of-the-pyramid business, perhaps beginning in the environmental and health realms.[10]

Demographics are also an argument for bringing together business and the BoP. The planet is getting more and more crowded. The world's population will increase by another 2 to 3 billion people in the next thirty years, and most of those new additions will be part of the BoP.[11] The magnitude of this growth in human population can be hard to comprehend. A way that I have found helpful is to consider the human population growth in the span of one lifetime, as illustrated in Figure 1.1. Imagine someone born in 1963, when world population was about 3.2 billion. By the time he or she turned fifty, the population on the planet had more than doubled: an increase of nearly 4 billion people in that half-century. Assuming this person lives for eighty-seven years, the population during his or her lifetime will have nearly tripled, with an additional 6 billion people having been added to the human head count in a single lifetime,.[12] And again, most of this growth will likely have occurred in the BoP socioeconomic segment.

As the Swedish multinational Tetra Pak and other companies have observed, some of those in the BoP segment may well move up the pyramid over time, thereby becoming even more attractive customers to these companies.[13] Of course, as some people move up the economic pyramid, others may

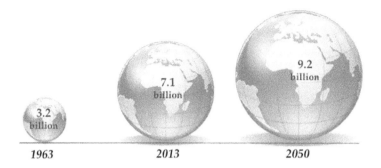

FIGURE 1.1 Population growth within one lifetime

suffer a reversal of fortune and fall back. But the larger point remains: The business opportunity is substantial now, and it will only get bigger.

The development community has to deal with the same growth numbers but with a different framing. The development challenge is already intimidating, and it will become more daunting. Since World War II, development agencies and donors across the globe have spent billion of dollars to alleviate poverty and improve the lives of people in developing nations. Certainly some of these efforts have led to important successes. The emerging consensus, however, is that despite their massive scale and their long histories, these efforts alone haven't done enough.[14] As Peruvian economist Hernando de Soto has argued, billions of people still primarily transact in informal markets and lack access to the benefits of globalization.[15]

Facing these challenges, the development community is increasingly seeking new approaches to carrying out their core missions of improving the social and economic well-being of the BoP. During the past half-century, business was often seen as part of the problem rather than part of the solution. As a result, philanthropic efforts, rather than market-based approaches, were the dominant approach to alleviating poverty in the developing world.

In recent years, however, a wide variety of players, ranging from government agencies to nongovernmental organization (NGO) leaders to foundations, have made concerted efforts to encourage more enterprise-oriented activities in BoP markets.[16] The private sector is seen a potentially valuable partner, impact investing has taken off, social entrepreneurs are supported across the globe, and the development community—with its substantial resources—has increasingly embraced impact enterprise as a new and complementary poverty alleviation strategy.[17]

In short, we see a convergence of agendas, as suggested in Figure 1.2. The development community wants new approaches for scaling impact at the same time that the business community wants new opportunities for future growth. Given their increasing alignment and complementary skills and resources, working together seems to offer the best opportunity to facilitate successful BoP impact enterprise development.

DEFINING A BOP IMPACT ENTERPRISE

Collectively we need an explicit definition of a BoP impact enterprise because the cast of characters involved is large, growing, and is sometimes quite passionate about what they seek to achieve. Therefore, too broad a definition will lead to confusion. Distilling this dialogue down to its essentials can facilitate more robust and productive conversations. With that in mind, here is my definition of *impact enterprise* for the BoP: *A BoP impact enterprise is one that operates in the underdeveloped market environments in which the BoP transacts, seeks financial sustainability, plans for scalability within and across markets, and actively manages toward producing significant net positive changes along multiple dimensions of well-being across the BoP, their communities, and the broader environment.*[18]

This definition recognizes that BoP impact enterprises can be an individual enterprise or an interconnected network of ventures, such as those found in franchise models and value chains. It also emphasizes the importance of seeking financial sustainability and endorses the idea of a financial return on investments made. Of course, this expected return—both the amount and the timing—can vary according to the specific goals of the entrepreneurs, investors, and other stakeholders of the enterprise. The point is that the enterprise must seek (and hopefully, achieve) a financial return that satisfies its owners and enables long-term financial sustainability.

The definition also recognizes that achieving impact requires enterprises to reach scale, which means they must grow beyond serving local consumers in a local market. This growth can be the result of serving more buyers and

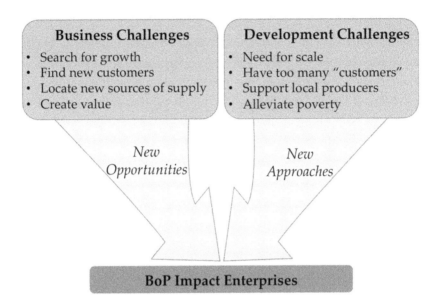

Business Challenges
- Search for growth
- Find new customers
- Locate new sources of supply
- Create value

Development Challenges
- Need for scale
- Have too many "customers"
- Support local producers
- Alleviate poverty

*New
Opportunities*

*New
Approaches*

BoP Impact Enterprises

FIGURE 1.2 Collaborating to build BoP impact enterprises

sellers with existing products or services offerings, providing existing buyers and sellers with new offerings, or reaching new consumers with new products or services. An interesting example of the last is BoP impact enterprises that can be a source of disruptive innovation that can then compete in wealthier markets higher up the economic pyramid.[19]

In a number of respects, the definition of a BoP impact enterprise aligns closely with traditional descriptions of business ventures. And this is important: BoP impact enterprises are like other business ventures seeking economic sustainability and scalability, and they face a number of familiar expectations. How can we surprise and delight those we seek to serve? How can we hear their voices? How can we create a sustainable business? What are potential sources of competitive advantage? Can we establish and maintain the right set of collaborations and partners? How can we create a value proposition that satisfies all stakeholders? The challenge for these enterprises is that they must address these questions in a different, unfamiliar, and underdeveloped market environment. This means that BoP impact enterprise leaders must focus not only on building their enterprises but also on creating the markets within which they operate.

The definition also acknowledges some other important distinctions. First, it implies that the enterprise's investors are not necessarily seeking to maximize profits. Instead, stakeholders may desire some mix of financial and social returns. Indeed, the definition gives explicit attention to the importance of a proactive approach to improving well-being. It recognizes that impacts can be both positive and negative and that the enterprise has an explicit goal to manage toward net positive outcomes across multiple dimensions. A second distinction is that microenterprises operating in BoP markets are not necessarily BoP impact enterprises because the former generally do not seek scale beyond the local market.

The challenge, and the opportunity, is to get ourselves all in sync with our definitions and aligning our motives. The central premise is *mutual value creation*—in other words, that enterprise strategies seeking financial sustainability at scale should also proactively manage toward generating net positive social returns as measured by changes in well-being

EVOLUTION OF THE BOP DOMAIN

The modern concept of the base of the pyramid was initially articulated by Stuart Hart and C. K. Prahalad in a 2002 paper, "The Fortune at the Bottom of the Pyramid."[20] This was followed by a paper by Prahalad and Al Hammond, "Serving the World's Poor Profitably," which also appeared in 2002, and by the first empirical analysis of success and failure, "Reinventing Strategies for Emerging Markets" by Stu Hart and me in 2004.[21] Also in 2004, Prahalad's groundbreaking book, *The Fortune at the Bottom of the Pyramid*, was published.[22] All of these emphasized the value of seeing the BoP as a source of business opportunity, combined with the promise of a scalable approach to reducing poverty, and highlighted the importance of adopting new strategies to succeed in these markets.

As interest in these ideas grew and evolved, the definition of the BoP came under some scrutiny. We have learned that debates over this kind of definition are useful, but only up to a point. For example, who is part of the BoP? Any line that one draws—such as the one I proposed at the outset of this chapter, which posits an annual per capita income of less than $3,000—is necessarily arbitrary (e.g., What's the practical difference between $2,999 and

$3,001?). Second, the BoP is a heterogeneous socioeconomic segment, and to think otherwise risks substantial overgeneralization. Third, any socioeconomic segment is defined by more than its income level. As I will discuss in a later chapter, poverty is a multidimensional challenge.

Over time, a rich array of complementary terms and approaches has emerged—for example, inclusive business, growing inclusive markets, pro-poor business, sustainable livelihoods, opportunities for the majority, impact investing, and shared value. They all start with the premise that launched widespread interest in the BoP: Business can play a greater role in addressing social issues, especially poverty. Collectively, their similarities far outweigh their differences, and they have taught us a great deal about the role of business in creating a net positive social impact for the BoP.

Through these various approaches, we have learned enough about BoP impact enterprise development to move both theory and practice from a BoP 1.0 model to a more robust BoP 2.0 perspective[23]—that is, from first-generation efforts, which focused primarily on introducing the BoP as a viable market opportunity that required thoughtful execution, to second-generation strategies, which emphasize the need to co-create this market, with a particular emphasis on innovation and engagement with the BoP in this process. This transformation in thinking has meant moving away from the original question—Is there a fortune at the BoP?—to a more useful one: How can we create a fortune with the BoP?

This transition in framing from finding a fortune *at* the BoP to creating a fortune *with* the BoP has ushered in a stronger focus on innovation. This means not just technological innovation, but—more important—business model, impact, and partner ecosystem innovation. Fortune finding was about motivation execution; fortune creating is about encouraging innovation. Table 1.1 captures the differences between these two approaches.[24]

If you read the left-hand column as a distillation of traditional market entry in the developed world, you are correct. I call it fortune finding. Simply stated, the market opportunities are already there and the challenge is finding them; once they are discovered, the perceptive entrepreneur devises a way to exploit them by marshaling familiar resources, minimizing and off-loading risks wherever possible, maintaining control and shunning unfamiliar partners, drawing on relevant precedents, executing effectively and efficiently, and monitoring the social impacts

TABLE 1.1 Fortune finding versus fortune creating

"Fortune Finding" *Execution Oriented*	*"Fortune Creating"* *Innovation Oriented*
Opportunities exist; identification is key	Opportunities are built; co-creation is key
Leverage expertise; reduce risk	Recognize ignorance; inspire creativity
Maintain control	Seek collaboration
Decision based on rigorous planning and analysis	Decision based on creating options to learn
Adapt existing models	Innovate new models
Manage implementation	Encourage experimentation
Minimize mistakes	Appreciate learnings
Monitor social output	Enhance social impact

of the enterprise—typically with an eye toward pleasing the kinds of socially oriented investors and organizations that might otherwise criticize them. There's nothing inherently wrong with this approach; in fact, it generally works well if the overriding focus is on minimizing change and achieving flawless execution.

I hope the right-hand column strikes you as something dramatically different. Fortune creating is far less about flawless implementation and far more about inspired innovation. Although there is always a need to balance innovation with execution, BoP impact enterprises, especially in their early stages, need to ensure they have a strong emphasis on innovation.

I expect that some of this terminology sounds unexpected, even odd. Be reassured; I explain all aspects of this approach in subsequent chapters, including how enterprise design and development can follow a fortune-creating orientation. And when I use the term *fortune creating*, I am talking about generating new value for both the enterprise and those it seeks to serve. For now, though, I simply underscore that innovation and enterprise development in collaboration with the BoP are both different and doable.

My description quickly turns into prescription for enterprise success—the three cornerstones that I introduced in the Preface. It seems clear that BoP impact enterprises will best flourish when their leaders have a set of guiding strategies and frameworks that are based on creating value with the BoP and are integrated with support and investment from the development community, government agencies, and other partners.

Clearly, attending to the needs of the BoP is a growing opportunity—and a growing challenge. For those of us interested in business-based approaches to poverty alleviation, this also means that the key question is no longer why businesses should do it, as summarized above, but how they should do it, the subject of the chapters that follow.

WHAT'S NEXT?

Given the interest and alignment across sectors, what's preventing the realization of the BoP promise—the flourishing of a greater number of sustainable and scalable BoP impact enterprises?

At least three substantial challenges present themselves. First, impact enterprises serving the BoP still face daunting challenges, including *value-creation* constraints (lack of raw materials, financial resources, production resources) and *value-capture* constraints (lack of market access, market power, and market security).[25] Successful BoP impact enterprises are those that overcome those constraints by developing capabilities that respond to realities on the ground. What are the strategies, frameworks, and tools that enterprise leaders can use to create and scale viable value propositions and innovative business models?

A second challenge has to do with mutual value creation. Most of the initiatives that have arisen have continued to focus on doing something "to" or "for" the BoP: the wrong mind-set. Success in BoP impact enterprise development requires a shift in this language, and the associated implications, to a focus on doing something *with* the BoP.

To do this requires overcoming the third challenge: bringing together two formerly independent domains. Businesses are accustomed to transacting with the wealthy in the formal economy; NGOs and other development sector entities have traditionally focused on providing resources to lower-income communities in the informal economy. The complementary nature of these two skill sets is a critical strength, but it's also a complicating factor.

How do two groups that have traditionally operated in very different ways, often regarding each other with suspicion, learn to collaborate effectively?

These challenges can be addressed. We need to apply the right tools purposefully and skillfully. Again, that is what this book is about and how I have organized it.

THE ROAD MAP

Can we generalize about what works when doing business in BoP markets? Based on my experience and research, as well as that of others focused on BoP impact enterprises, the answer is yes. We have learned enough now to offer recommended approaches for enhancing the success for BoP impact enterprises. As you will see, description quickly turns into prescription for enterprise success—the three cornerstones of frameworks to guide enterprise development, a path to creating value with the BoP, and an ecosystem of partners to support enterprise growth and market creation

My goal is to provide frameworks, tools, and strategies that are customizable. The BoP is a heterogeneous segment. The enterprises serving them come from different industry sectors, use a variety of different business models, and operate in different local contexts. To account for this diversity, my frameworks are designed to be generally applicable to all enterprises, while also enabling individual ventures to adapt them to their specific circumstances.

Chapters 2 and 3 address the lack of tools and frameworks for guiding enterprise development. In Chapter 2, I summarize the results of my work on internal design, that is, the configuration of variables (resources, metrics, structure, and problem-solving approaches) that interact in the process of developing a business model. BoP impact enterprises must ensure they sufficiently emphasize innovation. And at no time is this more important than in the initial stages of enterprise development when the leadership team is designing its business model. The team needs to enable a kind of business model R&D whereby the enterprise gets the configuration of internal design variables right.

Here I return to a key distinction: the difference between the fortune-finding mentality of traditional business development and the fortune-creating mind-set that is more likely to succeed in the BoP context. This difference may sound somewhat abstract, but it quickly gets down to practical kinds of choices that enterprises have to make. What financial and human resources do we need? How will we measure success? Who will we work with as colleagues and partners to solve the problems that inevitably will arise? These questions and others are addressed in the Business Model Innovation Framework, which guides venture leaders through the process of getting the internal design right.

I developed this framework after I had tracked the evolution of eighteen initiatives—mounted by six multinational corporations—that in many ways were also very much like start-up ventures. All were initially focused on BoP market entry. My research has shown that how these initiatives were set up was critical to their ultimate success. Enterprise leaders seeking to build BoP business models must understand the benefits and limitations of the resources they access, the metrics they are measured by, the structure and location they use, and the cross-boundary relationships they seek to develop. Getting all four of these design variables right is a prerequisite to creating a viable business model for BoP market entry.

After that model is in place, the next challenge is scaling, the focus of Chapter 3. Scale has benefits for all parties in BoP impact enterprise development. Obviously the business-oriented partners in the enterprise benefit from growth in revenues and profits; at the same time, the mission of the development community is better served when the enterprise can sustain and scale its social impacts, so the interests of the two constituencies in the partnership should be well aligned.

Nevertheless, scaling is where all too many enterprises come up short. One reason is that they fail to design for scale at the very beginning.[26] Another is that they fail to manage their pilots adequately. A third is that ventures fail to understand the sources of competitive advantage, and the capabilities required, for sustainability and scalability in BoP markets.

My prescription for enhancing scalability is summarized in a framework that focuses on three mutually reinforcing scaling imperatives: co-creating, innovating, and embedding (the C-I-E Framework). Co-creation is envisioning what the enterprise can be. This includes the hard work of invention, in which enterprises work with the BoP to craft solutions and seek to leverage what is right in the local marketplace. What is the relevant local value proposition, and what sort of business can we build together that advances that proposition?

Innovation takes the ideas generated in the co-creation stage out into the marketplace. Innovating generally consists of two concurrent activities: orchestrating effective experiments and building market opportunities. By asking a series of focusing questions—*What are we going to learn? Why this partner? Why that location?*—the enterprise homes in on pilots that will prove or disprove the value proposition. The good pilot is purposeful (meaning that it has clear goals), has appropriate metrics and incentives in place, and understands and manages risks, including the risks that it is creating for the BoP.

Understanding the potential for creating market opportunities is a key part of innovating for BoP markets. How can we boost demand among people who have not traditionally thought of themselves as consumers of a particular product or service? How can we reduce market inefficiencies that local producers face? How can we facilitate the development of and access to missing market infrastructure and other public goods?

Embedding, the last element in the C-I-E Framework, focuses on bringing the evolving activities of the enterprise into a coherent whole, again with a focus on making sustainability and scalability possible. Financial sustainability requires competitive advantage, which in mature economies tends to derive from internal-to-the-company assets. In BoP markets, by contrast, enterprises must also build competitive advantage by integrating its resources and activities with assets and organizations that exist outside firm boundaries. This necessitates developing and maintaining collaborations with a diverse set of partners.

Scaling also requires building and leveraging a capability in social embeddedness, whereby the enterprise develops the capacity to rapidly understand the opportunity in new BoP market contexts. Social embeddedness incorporates two key skills: the ability to efficiently access critical, market-specific information and the capacity to effectively interpret that information. The better the enterprise builds its capability in social embeddedness, the better able it will be to speed up the process of co-creating, innovating, and embedding that can generate sustainability at scale.

Chapter 4 explores the crucial yet still poorly understood goal of mutual value creation. Many impact enterprises claim to deeply understand what value they're generating for the BoP, but when pressed, they resort to either inspirational anecdotes or business-oriented output measures. We need to do better.

Understanding poverty alleviation outcomes is not a luxury or a cost of doing business to satisfy partner expectations; it is a necessity in the early stages of a venture, and especially as the enterprise seeks growth and scale. How else can a venture hear the voices of customers? How else can it enhance the business's value proposition and improve on the strategy that lies behind the business?

To get there, we have to more holistically define *poverty*, a word with multiple connotations. Poverty is more than simply the absence of economic well-being. According to the World Bank, for example, poverty comprises not only material deprivation but also risk, vulnerability, and powerlessness.[27] In other words, individuals and communities also must be able to help themselves and influence the world around them.[28] Furthermore, geographic, social, and other types of isolation can impoverish individuals and communities through a sense of powerlessness.

Framed holistically, these dimensions can be summarized as a lack of three types of well-being: economic, capability, *and* relationship. These are often found in combination, but substantial deficits in any of them alone can have devastating impacts on the lives of the poor. As presented in the earlier definition, BoP impact enterprises actively manage toward producing significant net positive changes along multiple dimensions of well-being.

To help would-be impact enterprises assess and enhance their value proposition, I have devised what I call the BoP Impact Assessment Framework, a tool that tracks changes in well-being. By design, it is holistic, interactive, actionable, and flexible, enabling enterprise team leaders to apply it in a wide variety of contexts. It asks two key questions:

- Who is being affected?
- How are they being affected?

The answers to these questions provide more than just a snapshot of today's reality; they also provide a forward-looking picture, suggesting ways to improve the net positive value proposition on the ground.

Consider the case of microfinance. Giving poor people access to credit is a powerful thing. At the same, though, they are being given debt. I'm certainly not saying, "Focus on the negatives." But I am saying that there are almost certainly positive and negative impacts out there to be found, and your understanding of both needs to be built into your assessment of the value creation opportunity. If the enterprise's value proposition is understood with sufficient rigor and thoroughness, the leadership team will be better positioned to craft strategies for enhancing the positive and mitigating the negative.

As it turns out, creating a more robust value proposition, like getting to scale, almost always involves close collaboration with development-community partners. BoP impact enterprises must create an ecosystem of partners to support their effort. This is the topic that I explore in depth in Chapters 5 and 6.

In Chapter 5, I start by describing the rich universe of potential partners, whom I refer to as scaling facilitators. These scaling facilitators use a variety of implementation models (e.g., accelerators, impact investing, last-mile distribution, and market systems strengthening) to provide support to BoP impact enterprise development. The challenge for the enterprise's leadership team is to develop a proactive and effective partnership strategy that maximizes access to the resources available from scaling facilitators and their associated implementation models. Toward that end, I introduce the Partnership Ecosystem Framework (PEF).

The PEF divides the partnership landscape into four quadrants—facilitating enterprise activities, enhancing enterprise resources, facilitating market transactions, and enhancing market environment—that capture the landscape of support that potential partners can provide. The result is a diagnostic tool that enterprise leaders can use to systematically understand their current partner portfolio and assess where the best opportunities lie for building a more robust partnership ecosystem.

Chapter 5 looks at the "who" of partnerships and Chapter 6 the "how." The kinds of collaborations described in Chapter 5 don't just happen; they have to be carefully developed. I have coined a phrase that captures the perspective that I feel must guide these partnering efforts: *collaborative interdependence*. The use of the term *interdependence* is purposeful, because I want to stress the difference from partnerships based on dependence or independence. In collaborative interdependence, both parties stop asking, "How can you help me?" and start asking, "How can we help each other?"

This isn't automatic or easy. Based on my observations and research and that of others, it seems clear that the BoP impact enterprise is wise to invest in the critical role of what I call the chief ecosystem director (CED)—the individual or team responsible for this delicate management process.[29] For a start-up venture, resource constraints may mean that this role isn't a full-time position. Even so, having someone who is explicitly responsible for developing partnerships is crucial. By designating a senior individual or team as responsible for developing a set of key partnerships into an effective whole, the enterprise puts appropriate weight on an all-important process. The CED strategizes how to extend the enterprise's partnership portfolio to fill specific gaps in enterprise development or market creation.

In a sense, the CED's job is about effectively managing the partnership content and process. This includes identifying and overcoming both internal challenges and cross-sectoral tensions: What resistance exists inside the enterprise, and how can it be overcome? Are there stereotypes and preconceptions that have to be overcome? Are biases against grant capital and other types of subsidized support getting in the way of progress? Are some behaviors of potential partners difficult to understand or explain? I attempt to provide the CED with strategies and responses to address these and other potential roadblocks and, more important, convey a way of approaching, building, and managing a robust portfolio of partners.

Chapter 7 summarizes the ideas, tools, and frameworks presented in the previous chapters and highlights the importance of continuing this learning journey. The BoP domain is at an inflection point. We have seen the promise of sustainable, scalable BoP impact enterprises, but we have more to do to truly deliver on that promise. We must continue to draw lessons from the experiences—the successes and the frustrations—of enterprises operating in the field. We must continue to bring good data and good thinking to bear on the right questions and identify what works and what doesn't.

LOOKING FORWARD

The lessons in this book are important ones for both business leaders and development professionals. The linking of two formerly independent domains—the business world and the development community—creates unprecedented opportunities to build businesses and alleviate poverty in BoP markets concurrently and to do both better than they could have been done alone.

The opportunity is substantial, but it requires new mind-sets; new metrics, resources, and problem solving; new business models; new skills and capabilities; new understandings of mutual value creation; and new partners and partnership approaches. It requires a value proposition that satisfies both the impact enterprise and the BoP and a willingness to revisit and enhance that value proposition on a regular basis.

We must also ensure a sense of urgency. The poverty that the BoP faces is a large and looming threat to any visions we might have of an equitable and peaceful society, today and in the future. Let me state that belief more strongly: *Poverty is society's greatest challenge, today and tomorrow.*

I take nothing away from the seriousness of other important issues, such as climate change. But are we comfortable with the prospect of literally billions of people standing on the outside of affluence, looking in? As the inequities in our global society become more and more visible to the BoP across world—through the miracles of modern technology, including all those cell phones—will those many billions be comfortable with their opportunities for a better life? What will tomorrow look like, and will that vision of the world satisfy enough people?

To really address the problem—to tackle poverty in all its complexity—we need to make business work better for the BoP. The key question for both business leaders and development professionals is no longer: Are BoP impact enterprises worthy of investment? It is now: How can we make investments in BoP impact enterprises perform better? How can we fulfill the BoP promise?

That's what this book is about.

2 ENABLING BUSINESS MODEL INNOVATION

This chapter focuses on the customizable tools and frameworks to guide BoP impact enterprise development. It explores internal design—that is, how enterprise leaders can configure key internal design variables to maximize the likelihood of success. It thus addresses organizational rather than technological challenges.

This chapter offers three important lessons. The first is that an enterprise building a business model—in other words, the logic for how it creates, provides, and captures value[1]—capable of serving the BoP must ensure a proper focus on innovation and avoid the understandable tendency to overemphasize execution. Business model innovation implies research and development and an associated emphasis on experimentation and learning. So at the outset of BoP venturing, it's important to think about engaging in business model R&D.

The second lesson is that BoP impact enterprise leaders must recognize that there are different types of business model innovation, and they must be able to identify which is most appropriate for their situation. Innovation in business models can involve an entire business model or only some specific components of it. While both approaches can yield valuable insights in moving the business toward success, enterprise leaders must identify the right approach for the circumstances they are facing.

Finally, to innovate successfully, leaders of BoP impact enterprises must get the internal design right. By *internal design*, I mean the configuration of enterprise-specific variables—resources, metrics, structure, and problem-solving approaches—that interact in the process of developing a business model. Different configurations lead to different innovation opportunities.

I've worked with and researched a great many BoP impact enterprises and can say with a high level of confidence that I can look at the internal design in front of me—be it of an entrepreneurial venture or an initiative within a larger company—and tell pretty quickly whether it is set up for success. If enterprise leaders do not properly emphasize innovation, do not recognize differences in the types of business model innovation, and do not create the appropriate configuration of internal design variables, the resulting business model will almost surely not succeed in BoP markets.

Perhaps any claim about predicting success seems overly bold, but I think that after reading this chapter, you will agree that some kinds of outcomes can be foreseen.

FIRST: DESIGNING BUSINESS MODELS FOR INNOVATION, NOT EXECUTION

It is probably worth restating here one of the key points of Chapter 1: Success with the BoP begins with how you frame your initiative—in other words, your mind-set going into the venture. All too often, companies have approached the BoP with a fortune-finding mentality. I liken this mind-set to a gold rush: The ore is in the ground; all we have to do is find it and exploit it. Fortune finding is about identifying an opportunity, leveraging what you already know, and executing effectively. It emphasizes rigorous planning and careful implementation while minimizing the need for change—and, of course, curtailing any deviations from the initial plan.

A better mind-set for the BoP is fortune creating. This involves collaboration—co-creation—with partners formal and informal, inside and outside the enterprise. Fortune creating is about recognizing what you don't know and figuring out how to acquire that missing knowledge. It's less about execution—although good execution is ultimately important to every business—and more about inspiring creativity, encouraging experimentation, and, especially, enabling innovation.

In comparing the two approaches, I sometimes cite the example of a cash flow statement. After getting my MBA in the 1980s, I was a senior consultant in business valuation for Deloitte Haskins & Sells (now Deloitte Touche Tohmatsu). We developed cash flows to assess the value of businesses in a wide variety of industries. I found it an illuminating experience. Once I understood the mechanisms for developing a cash flow statement, I realized that the final results depended heavily on the assumptions made about the future. The better those assumptions were, the more confidence I could be in my cash flow statement.

Cash flows are especially insightful when the future can confidently be modeled from past experiences. This is particularly true when you envision only modest or incremental changes to what has gone before. Thus a cash flow statement tends to be most helpful when you are fortune finding (and when your assumptions are likely to be pretty good) and less reliable when you are innovating in the fortune-creating mode.

Fortune creating, and the innovation associated with it, may benefit from a staged investment approach that is something like the logic you might apply to investments in technology development. The initial goal isn't to predict returns; it is to facilitate innovation. The objective is to create options—decision points—for potential further investment.[2] The financial model is based on having the resources needed to test different experiments and then to invest further only if these initial experiments yield positive outcomes.[3] The issues then are what resources are needed to build an initial version of the business approach and what outstanding issues will be answered when conducting pilot tests in the marketplace. The outcomes of these experiments will generate new insights into whether the approach is potentially viable and what investments are needed to continue the innovation process. The idea is to link future investments of resources to innovation outcomes.

A CASE IN POINT: NIKE'S WORLD SHOE PROJECT

I'll ground this discussion in a real-world case study of sportswear maker Nike's effort to create an athletic shoe that would be affordable and attractive to the BoP.[4] You will see that the World Shoe project suffered from a number of missteps. Most damaging, the team running the project viewed their primary challenge as one of execution as opposed to innovation: The team thought that once they had the right shoe, wrapping a business model around it would be easy. That assumption couldn't have been further from the truth. As in many other BoP impact enterprises, developing the technology—in this case, creating a low-cost shoe—was the easier part; building the business model proved to be a much greater hurdle.

Nike is one of the world's most successful manufacturers and distributors of sportswear, and its iconic "swoosh" is one of the best-known trademarks in the world. The company was founded in the early 1960s by Phil Knight, a former track star and Stanford Business School graduate. The business proved an astounding success, with revenues growing from $60,000 in 1972 to nearly $9 billion by 2000. In that same year, Nike controlled an amazing 45 percent of the U.S. athletic shoe market.

But Tom Clarke, Nike's president at the time of the World Shoe, suspected that trouble lurked behind those numbers. Soaring revenues had flattened out, and the company's profits and stock price had sagged. And although the company was celebrated for its skill at international sourcing, enabling it to sell shoes that were mostly manufactured overseas profitably in the United States, it was far less adept at selling in less affluent markets. In particular, Clarke was looking at China. Only a small percentage of that country's estimated 1 billion "exercising people" (as one survey phrased it) could afford a high-end Nike running shoe. Could Nike create a shoe that could serve the bottom 80 percent of the market, which the company was not reaching with its existing product line?

There certainly was evidence to hint at a substantial new market. For one thing, counterfeit sales of Nike footwear and apparel continued to thrive. Nike estimated that more than 2.2 million imitation Nikes were being sold annually, representing $70 million in lost revenue.

With these challenges and opportunities in mind, Clarke asked colleague Tom Hartge, director of emerging market footwear, to launch the World Shoe Project, with a goal of developing a footwear line exclusively intended for low-income markets in Asia, Africa, and Latin America. Hartge was a longtime veteran of Nike and was well respected internally. To offer him support, the World Shoe team was closely integrated with both the Footwear and Asia-Pacific departments.

Working collaboratively with designers at headquarters and the local factories in China that produced Nike's high-end shoes, the team was able to fairly quickly develop a shoe with a factory price to Nike of about five dollars.

The real challenge for Nike arose in coming up with a viable strategy for the new product. As Hartge would later caution other aspiring BoP impact enterprise leaders: "Don't underestimate the difficulty of trying to embrace a new business model."

Once the technology was developed, the team saw the World Shoe effort as primarily an execution challenge—and this, as it turned out, was the initiative's fatal flaw. "I really felt that if we just figured out the product-creation part of the formula, which is usually the toughest part, then the rest of it would come easier; and in fact I now think in hindsight this was the easiest part of the thing. We know how to make shoes....What we don't know how to do is a lot of this other stuff, certainly in conditions we have never been in before.... It almost exponentially got harder once [we got the shoe]," Hartge later confessed.[5]

The retail price point, fifteen dollars, was based on Nike's traditional margin structure, which emphasized selling high-priced shoes to those who could afford them. While World Shoe's stated intent was to measure performance by the number of shoes sold, an underlying emphasis on high gross margins, embedded in the company's internal measurement systems, permeated the project.

Many functional activities for the World Shoe project emphasized execution over innovation. Manufacturing, for example, was assigned to existing lines in two of Nike's dedicated factories in China. While this minimized the need for new capital expenditures, it also led to a rigid production process restricted by predetermined run times and order levels. Although the team benefited from the company's capabilities in shoe design, they did not actively engage potential customers in these efforts. In addition, the World Shoe team was not given a budget for marketing and distribution. Instead, the team leveraged Nike's existing approach to local distribution, including relying on the company's network of Chinese-based retailers, which were primarily located in the largest cities. Marketing was done by the local regional managers, who were more incentivized to sell high-end, high-margin Nike shoes than the lower-margin World Shoe.

In ensuing months, the World Shoe Project languished, mostly relegated to the large cities where it was launched. Rather than reaching the BoP, the

World Shoe proved most attractive to customers in the middle of the pyramid who could not afford top-end Nike products.

Philosophically, Nike had been behind the World Shoe. CEO Phil Knight declared himself to be a big fan of the project. His colleagues further down in the organization maintained that the World Shoe was "ahead of its time" and that it was "the right model at the wrong time."

I would argue the exact opposite: It was the wrong model at the right time. Without really exerting itself, Nike proved it could produce a five-dollar pair of shoes. It proved it had the wherewithal to invest in a new team and launch a new product line. What it *didn't* have was the right business model. Simply put, the World Shoe failed in its business model development. In the end, the business model emphasized execution, not innovation—not a recipe for success in BoP markets.

KEY DESIGN VARIABLES:
ALONE AND IN COMBINATION

My goal in working with BoP impact enterprises is to facilitate successes by helping to transform ideas, resources, and strategizing into viable enterprises. In that spirit, BoP impact enterprise leaders must recognize two things. First, there is more than one way to go about the business model innovation process. Second, the team must recognize and manage the key internal design variables that influence the process, including understanding how different configurations of business variables support (or hamper) different types of innovation.

These observations and the prescriptions that follow draw on my multi-year analysis of eighteen initiatives that were all originally conceived as BoP impact enterprises. (As you will see, that's not where they all wound up.). These initiatives were sponsored by six multinationals, all of them large and experienced U.S.-based firms intending to enter BoP markets through corporate-initiated, wholly owned greenfield initiatives. And while I will first speak to internal design from the perspective of large transnational companies, these findings apply to almost any type of BoP impact enterprise, including entrepreneurial start-ups, social enterprises, initiatives developed by non-profits, and ventures by companies based in the local country. They apply whether the enterprise is designed to serve BoP consumers, BoP producers, or both.

I also dig more deeply into the experience of two other BoP impact enterprises—one that proved adept at building a business model that emphasized innovation and did reach the BoP and another that did not. I compare these companies' experience to Nike's and explain why things went the way they did.

Business Model Innovation Framework

In my study of these eighteen multinational-based initiatives, I identified three metrics of success: whether the initiative launched; whether that launch actually targeted the BoP; and the type of business model innovation that was facilitated.[6] I found that four design variables were particularly influential in predicting the outcome, as presented in what I call the Business Model Innovation (BMI) Framework summarized in Figure 2.1.

As the figure indicates, enterprise leaders seeking to build BoP business models must attend to the resources they can access, the metrics by which they will be measured, the problem-solving approach they will use, and the organizational structure within which they operate. Getting all four right is a prerequisite to building a viable business model. Achieving the kind of business model innovation needed for successful BoP market entry requires understanding how each of these variables needs to be tailored to a specific market objective.

Resources

Two types of resources (at the upper left of the figure), human and financial capital, play key influencing roles. In both cases, it is not just the amount but also the type of these resources that matters.

As an enterprise leader, you have to think carefully about the human resources—the talent—that you will need to build a viable business model. While it is always tempting to assemble a team that consists mainly of excited and motivated colleagues—the people who really want this effort to succeed—that isn't always the best strategy, since that team isn't likely to have the skills and knowledge needed to execute successfully in the BoP space.

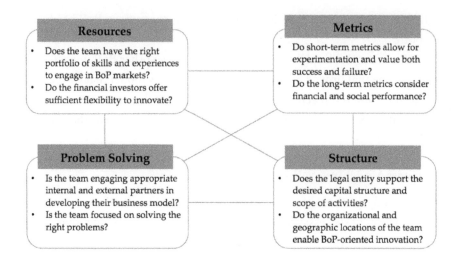

FIGURE 2.1 Business Model Innovation Framework

Would-be BoP leaders are wise to remember that developed world expertise and entrepreneurial traditional wisdom are insufficient, and maybe even inappropriate, for BoP markets.

It's an apparent paradox: The enterprise leader and his supporters bring ideas and enthusiasm to the BoP and see themselves as change makers with a purpose. But all too often, this combination of energy and commitment masks a misplaced confidence. Expertise developed in top-of-the-pyramid, developed world markets has limitations in a BoP context. In fact, implicit biases about the BoP and how to serve them can be damaging, even fatal, to the enterprise's prospects. Furthermore, and a very real danger, is that this type of team also often lacks humility about what they don't know. Understanding what you don't understand is a key component in building an effective team.

Enthusiasm is not a substitute for relevant experience and knowledge. The team will need a portfolio of skills, including both general business acumen and context-appropriate expertise regarding BoP market environments. A team that is steeped in business as usual will need to add specialized BoP resources. They must have the capability to gain a deep sense of the local context—the BoP markets and ecosystems around them—and to partner with development and nonprofit organizations that have experience in this environment. Augmenting this type of team with some outsiders, including one or more people with strong BoP credentials, is crucial if the enterprise is to understand the local context. Conversely, a team that is primarily versed in the challenges of the BoP or in development issues needs to seek out colleagues who understand business and the challenges of building economically viable enterprises.

The team must also be able to innovate effectively. Again, humility is a saving grace. Professional experience gained in corporate venturing or entrepreneurial endeavors, for example, may contribute a great deal to success in traditional developed world contexts; it may have much less connection to success in interactions with the BoP, and, in fact, overreliance, explicitly or implicitly, on these experiences can restrict the opportunity for innovation.

The team must also truly embrace an entrepreneurial orientation.[7] The initial stages of BoP impact enterprise development are often intense, and the team will likely go through a lot of anxiety in bumping up against some things that work only partially and other things that don't work at all. In addition to having steady nerves, the leadership needs to know when to let go of one approach and try a different one. The team cannot afford to love their initial ideas so much that they are unwilling to learn and innovate when the evidence suggests that the current approach isn't working.

In addition to addressing the talent questions, the BoP team also needs to carefully consider the type of financial resources that it seeks to start the enterprise. The initiatives in my study tended to rely on two types of financial resources: funding that came with the expectation of short-term returns or some sort of "patient" capital that had longer-term return expectations. To support business model innovation, the enterprise team generally requires money on which financial returns are not demanded immediately and capital that understands the realities of investments in innovation.

True learning grows out of experimentation, and good experimentation necessarily has false starts and failures. This creates the need to invest in options that allow learning and course corrections at appropriate junctures. Experiments that are working will receive additional resources to further the model's development, and those that are not must be redirected. Innovation-oriented capital understands the need for this learning journey.

BoP impact enterprises can seek this patient capital from external and internal sources. Externally, a growing number of nontraditional funding sources, such as impact investors, angel investors seeking social impact, and development community organizations and foundations, are interested in providing patient capital to these types of enterprises.[8] Company-incubated enterprises can also look inside organizational boundaries to top-level managers with budget authority to provide what some companies call "market support funds," dedicated to driving specific strategic initiatives that don't have an immediate financial return. Alternatively, in large companies, enterprise leaders can turn to corporate social responsibility or even corporate philanthropy departments to provide some initial seed funding to support pilots and experiments, knowing that this is not a sustainable source of capital.[9] To access these types of investments, enterprise leaders must show how combining patient capital with the power of enterprise can engender a mix of financial and social results that traditional internal and external sources of capital alone could not accomplish.

A word to the wise: Access to capital is good; access to the right capital is much better. As we saw in the case of Nike's World Shoe, investment capital that requires a short-term return can drive a BoP impact enterprise toward an emphasis on business model execution, which can lead to a focus on more familiar, middle-of-the-pyramid markets.

Metrics

A closely related issue in the model is **metrics** (the upper-right quadrant of Figure 2.1). The desire to measure success in terms of short-term financial returns is well known to anyone who has worked in the corporate or investment worlds. You can't go for very long without being asked how your efforts will affect next month's or next quarter's return. Yet these traditional go-to-market metrics may be misguided here. Treating a BoP impact enterprise like more traditional market entry efforts is generally a prescription for failure. BoP markets, as noted, are fundamentally different from those found higher up the economic pyramid. New initiatives must innovate and learn before they can execute and grow. Standard financial measures of return on investment, return on equity, and so on can be particularly counterproductive at an earlier stage of enterprise development because they encourage a focus on the short term.

BoP impact enterprise leaders must remember that companies of all sizes do invest in ways that are designed for long-term payout, and these investments can be very large sums. This kind of investment, though, is usually focused on technological R&D, particularly emerging technologies. The returns from these investments tend to be measured in years rather than months. The challenge in the BoP context, regardless of whether this is a corporate-led initiative or a start-up enterprise seeking outside funding, is to use these same kinds of R&D-oriented yardsticks to facilitate business model innovation.

My first prescription is to proactively set your own metrics rather than let someone else set them for you. What should your business model innovation metrics look like? Most important is that they should emphasize (1) short-term experimentation and a willingness to value the learnings that come from success and failure and (2) attractive long-term financial and social performance goals.

Shorter-term metrics should focus on factors that demonstrate progress toward different, but still valuable, measures of success—for example: experiments launched; hypotheses tested; lessons learned; partnerships established and sustained; and value created for local customers, producers, and other stakeholders. Longer-term metrics can, and in many cases should, be more traditional: revenues, profitability growth, and so on. The long-term financial goals of the enterprise must emphasize sustainability at scale from the very beginning. From the business's point of view, this is what will make the investment in short-term learning worth the time and money.

Equally, the enterprise's long-term metrics should include net positive increases in local well-being and value creation. Among other things, this is the carrot that will help ensure that the enterprise's social impact–oriented partners see value in their investment of resources and support. (I discuss assessing and enhancing social impact in much greater detail in Chapter 4 and the who and the how of building a partnership ecosystem in Chapters 5 and 6.)

Structure

Structure in the BMI framework (the lower right quadrant in Figure 2.1) includes the choice of legal entity. In the case of enterprises launched within incumbent organizations, this also corporates what could be described as the location within the larger organization.

For all BoP impact enterprises, the choice of the legal structure is a critical issue. It can facilitate or—if the enterprise leader is not careful—restrict the opportunity to achieve the goals of the business. For example, decisions about priority of activities, scope and scale of operations, speed of growth, and desired levels of profitability and risk can influence decisions about capital structure.

Legal entity choices, moreover, can influence capital structure options. Nonprofit organizations, for example, often have an easier time accessing philanthropic donations but cannot offer equity stakes (at least in the United States). For-profit organizations can receive equity injections but can't offer donors the tax benefits associated with charitable contributions. Tax-exempt nonprofits generally don't pay income taxes (although they may be required in some jurisdictions to pay value-added tax or other taxes) and can't offer dividends. For-profits can share their financial gains with their shareholders but do pay taxes on their net profits. As a result, enterprise leaders must recognize that different legal entities are more or less attractive to specific potential investors.

New types of legal entities seek to balance the benefits of for-profit and nonprofit organizations. In the United States these include benefit corporations, low-profit limited-liability companies (LC3s), flexible purpose, and social purpose corporations. Each of these entities comes with its own strengths and limitations, all of which require careful consideration by the enterprise leadership team. It's worth noting too that these entities are not recognized in all states.

Start-up enterprises generally have greater flexibility in the choice of legal entity that they can choose to adopt and are not constrained by an incumbent's existing status. Incumbents, however, can still consider setting up a separate legal entity to help facilitate their efforts at BoP impact enterprise development.

Both start-up ventures and enterprises embedded in incumbent organizations, for example, can take a hybrid route, using both for-profit and nonprofit entities to leverage the best of both options.[10] This can be a particularly fruitful approach because it allows the enterprise to access different sources of capital for different uses. There are some challenges, however, in setting up and managing such a hybrid structure. For entities established in the United States, a nonprofit can own a for-profit, but a for-profit cannot own a nonprofit; it can have only a contractual relationship with the nonprofit. The respective entities must also maintain an arm's-length relationship, as represented by independent decision making. This has implications, for example, for the composition and overlap of the members of the respective boards that govern these entities.

Given the complexities of legal entity selection, having access to a lawyer can be crucial in creating the structure that best enables an enterprise to achieve its BoP vision.[11] As Deborah Burand, a former colleague at the University of Michigan Law School, puts it, "Lawyers are your friends, and you need access to them as part of your venture team.[12] Legal entity selection has far-reaching, long-term consequences since these decisions are generally difficult to reverse once executed.

Enterprise leaders must also understand what kinds of organizational structures give the new venture the best chance of success. One component of that larger issue, a component that is relevant to all types of BoP impact enterprises, is where the team will be physically located. At least some members of the team need to spend significant time in the local BoP context. Is the team primarily based in a developed or a developing market context? If in the developing world, does the team's location (e.g., urban or rural) match the characteristics of the proposed BoP market?

In addition to their geographic location, BoP impact enterprises incubated inside an existing organization must consider their location within the broader corporate structure. Researchers and business practitioners alike have thought a good deal about the business incubation process. A common theme that emerges is that the new entity needs to be both protected and connected.[13]

The new enterprise has to be shielded to some extent from the typical pressures and demands found in the day-to-day routines of most organizations. Enterprises incubated within an incumbent organization that lack this kind of protection often must contend with a compressed time line and face demands for short-term financial returns. (This is one reason why corporate R&D centers are rarely co-located with headquarters.) The remedy is to place the fledgling BoP investment in a location that provides internal white space—a sort of corporate greenhouse where it can be protected from the pressures of short-term expectations.[14] Think of the BoP business model development white space as a zone of corporate R&D—at least at the outset. Just like investments in technology, companies must see their BoP initiatives as having long-term returns. And just like technology-oriented research, investments in BoP business models should be made based on the opportunity to innovate and the potential to translate those innovations to market reality.

The company's top management can play an important role in facilitating this type of protection. A colleague with substantial experience with BoP impact enterprise explained to me:

> Often the operating mind-set of the parent organization can transfer into the BoP venture, resulting in mediocre achievement or the venture not achieving its full potential.
>
> My first boss here didn't review my work in detail for about a year and half—only casual interaction and chats on how things are. One day I approached him and asked him why he doesn't review me, and I was amazed to hear his answer. He said, "Your vision for this business is way higher and bigger than mine. If I review you, my worry is that I may bring you down to my level." Whether your boss in an incumbent firm or your investors in a start-up, these kinds of people are gems who can make a big difference.[15]

While protection is important, an R&D-oriented endeavor also has to have its finger on the pulse of the business. Protection and connection need to be balanced, and that balance almost always changes over time. At an early stage, the relationships and connections to the business need to be frequent and robust but remain relatively informal.

One way of thinking about this is the difference between a board of advisors and a board of directors. The good ideas that have been generated in the protection of white space must stay connected to the corporate mainstream so that future innovation can be paid for. When discussing this with enterprise leaders in large companies, I often use the phrase "formally isolated and informally connected." Keeping the enterprise informally connected becomes a particularly important role for the leader.

Problem Solving

Problem solving, in the lower left quadrant of the BMI framework of Figure 2.1, is my shorthand for a multidimensional challenge: boundary spanning within and across the organization through the creation of internal and external relationships. The key issues are: Who are we talking to and what we talking about as we attempt to define and solve key problems? And whose problem or problems are we actually solving as we go through this process?

For BoP impact enterprises incubated within an existing organization for-profit or nonprofit, this means problem solving with partners both inside and outside the organization. For start-ups, this may require even greater external boundary spanning, as the pool of internal candidates is likely to be much smaller. In either case, successful boundary spanning requires rich and robust two-way conversations with individuals and organizations that are not necessarily part of the enterprise's formal relationship network.

Internally, especially for BoP impact enterprises incubated within a larger organization, leaders must be sure they are reaching out to people beyond their relatively small core group. This becomes particularly important if the enterprise is embedded in a white space that provides structural protection. When this happens, formal connections and interactions within the organization are limited by design. While this helps enable and maintain an innovation orientation, it also means that enterprise leaders must share with and learn from colleagues with whom they have only an informal relationship. This boundary spanning should focus on both adding technical expertise—marketing, legal, manufacturing, and other functional departments—and building internal legitimacy with key business units.

Similar to technology R&D efforts, when the initiative is ready to emerge from its white-space protection, it must be seen as integrated into the broader strategy of the organization. This early and ongoing attention to building informal boundary-crossing relationships helps ensure that the BoP impact enterprise has taken into account the operating realities of the larger organization or a key business unit of it. These boundary-spanning efforts can be extremely important in the event of an anticipated or unanticipated transition. If the enterprise needs a new home, the enterprise leadership team will already have had an opportunity to share and refine its internal value proposition.

Externally, the key problem-solving issues already introduced—the people you are talking to and what you are talking about—become relevant for both start-ups and new initiatives within existing organizations. In terms of *who*, enterprise leaders must be sure they are having a rich set of conversations with a diverse set of colleagues—for example, from development organizations, foundations, and other groups that may have a lot of experience in BoP markets.

This may sound easy in theory but proves difficult in practice. How do you have productive conversations about business model innovation with people who don't readily accept the idea that business can be part of the solution to social issues? The answer lies in having open and honest discussions with these individuals—a process that takes time, energy, and commitment. Unfortunately, it is often sidestepped, overwhelmed by the crush of daily activities or the hubris of the leadership team.

Why is it important for the BoP initiative's leadership team to cross organizational boundaries and build bridges with outsiders? Consider these challenges: Inadequate or inaccurate information, as well as limited and informal infrastructure in BoP markets, can inhibit enterprise development. Gaining an early and deep understanding of how to leverage the opportunities and avoid the pitfalls of these markets is crucial for speeding up the time required to build a viable business model. Indeed, convincing relevant partners to share their knowledge and perhaps resources is absolutely essential to success.

This also leads to the question of *what* these problem-solving interactions are focused on. Whose problems are being solved? Potential advisors from the development community are likely to have different performance goals. They seek social value creation and are looking for opportunities to extend and enhance their own projects. That does not necessarily imply a conflict of interest, but it does mean that enterprise leaders must be thoughtful about the external interactions they are developing. They must understand their partners' goals and how sharing information, knowledge, and ideas can create mutual value. That said, they also must be wary of spending too much time solving their partner's problems. Investing time and energy in a partner's socially oriented projects may be a fast way to take action and generate a compelling story for public consumption, but these efforts are likely to generate only limited knowledge about the enterprise's specific business model innovation challenges.

Furthermore, and perhaps most important, listening, learning, and actively engaging with the BoP is necessary in creating a viable business model. *The BoP is not part of the problem; it is part of the solution.* Engaging with the BoP from the earliest stages of business model innovation is a key part of the problem-solving process. As I discuss in the next chapter, this is often easier said than done. Yet any fortune in these markets must be created with the BoP, and an enterprise's boundary spanning must include active engagement with the BoP in the problem-solving process.

DESIGN VARIABLES IN ACTION

There is not just one type of business model innovation. Innovation efforts can have different goals, and this can influence the configuration of design variables within the BMI Framework. In my study of the eighteen multinational-based initiatives, I assessed how different configurations influenced the type and success of business model development.[16] I found that those eighteen differed along three important performance dimensions:

- Did the initiative stay true to its intended BoP orientation, or did it shift during the design stage to a middle-of-the-pyramid effort?

- Did it actually launch?

- For the BoP initiatives that launched, was the launch design focused on testing the entire business model or testing only some components? In other words, was it shaped in a comprehensive way or conceived as a means of testing only a subset of the overall business model?

While all eighteen were initially intended as BoP initiatives, only fourteen maintained their focus on BoP markets; the remaining four shifted to middle-of-the-pyramid markets. (The World Shoe case has already demonstrated how one venture made that shift.) All four initiatives that made this shift from BoP to middle of the pyramid actually launched, while only nine of the fourteen BoP initiatives got out of the starting gate. The five that didn't launch were shelved because management decided that their efforts, including their configuration of design variables, were not going to lead to viable business models.

The importance of the third dimension, the scope of the launch test, became apparent during the course of my study. I found two broad types of business model innovation, distinguished by the learning goals that guided them. One group had a primary goal of testing the entire business model, and so those initiatives were launched in a comprehensive way, with all the necessary components in place to carry out a fair and comprehensive market test. The initiatives in the second group were designed primarily to generate learnings about specific components of the business models—for example, whether local distributors could be signed up in adequate numbers or whether the agreed-on outreach strategies could be made to work. Other components, such as financing approaches or pricing strategies, were saved for later.

What happened? The four initiatives that transitioned to middle-of-the-pyramid markets wound up deemphasizing innovation in their business model development efforts. Instead, they envisioned only incremental changes to their existing business models and ended up focusing on execution, as in the World Shoe case. The nine launched initiatives that remained focused on BoP markets retained an innovation-oriented approach to their business model development efforts. Three of these initiatives relied on a comprehensive model, whereas the other six embraced a component approach.

For some impact enterprises, component innovation is a first, and perhaps key, step in developing a comprehensive business model suitable for the BoP context. If your team first tests using a component approach, that can provide insights into specific aspects of a business model. Moving to comprehensive innovation—in other words, implementing the full business model—is then likely to be smoother because you will have field-based experience with some aspects of the design.

Developing this type of phased approach to innovation can prove more challenging to start-ups, especially if they have not built this learning process into discussions with their funders and other stakeholders.[17] If they haven't allocated sufficient resources for business model innovation, they may be forced to test the full model, which may require innovating across multiple components simultaneously, an approach that likely will increase the difficulty of managing the innovation process.

The three approaches to business model development—business model execution, component business model innovation, and comprehensive business model innovation—required three different configurations of design variables to achieve launch. In all cases, aligning the four design variables introduced in Figure 2.1 was critical in determining the type and success of business model development. Certain configurations of design variables almost inevitably lead to a transition from BoP to middle-of-the-pyramid markets. The differences in the design variable configurations also determine whether a BoP initiative engaged in comprehensive or component innovation. And as the failed initiatives in my study demonstrated, initiatives that did not achieve an effective configuration did not launch.

Not unexpectedly, metrics and problem-solving strategies played an important role in determining the type of business model developed in these initiatives. Business model execution occurred with the combination of metrics that emphasized short-term growth and limited internal and external boundary spanning. These initiatives primarily accessed "impatient" capital and did not require structural protection. I stress that shifting in focus here from BoP to middle-of-the-pyramid markets shouldn't be considered a failure if that shift grows out of the business model development process and represents an informed assessment of a given enterprise's best chances for success. Some ideas are well suited for the BoP; others are not.

Both component and comprehensive business model innovation required learning-oriented metrics and high levels of external boundary spanning. Only comprehensive business model innovation, however, involved substantial internal boundary spanning. Because these initiatives were testing the full business model, their leadership was especially interested in connecting more closely with the rest of the company. Comprehensive business model innovation in particular also benefited from structural protection in the form of internal white space, not surprising given the high level of internal interactions.

A key lesson from this analysis is that enterprise leaders need to pay close attention not only to the individual design variables in the BMI framework but also to the integration among these variables. A mismatch between, for example, the level of internal boundary spanning and the amount of structural protection may lead to an initiative that can't deliver on its metrics.

A SECOND CASE IN POINT: CEMEX'S PATRIMONIO HOY

Now we'll look more deeply at the business model design challenge with a second BoP enterprise. This initiative was launched by a Mexican multinational CEMEX, which operates in what might seem like an unlikely sector for BoP entrepreneurship: the cement business.

CEMEX was founded in 1906 as a regional Mexican cement producer.[18] In 1996, with the acquisition of Colombia's Cementos Diamante and Samper Companies, CEMEX became the world's largest cement producer, and its 2005 acquisition of the U.K.-based RMC Group Plc made it one of the world's largest producers of ready-mix concrete. By 2013 CEMEX had revenues of over $15 billion. It was one of Mexico's largest companies and perhaps its most globally oriented, with operations in more than fifty countries and trade relationships in more than one hundred.[19]

Its BoP story begins during the Mexican economic crisis, which cut deeply into CEMEX's sales in Mexico.[20] At that time, the plunge in Mexican cement sales was particularly ominous for CEMEX, which derived some 60 percent of its total revenues in that market. The head of CEMEX-Mexico, Francisco Garza, asked his executive team to look behind the dismal numbers in all of their markets, in hopes of discovering some new path forward. As it turned out, one apparent answer could be found close to home. Although cement sales to major contractors had plummeted by as much as 50 percent, sales to low-income customers engaged in small-scale construction had fallen by only 10 to 20 percent.

Collectively these low-income customers were a force to be reckoned with. They built about half of Mexico's homes every year, with substantial room for growth. According to the Inter-American Development Bank, Mexico faced a 20 percent housing shortfall—meaning that 750,000 new homes a year needed to be built to catch up and keep up with the country's fast-growing population—and half of those homes would be built in the low-income, informal sector.[21]

Some 2 million low-income families, comprising about 10 million people, lived in *colonias populares* (unplanned, informal settlements surrounding Mexico's major cities). They accounted for as much as 25 percent of Mexico's urban population. They lived under crowded conditions—four or five people often sharing one- and two-room houses—and added onto those houses, often room by room, when time and money allowed.

An internal team led by Hector Ureta, head of the auto construction division, was appointed to learn more about this possible opportunity. It was created under and funded directly by CEMEX's corporate executive committee. Garda put the budding initiative within an internal white space, a protected place with time and resources to grow. To facilitate this, the team was located not in corporate headquarters in Monterrey but in Guadalajara, where the company had a much smaller presence and the team could more easily spend time in a BoP market context. Furthermore, the initiative was not expected to meet the company's short-term economic metrics. Rather, its initial task was to experiment with designing a business model that both addressed Mexico's critical social need for additional high-quality housing in low-income communities and would also make money for the company in what seemed like a potentially huge and profitable market. The initiative would continue only if it showed a path to profitability.

To hear the voices of customers, the team first turned to CEMEX's distributors.. What the team heard from them was not surprising: The cement market was ferociously competitive, pricing was everything, and there was no way for CEMEX to increase its market share. But it also became clear that because the distributors wanted to maintain their middleman role, they weren't necessarily telling CEMEX's team everything. As a result, the team decided to conduct its own in-field research.

Ureta realized that conventional business methods and mind-sets would be unlikely to help CEMEX forge stronger relationships with the low-income sector. He therefore urged his team to challenge their beliefs and—in a startling departure from the prevailing corporate culture—made a "declaration of ignorance" on behalf of himself and his colleagues. This was intended to signal to the residents of the colonias that the team knew that it understood almost nothing about life in those neighborhoods but that it was willing to learn. This was also an internal signal that allowed the team to establish success metrics based on learning and experimentation.

Team members began making extended trips to the colonias, talking to family members and community leaders. They learned, among other things, that local people added rooms to their homes in a relatively unplanned and inefficient manner. Home builders often took four to five years to add a room to their home, with 30 percent of the materials being wasted due to poor construction practices, theft, and spoilage from exposure to wind and rain.

The team's first response was to create a new product—a smaller, 25 kilogram bag of cement—on the theory that providing the product in smaller, lower-priced packages would increase sales as well as help prevent spoilage, waste, and theft. The product was a failure, in part because cost was only one part of the larger puzzle and because in the colonias, having large bags of cement outside one's house was a sign of prosperity.

After a second round of more intensive field-based research, CEMEX dramatically changed the nature of its initiative to more effectively respond to home-building challenges in the community, such as low levels of saving, lack of access to financing, limited construction knowledge and planning skills, and difficulty in accessing quality building materials. Rather than emphasizing selling cement, the goal now was to build new and expand existing houses with local partners (*socios*). To achieve this, the company offered financing—first providing funding through groups and later directly to individuals. It made installment plan payments simple by setting up service centers within the colonias. It also supplied appropriate materials at fixed prices and offered to store purchased materials until they were needed. And finally, it provided architectural advice, with an emphasis on helping the socios understand the full complement of building activities for each project. At this point, the parent company renamed the initiative Patrimonio Hoy (patrimony today), implying that socios could build today while investing for their future generations.

This model was continually refined over the next two years as the enterprise team engaged in business model innovation efforts. The result was a completely new business model within CEMEX. The parent company's main business focused on selling to fewer customers at high margins; Patrimonio Hoy, by contrast, emphasized selling to many customers at low margins.

By being based in Guadalajara rather than at corporate headquarters, the team could build deep relationships with the local community and their partners, a key aspect of their business model development success. As Ureta explained,

> You literally have to live over there, for them to see you that are you part [of the community]…you have to co-invent, to co-design with them. We did that. We spent almost two years adjusting our first version of the Patrimonio Hoy program…but we were co-inventing with them. Come over; have a fresh glass of Coke, some chips. With the women of the community, we would say why isn't this working? Why? They helped us to co-invent the whole thing.[22]

And the social performance? According to Patrimonio Hoy, the quality and functionality of the rooms and homes built by the socios improved as the time and cost associated with building went down. Local building time for a room declined from four years to one and a half. Socios enjoyed a 33 percent savings thanks to reduced spoilage and theft. The initiative has also received a number of awards for the social impact of its model and has generated substantial favorable press coverage for the company.

The business results were good as well. In 2004, Patrimonio Hoy reached breakeven and was self-sustaining. By 2011, the initiative served forty-five cities through Mexico and had revenues of $45 million. In 2014, Patrimonio Hoy had achieved national coverage, serving fifty-six cities across twenty-nine states. The program has since expanded into Colombia, Costa Rica, the Dominican Republic, and Nicaragua.[23] Over a decade of operations, it has served more than 450,000 families—some 2 million individuals. By selling an additional 60,000 tons of cement per year, the initiative also generated an incremental $6.5 million for CEMEX.[24] Patrimonio Hoy's current challenge is to achieve greater scale—a key focus in subsequent chapters of this book. But CEMEX continues to see Patrimonio Hoy as a profitable and valuable BoP impact enterprise and a successful effort at business model innovation.

LEARNING FROM THE REAL WORLD

We have looked in depth at two companies and seen how business model innovation efforts played out in their respective BoP experiences. Now I add one more company's real-world experiences to broaden our base for extrapolation. I'll call the company, a large pharmaceutical enterprise, Mondophysic.[25]

A few years back, I was invited to work with a team of top managers launching a new initiative at Mondophysic. Like others in the industry, Mondophysic focused on serving the top of the pyramid. The BoP faced a different set of health issues, and the company was not well positioned to address them. But the company saw the BoP as a new market opportunity that was worthy of further attention, and decided to invest several million dollars to build a team focused on creating commercially viable strategic approaches to serving the BoP.

The person tapped to lead the team appeared to be extremely well qualified for the job. She was a medical doctor who had worked for Mondophysic for a number of years and was well respected internally. Applications poured in from others around the company who were interested in joining the team. As a result, the team soon had skilled leaders from across several key disciplines within the company, including strategic planning, commercial procurement, information technology, new product access, accounting, and legal. Although this new team was attached to one of Mondophysic's major divisions and overseen by the president of that division, they were also given substantial freedom in terms of what they could do. Their metrics were purposely left relatively undefined, particularly in the short term. Over the long term, the initiative was expected to be profitable.

What could be better? They had money, a talented team, a strong connection to an interested business division, and freedom to explore. But it is what they *didn't* have that doomed the team. For one thing, the team itself—while extremely talented by internal standards—lacked members with deep knowledge about BoP markets and the development community and nonprofit organizations that served this segment. To their credit, they were quick to realize this and were soon en route to Africa and Asia in search of potential partners.

There, they met with a variety of reputable and well-recognized players and built initial collaborations with a number of them. But as it turned out, those relationships—and the associated problem-solving focus—were primarily one-sided, emphasizing the needs of their partners. Mondophysic, for example, provided much-needed equipment and resources to support a rural health center network. This was admirable in and of itself, of course, but when I asked the team what the purpose of this partnership was, the answers I got back were ambitious in scope but notably vague in detail. The value proposition of these partnerships, they told me, was to test a holistic business model to increase demand for health care services and combine provision of health care with access to quality drugs. This and other similar partnerships were about getting out into the field—learning what worked and what didn't and building skills and knowledge to support future endeavors.

Yes, getting out into the field was an important objective—especially for a team primarily based in the United States and with only limited experience in BoP markets—but it was not sufficient for these collaborations. I strongly encouraged the team to consider a more focused set of outcomes and recommended that they also clearly identify which aspects of a new business model they would be testing. We discussed how this could be designed into the projects.

Around the same time, the team was starting to feel some internal pressure to demonstrate progress. To avoid delays in implementation, they decided to continue with their initial set of projects as currently framed. But these projects were run and controlled by the partners. The company team made regular visits but didn't maintain their own people on the ground to absorb the lessons that were there to be discovered. The bigger issue was that they weren't learning enough about building a business model that would work for Mondophysic. Given the project design, as a team member later reflected, the partner was either not willing to collaborate, or was incapable of truly collaborating, on the co-creation of a new model.

Another lesson was clear, to me at least: The initiative's lack of clear metrics was actually causing a narrowing of focus rather than facilitating freedom of action. Having failed to define a clear set of learning metrics, the team had difficulty demonstrating progress against its mandate of developing a financial sustainable initiative targeting the BoP. While Mondophysic's top management continued to support the endeavor, they also wanted to know where the team was heading and how it was progressing toward those goals. Given their relatively limited knowledge of the space, the team was initially reluctant to put forward a set of learning-oriented metrics. But business, like nature, abhors a vacuum, and soon enough, metrics were being imposed on the team. Because of the team's close connection to the business division, these metrics increasingly began to emphasize revenues and profits.

As a result, the opportunity to learn and innovate was fast disappearing. The ongoing field-based projects weren't designed to provide a financial return or yield a clear-cut set of learning outcomes that might highlight a potential pathway to profitability. The team began to focus more intensively on shorter-term procurement-oriented opportunities that emphasized winning large tenders to provide substantial quantities of existing drugs to developing countries. This was more familiar territory, and the challenge became more oriented toward execution. But this increasing emphasis on execution—and the subordination of innovation—spelled the beginning of the end of efforts to create an innovative business model specifically designed to serve the BoP.

PUTTING IT ALL TOGETHER

What can we learn from the very different experiences of Nike, CEMEX, and Mondophysic?

The first point to stress is that the three companies started with very similar jumping-off points. All three were powerhouses in their respective fields. All three were dealing with stagnating or fluctuating sales in their primary markets, and all sought to cultivate a new market opportunity—low-income consumers in developing countries.

But that is where the similarities end. Their respective approaches to designing BoP-oriented business models could not have been more different, as summarized in Table 2.1. Looking back to the design variables introduced in the BMI Framework, it is easy to understand why Nike wound up with a middle-of-the-pyramid initiative, why CEMEX achieved what all three companies originally had hoped to achieve—the successful launch of a BoP

TABLE 2.1 Comparing business model innovation success

	Nike (World Shoe)	CEMEX (Patrimonio Hoy)	Mondophysic
Structure	Integrated closely with country operations	Protected; provided white space at corporate level	Protected; provided freedom within division
Metrics	Adopted traditional internal metrics; used established margins; focused on short-term returns	Avoided traditional internal metrics; developed long-term learning-oriented metrics	Avoided traditional internal metrics; did not develop specific learning-oriented metrics
Resources	Negotiated for piece of operating budget; team started with limited BoP knowledge; product and model based on top-of-the-pyramid expertise	Access to internal patient capital; team started with limited BoP knowledge; spent more than a year in local community	Access to internal patient capital; team started with limited BoP knowledge; regular visitors to local communities
Problem solving	Close formal connections internally; relied on familiar external partners	Informal internal connections; "declaration of ignorance;" co-designed business model with local partners	Informal internal connections; recognized "ignorance;" local partnerships focused on partners' problems
Outcome	Incremental change to existing business model; reached middle of the pyramid, but not in sufficient volume	Achieved business model innovation; developed a new and profitable business model focused on BoP	BoP business model did not come together; sought opportunities to win tenders using existing products

impact enterprise—and why Mondophysic wound up with a collection of short-term procurement opportunities.

Nike went with the incremental and the known and applied its traditional metrics to its World Shoe initiative, with the predictable result of incremental innovation and an emphasis on execution. CEMEX, by contrast, protected its

BoP impact enterprise, accessed patient capital, declared ignorance while also developing a clear set of learning-oriented objectives, and initially focused on testing components and then the full business model. The result was that the Patrimonio Hoy initiative was successful in its efforts at business model innovation. Similar to CEMEX, Mondophysic protected its BoP initiative, provided patient capital, and created freedom to innovate. With the best of intentions, the Mondophysic team recognized their "ignorance" and sought greater knowledge about the BoP market opportunity by entering into a set of new collaborations with local partners. Their metrics, however, remained relatively ambiguous, and the new problem-solving collaborations provided far more benefits to the partners than to the company.

Nike assumed that a technological solution would get the company most of the way toward a BoP success; CEMEX, after a false start or two, realized the importance of co-creating a business model with the BoP and its partners. Mondophysic learned a great deal about the BoP context but failed to acquire sufficient knowledge to address the challenges of developing a new business model. Part of the problem was mismatch between the time it took to learn and the team's metrics. As a senior Mondophysic leader later told me, "The window of management openness to try out things shut faster than we were able to get action off the ground. Our protection ended."[26]

There is a critical difference between good intentions and good outcomes. I underscore that all three of these companies were populated by good people with good intentions. All three companies had demonstrated the ability to grow and innovate in the past, which gave corporate leaders confidence as they approached the BoP context. But only CEMEX brought together the appropriate configuration of resources, structures, metrics, and problem solving tailored to facilitate innovation; it was the only one that could claim to have achieved success in business model R&D.

This brings us back to the opening premise of this chapter: that successful BoP impact enterprise development depends on innovation, and business model innovation in turn depends on effectively using the BMI framework by understanding how each internal design variable needs to be tailored to generate the right configuration. While there may be other influential variables that come to bear on specific enterprises, the BMI framework captures how to shape the four internal design variables most critical in achieving business model innovation and, ultimately, building an BoP impact enterprise. While the examples in this chapter compared multinational corporations' initiatives, this model applies to all types of BoP impact enterprises, ranging from entrepreneurial start-ups to new initiatives in large multinationals.

In fundamental ways, business model innovation in the BoP context is similar to the R&D process that sustains technological development in the middle and top of the pyramid: build the right team, seek protection from short-term financial metrics, pursue patient capital, and value innovation and the opportunity to develop and test new models—ideally learning as you go and remaining open to midcourse correction as new information becomes available.

Business model innovation and its associated R&D emphasis is a challenging undertaking in the BoP context. It requires careful attention to ensure that the initiative retains an innovation orientation in the face of internal and external pressures that emphasize execution. It uses metrics that reward both generating learning and demonstrating progress toward economic viability. Problem solving is accomplished with a cast of often unfamiliar characters from outside the organization who generally have their own set of problems to solve. Perhaps most challenging, it requires humility—a declaration of ignorance—about what we don't know that helps enable the enterprise team to embrace and retain an innovation orientation.

Hard and complicated work? Yes—but tailoring the four internal design variables to shape the right business model is well worth the effort, because it sets you up for success in achieving sustainability and scalability. Indeed, the decision to launch an initiative is just the beginning of the journey. Innovation and learning continue as the initiative—the BoP impact enterprise "in the making," if you will—moves through subsequent stages of development, the topic of the next chapter.

3 BUILDING FOR SCALE

Scaling—growth based on an economically sustainable business model—is the stage of evolution in which all too many BoP impact enterprises come up short. While we see many pilots launched, few of these achieve sustainability and scalability.[1] Pilots and small-sized ventures are fine in and of themselves and can have important local impacts and generate useful insights into opportunities for innovation. But without a path to scale, these efforts will not attract sizable investments, and they are unlikely to play a substantial role in poverty alleviation.[2]

In Chapter 2, I introduced the BMI Framework, aimed at helping BoP impact enterprises create the configuration of internal design variables needed to develop innovative business models for the BoP context. In this chapter, we look at the strategies and skills that these enterprises must develop in order to move from planning to piloting to scaling.

Given the magnitude of the opportunity, with trillions of dollars in transactions by BoP consumers and producers annually in the balance, scaling is obviously an attractive business strategy.[3] And in light of the magnitude of the challenge—billions of people in the BoP facing poverty on a daily basis—scaling is an imperative for the development community. Finally, we have seen good evidence, in industries ranging from mobile phones to agriculture, that scaling and achieving the BoP promise is possible.[4]

We have enough experience now to know how to build better BoP impact enterprises.[5] What has been missing to date is the identification and articulation of a set of strategies that can help enterprise leaders enhance the likelihood of building sustainable, scalable enterprises. I have identified three key strategic imperatives that can increase the likelihood of enterprise sustainability and scalability. These imperatives apply across different business models, industry sectors, and geographies. Of course, the specific details on execution vary according to specific circumstances, but the core principles remain consistent.

The three imperatives, which I call the "C-I-E scaling strategies," are co-creating, innovating, and embedding, as depicted in Figure 3.1. Each of these imperatives consists of two scaling strategies that are particularly valuable in different parts of the development journey. Understanding and executing against each these six scaling strategies can help any enterprise better achieve sustainable growth. Of course, additional strategies can be called into play, but these six are the critical jumping-off points that are particularly relevant to BoP impact enterprises. Figure 3.1 also points to the importance of assessing, ensuring, and enhancing mutual value creation, respectively, as the enterprises embraces each of the strategic imperatives. (I leave a detailed discussion of this key theme until Chapter 4.)

Although I portray the C-I-E scaling imperatives in a linear way to highlight the direction to head in, this process may become an iterative one for many BoP impact enterprises. Enterprise leaders may find that the outcomes from innovations in the piloting stage, for example, may require further co-creation. Similarly, results from efforts to scale may point to a need for additional innovation and more piloting. Depending on the scope of their activities, an enterprise also can be engaged in multiple stages across different operating contexts. Furthermore, while the framework presents each of the scaling strategies separately, they constantly overlap and reinforce each other. But to generalize, in different stages of enterprise development, different scaling imperatives and associated strategies tend to predominate.

CO-CREATE: ENVISIONING THE BOP IMPACT ENTERPRISE

Co-creating means what its name implies: working with others to invent solutions and create value.[6] It emphasizes the importance of engaging, connecting, and empowering customers, suppliers, and local partners to jointly create a value proposition. Co-creation takes patience and a willingness to collaborate. This perspective is well captured by an old African proverb: If you want to go fast, go alone; if you want to go far, go together.[7] Co-creation

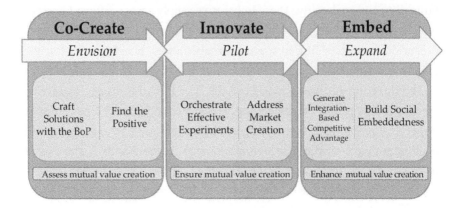

FIGURE 3.1 Co-Create, Innovate, and Embed scaling strategies

also emphasizes that in driving a successful outcome, it matters not only who is engaged but also how they are engaged. In BoP markets, this issue of "how" becomes especially relevant. In particular, this involves how we frame our interactions with the BoP and interpret the market environment in which our transactions with the BoP will occur.

Crafting Solutions with the Base of the Pyramid

When serving higher-income markets, most enterprise leaders recognize and value the insights of their customers, as evidenced by their intensive focus on lead users, focus groups, user communities, and other similar data-gathering approaches.[8] BoP markets, in which market data are often very limited, would seem a natural location for substantial interaction with local customers, suppliers, and entrepreneurs. Yet this is rarely the case.

Certainly access to the BoP is challenging, but that doesn't seem to be the main stumbling block for most enterprises. Rather, it is that BoP impact enterprise leaders and their team often carry a set of embedded—and incorrect— assumptions about the BoP and their ability to co-create with the enterprise team: They don't value the voices of the BoP. As a result, they don't engage these individuals (and the markets they represent) in ongoing and meaningful ways, which necessarily means that the BoP are not active participants in the crafting of the enterprise's products, services, and business models.

To envision the enterprise, business leaders must truly respect the BoP community and view them as key contributors—and indeed, business partners—in the development of the budding enterprise. Their shared goal must be to develop a local relevant value proposition based on a deep understanding of desired functionalities and unmet opportunities and to shape a business that conforms to that understanding.[9] To illustrate this point, let's first conjure up the opposite circumstance in a scenario that features you and me as its central players. Although the scenario is fictional in its details, it is an all-too-common reality in the field.

We start the day in our four-star hotel in, say, Nairobi. After a hearty breakfast, we get in our Land Rover and head out to the field. The traffic is heavy, and it takes a while to get out of the city. We then stick to the main roads, since going off-road adds considerable travel time. Eventually we arrive at a previously identified local community that we feel is representative of those we want to work with. Our arrival doesn't go unnoticed; in fact, it soon becomes clear that we are today's center of attention. We are surrounded by people who seem excited to see us, and we are escorted to the local leader's house.

Feeling as if we now have to do something to justify all this attention, we settle into our chairs, exchange pleasantries, and fairly quickly launch into a description of the proposed enterprise. Over the course of the next hour or so, we carefully explain what we propose to do and why this will be a good thing for the community. Our local translator helps out as needed.

While we are rarely interrupted, a few comments and questions do come up, especially early in the conversation. We are very pleased to be able to quickly demonstrate that we have already considered these issues and detail how we have appropriate embedded solutions in our business model. To ensure a good dialogue, every once in a while, we ask, "Well, how does this sound?" People nod and smile, and say, "Yes, yes; that sounds good."

As we wrap up our description, we notice that it's starting to get late. Since we don't want to be traveling after dark, it's time to head back to our hotel in the city. Before leaving, though, we do a final check-in with the community: "Do you have any final thoughts to offer us to improve our business model?" The polite response is that the community appreciates our interest in them and looks forward to the launch of the enterprise. Our hosts wave good-bye as we settle into the Land Rover for the long ride home. Back on the main road, we shake hands all around and congratulate each other: "Success! We have shared our business model, heard the voices of the BoP, and they support our approach."

I think you see my point: Designing a business model from afar and then looking to secure local support is a flawed approach. For one thing, the power dynamics are out of balance, strongly favoring the perspective of the enterprise team. They will be the ones who decide whether and how to engage. And this approach is really geared toward seeking approval, not feedback. Yet it is a trap that all too many BoP impact enterprises still fall into, even if their particular scenarios are not as exaggerated as the example. If we were serving the top of the pyramid, we would never develop a model without a robust conversation with potential customers and suppliers. We must instead ask: How are we viewing and treating our future consumers, producers, entrepreneurs, and partners? Do we have sufficient humility? And what approaches can we adopt that better enable us to co-create a business model with the base of the pyramid and other key local stakeholders?

In response, I offer two core activities to engage in to successfully craft solutions with the BoP: ensure that our perspective of the BoP is based on respect and dialogue, and establish interaction guidelines for collaborating with them (see Figure 3.2).

To check the perspective, we must first surface any embedded assumptions—preconceptions that you bring to the table, consciously or subconsciously. To see what I mean, take a moment to try this exercise: What are the first three words that come into your mind when you think about the base of the pyramid? Have these in your mind before you read further.

Are they words like *poor, isolated, undereducated, underresourced,* or *disorganized*? All of these words point toward what the BoP doesn't have. But when the focus is on what a person or a group doesn't have, our tendency is to reach out—to "help" them. While laudably empathetic, this is fundamentally the wrong approach for co-creation. If we are here to "help" the BoP, that suggests we know what to do. It also sets up a relationship in which we are the experts, and they are the lucky recipients of our expertise. We are the benefactors and they are the beneficiaries.

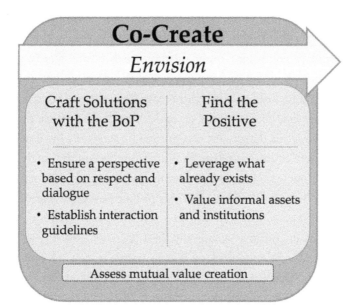

FIGURE 3.2 Co-Create: scaling strategies

Think again about words to describe the BoP. How about instead *intelligent, ingenious, thoughtful,* and *creative*? In my experience, this is a much more accurate framing of the BoP, and it's a framing that you can act on. As Hector Ureta from CEMEX's Patrimonio Hoy said, "The base of the pyramid are always in the optimal corner of the solution."[10] Fundamentally, you can't engage in the co-creation of opportunities if you believe that you are the sole or main source of wisdom. You have to recognize that the people who comprise the BoP are as intelligent as you are and have much to contribute to the process as advisors, colleagues, and partners. They can't do it without you, and you can't do it without them.

This is a shared endeavor, neither top-down nor bottom-up. The BoP must participate in developing your value proposition and can provide expert advice on key product and service functionalities, as well as critical insights on building a viable business model. As such, enterprise leaders must adopt a perspective of respect and dialogue at the earliest stages of envisioning what their venture will be.

A second critical core activity is to set interaction guidelines for how the enterprise will co-create with the BoP. Too many enterprises claim they are actively collaborating with the BoP, when in fact their interactions look much like my example that highlighted the difference between seeking approval and encouraging feedback. To put substance behind the words, I strongly encourage the enterprise leadership to carefully develop, and then clearly present, these guidelines to their entire team, regardless of whether they are local or international. Just because someone is from the host country doesn't necessarily mean this person respects or even understands the BoP.

This may seem counterintuitive: They are from the country, so the assumption is that of course they understand their less privileged fellow citizens. Not necessarily! When I'm challenged on this point by enterprise leaders, I tend to ask them, "Exactly how well do you know the inner-city residents or the rural poor in your country?" Generally the answer is, "Not very well." Think back to CEMEX's Patrimonio Hoy BoP initiative to develop housing solutions in Mexico. That enterprise began to gain traction only when its leaders made a declaration of ignorance.

Of course, the enterprise leadership team can and should choose interaction guidelines that work best for their team. When asked for advice, I recommend the three interrelated approaches: Be patient, stay longer, and come back.[11] These guidelines put an appropriate focus on the commitment, depth, and length of the interaction, and there are several payoffs to following them. The first, of course, is the recognition that it takes time and effort to develop a relationship based on trust and honest dialogue. The second is the fact that trust building can occur only over extended interactions. When you take the time to listen and learn, you are demonstrating respect, the foundation for developing a shared understanding.[12]

Finally, if you are not there on a regular basis, you don't know what you don't know. (Think of it as school: If you miss a class, you can't know for sure what you missed.) Just being there generates learning opportunities. Relationships built on commitment, respect, and a shared sense of purpose offer a strong foundation for co-creating in BoP markets. Your whole team has to embrace this perspective, and that is why having explicit guidelines for interaction is so crucial.

Finding the Positive

While developing meaningful and long-term relationships based on co-creation is critical in framing individual and organizational interactions, BoP impact enterprise leaders must also carefully consider how they assess the local context. Refer again to Figure 3.2. To adopt a co-creation perspective about the local context, enterprise leaders must focus on seeking out the good—in other words, finding the positive.

In all too many cases, enterprise leaders entering BoP markets spend a lot of time talking about the problems they may encounter: "There is no contract enforcement." "There are no property rights." "There is no rule of law." "How can I possibly operate in such an informal setting?" Perhaps it would better, they say, to wait until the market develops further or to seek out markets that are more formal and more familiar.

While that approach might seem to make sense, it also carries with it two embedded assumptions. The first is that these market environments generally have insufficient assets to support enterprise development, and the second is that the development trajectory of these markets is toward a more familiar, Western-style model. Neither of these assumptions is necessarily realistic, and in any case, they preclude a more productive approach to assessing opportunity. Rather than focusing on what is not there, I always encourage people to stand this approach on its head and instead ask, "What is here now?" This framing then becomes the basis for co-creating within the local context.

For example, taking my cue from Peruvian economist Hernando De Soto, who writes thoughtfully on the subject of property rights, I ask those "mindset-challenged" entrepreneurs if they've ever walked around in at night in any the rural communities they propose to work with.[13] If so, what did they hear on that walk? The answer, almost certainly, is dogs—lots of barking dogs. I often heard them when I was working in Malawi and Indonesia. And what's interesting is that as I walked down a road past a house, first one pack of dogs would raise a racket. As I went farther along the street and came to another home, that first pack of dogs would stop barking, and another one would start up. Even in the informal economy of BoP markets, in other words, there are recognized lines of demarcation. Be assured: If the dogs know the property boundaries, then, by analogy, so does the community.

The people in those neighborhoods understand a lot about local social, legal, and ethical boundaries. The BoP may not be able to invoke their "property rights" in the same way that you can in a more developed market—mainly due to the lack of formal recognition and enforcement mechanisms—but they are attuned to where those boundaries are. Just because you can't see local institutions doesn't mean they aren't there. This implies two core activities for finding what is right: emphasize leveraging what exists, rather than fixing what does not, and value informal, as well as formal, assets and institutions as opportunities for co-creation.

An interesting and familiar example comes from the field of microfinance. Many microloan programs targeting the BoP often rely on group lending and peer pressure to help ensure loan repayment. If one person in the group defaults, no one else in that group is eligible for a future loan. In other words, instead of depending on the kinds of physical collateral that are often lacking in these markets, microfinance relies on social collateral, which is often abundant. It works. When used in low-income markets in the developing world, this approach to collateralization has created excellent payback rates that can match those of banks in the developed world.[14]

CARE, PEACE, and Pioneer: Seeds to India

With these frameworks and guidelines in mind, let's take a sustained look at a concrete example of co-creating a business that involved figuring out a way to get high-productivity seeds into the hands of village farmers in India.

Although domestic agriculture is critical to sustaining India's huge population, currently estimated at over 1.2 billion people, farming in that country can be a tenuous occupation.[15] Landholdings are typically small, which limits incomes. These smallholder farmers are generally compelled to borrow at high rates of interest to purchase supplies for the growing season. Often lacking effective means of irrigation, they depend heavily on favorable weather.

All of these factors combine to leave little margin for error and reduce the farmers' willingness to explore investments that might have the potential to increase output but only by increasing risk. The stakes are high: The failure of any input (seasonal rains, seeds, fertilizers, or prices) can trigger disaster. The more they invest prior to harvest, the more they stand to lose if the harvest fails. If disaster strikes, the farmer may have to sell some of his or her few assets, such as livestock, a tremendous setback. If they can't pay off the loan, their opportunity to borrow money for farm inputs in the next season is greatly diminished. In the most severe situations, these farmers commit suicide.[16]

One chronic challenge for Indian farmers is low productivity, and that is often the result of low-quality seeds. In traditional Indian agriculture, seeds from the previous harvest are set aside and planted the following year. This process is often managed on the community level, with village "specialists" identifying the best seeds from the harvest and farmers then bartering with their neighbors to procure those seeds. The community-based system was reasonably predictable and reliable, and although it had its limits, especially in terms of productivity, it was in many ways preferable to purchasing commercial seeds, which—while promising higher productivity—were more costly and in recent decades had been plagued by counterfeit products.

Into this setting came what seemed like a strong trio of partners: an international nongovernmental organization (NGO), an India-based nonprofit, and a major U.S. seed manufacturer. The NGO was CARE, an international relief and development organization that operates in more than seventy countries around the world, fighting poverty and promoting economy opportunity through self-help efforts.[17] CARE had been in India since 1950 and through its work in eleven Indian states knew the key players well. The Indian nonprofit that CARE partnered with on the seed project was PEACE (People's Action for Creative Education), founded in 1986 to help India's rural poor, and more recently a source of microfinance for women in self-help groups (SHGs) in more than one hundred Indian villages.[18] The SHGs from multiple villages are aggregated into mutually aided cooperative societies (MACs), legal entities that enable SHGs and other groups to enter into agreements with partners from the commercial and social sectors.

The seed manufacturer was the U.S.-based Pioneer Hi-Bred International, since 1997 a subsidiary of chemical giant Dow and a seller of seeds in nearly seventy countries. In a typical year, Pioneer's revenues were on the order of $3 billion, and its R&D expenditures (in its ninety research facilities worldwide) approached $600 million.

In a complex sequence of events, CARE facilitated a partnership between Pioneer and PEACE whereby Pioneer seeds would be introduced to the villagers through PEACE. That process should have been a great opportunity for co-creation—but it didn't always turn out that way. In envisioning the initiative, representatives from CARE, Pioneer, and PEACE would meet with the local SHGs, with the leaders of the relevant MAC also in attendance. But the dialogue was constrained by the fact that although women are the primary focus of the SHGs and are often the sole or primary receivers of microcredit, men tend to make the important choices pertaining to their farms. Further complicating things, women often will not speak openly in the presence of men. In some cases, moreover, the MAC representatives, who ranked higher in the social structure, tended to dominate the discussion. Finally, key local stakeholders who played an important role in farming activities, such as distributors and buyers, were not actively engaged in the conversation.

Recognizing the challenges associated with testing the entire model, Pioneer decided to provide the seeds for free to PEACE to make initial pilots more feasible. This allowed PEACE considerable flexibility in responding to the financial constraints that local farmers face. As it turned out, PEACE decided it was inappropriate to set a precedent of free seeds. Instead, it charged farmers a close-to-market price for the seeds they agreed to take, but it didn't require repayment until after the crops were harvested. This pricing approach put Pioneer's products above those of the Indian seed manufacturers, a strategy that would work in the long term only if Pioneer's seeds outperformed those of its Indian competitors.

The implementation of the project was plagued by difficulties—problems that I ascribe to an inadequate level of crafting solutions with the BoP. For example, farmers felt that they had to buy at least some of their seeds from local merchants because they were dependent on those same merchants for a host of other goods and services: fertilizers, pesticides, seeds, credit, marketing of crops, and so on. If they stopped buying seeds from these distributors, there was a very real threat that these merchants would not sell them the other supplies they needed. Even so, the incomes of those local merchants did drop, and retaliation against the farmers was not uncommon.

The partners also did not account for the positive in the co-creation process. The local farmers had been surviving for generations, albeit with some clear limitations, using the existing farming model. Encouraging change would require a clear demonstration of the benefits of the new seeds. Assessing the program, however, turned out to be complicated. Without many demonstration gardens, measurable changes in productivity would mainly come from the farmers themselves. In some cases, the seeds arrived behind schedule. Some farmers hedged their bets, using seed from more than one source, and since many of these farmers declined to separate the two crops, head-to-head productivity comparisons were not easy to make. In some cases, the monsoon season was late in coming; in others, heavy rains washed away the crops, thus ending the experiment. Anecdotally, it appeared that the Pioneer products outperformed their local competitors, but the outcomes and the associated feedback to the farmers were mixed. After the first year of piloting, not much progress had been made.

To the partners' credit, they responded well and redesigned the initiative with a greater focus on co-creation with the local community and the local context. But a year had been lost, and without sufficient resources and a longer-term commitment by the partners, the initiative could have easily ended then.

INNOVATE: PILOTING IDEAS IN THE MARKETPLACE

The co-creation process is about the BoP impact enterprise team appreciating and leveraging the capabilities of the BoP and the assets of the market environment around them. The outcome, when successful, is a collaborative vision of the value proposition that a scalable and sustainable enterprise can generate and how it will deliver on this promise.

These co-creation efforts are a process of invention. Key information is shared, learning occurs, and new ideas are crafted. At this stage, the second strategy in the C-I-E Framework, innovation becomes crucial as we take what was invented during co-creation and apply in the BoP marketplace.[19]

While we might be justifiably proud of the novel ideas envisioned during the co-creation process, the likelihood that the initial designs are right on target is quite low, as demonstrated in the global seeds case. Furthermore, there are almost surely pieces of the business model that we still need to better understand. The challenge is to innovate in a productive and useful way. I should note that while innovation takes prominence as we move into a piloting stage, the enterprise should continue to interact, share learnings, and co-create with the local community, as well as seek to better understand the local context. In addition, pilots should be developed with an eye toward the strategies that become critical in the scaling stage, and that means examining the opportunities for generating integration-based competitive advantage and building a capability in social embeddedness as part of the outcomes of the pilot.

I divide the innovation imperative into two elements: orchestrating effective experiments and addressing market creation (Figure 3.3). The former focuses on the enterprise itself and the latter on the environment in which the enterprise will operate.

Orchestrating Effective Experiments

Enterprises can test all their business model or just parts of it. Yet many enterprise leaders fail to truly understand that innovation involves learning and possibly failure. Furthermore, too few enterprise leaders recognize that innovation is a process of experimentation that should be effectively managed. They assume that they can avoid most of the pain of innovation and learning, either because they believe their pilot is actually ready or nearly ready for scale or because they don't appreciate the importance of understanding how to conduct effective experiments.

My research on BoP impact enterprises indicates that effective experimentation relies on three enabling principles. The first is a clear articulation of what will be learned through experimentation. When I work with a company at this stage, I start by asking a series of pointed and interconnected questions: What exactly will we be learning? What hypothesis are we going to test? How will we know whether we are successful? What organizations should we partner with in this effort, and why? In which locations should we conduct this experiment?

It's amazing to me how many businesses get far down the road on their learning journey without good answers to these basics. I hear comments like, "Well, this organization stepped forward, so we went with them." Or, "This potential partner was well known, and we wanted to get them to support us." Or, "I'm relying on my partner to structure and oversee how this is rolled out in the field."

FIGURE 3.3 Innovate: scaling strategies

"So," I tend to respond, "how are you going to learn what you need to know if you don't carefully track both the design and implementation of your field-based pilot activities?"

The second enabling principle for effective experimentation is valuing and managing failure. Successfully testing specific hypotheses requires truly embracing the concept of learning, which means recognizing and benefiting from failure. To increase its chances of success, the enterprise may well want to plan a series of integrated experiments, designed to test the viability of various aspects or iterations of the design, and expect varying degrees of success during this journey—the approach that CEMEX turned to.

Here, some terminology may prove helpful as we proceed. It is important to clearly distinguish between a pilot and a project. A *pilot* is an initiative that is consciously designed as a learning vehicle. Pilots may not survive the test of time, and that is okay. The idea is to generate a process of trial-and-error that leads the team toward a more viable initiative, and this requires having metrics in place that value learning. In his book on lean start-ups, Eric Ries highlights the value of fast experimentation and associated learning and argues that these efforts should be carefully managed, which includes having the right metrics in place.[20] Through these efforts, companies are committing to learning, but not necessarily to the specific pilots they have launched.

A *project*, by contrast, is a commitment on the part of the sponsoring company to a particular activity that it will continue investing in for an extended amount of time. In many cases, projects are philanthropic in nature, designed to deliver social outcomes based on a fixed or an ongoing source of funding. These types of philanthropic projects are certainly admirable, but they are not specifically designed to produce learnings or to end if the learning opportunity ends. In projects, implementation overshadows experimentation.

So in theory at least, there is an important and useful distinction between pilot and project. In the real world, and certainly in the world of BoP impact enterprise development, the danger is that even without a conscious or explicit decision, pilots can morph into projects. Escalation of commitment or a misplaced sense of obligation can cause enterprise leaders to prop up well-intended pilots that are failing. Maybe the leadership has either invested so much in the pilot personally and professionally that they find it difficult to stop. Or maybe they feel committed to delivering the social benefits that a pilot-turned-project can deliver. Piloting, however, is not about achieving social responsibility goals; rather, it is a step on the journey toward creating a BoP impact enterprise that is sustainable at scale. Turning a learning-oriented pilot into a commitment-oriented project—which, by tying up financial and managerial resources, prevents investment in other, more viable ideas—can be counterproductive on many levels. Enterprise leaders must recognize the difference and act accordingly.

What makes a good pilot is purposeful planning, correctly valuing failure, and assessing and managing risks. Being purposeful means clearly articulating the goals of the pilot. These should be about successful experimentation, not sustained impact. Correctly valuing failure means that success is measured by opportunities for learning, as discussed in Chapter 2. Your metrics must support your innovation goals. You work with your team and local partners to avoid inappropriate escalation of commitment, maximize the value of learnings, minimize the allocation of blame, and ultimately act on what is discovered during the pilot to create a more viable enterprise with impact.

Something that may—indeed, should—be troubling you is the idea that we are "experimenting on the BoP." This is fundamentally the wrong perspective. We experiment *with* the BoP, and never *on* the BoP. This requires that enterprise leaders understand and manage the risks present in their piloting efforts, and it leads to the third enabling principle for orchestrating effective experiments: ensuring a soft landing for the BoP when the experiment ends.[21] This does create some particular challenges for BoP impact enterprise leaders because some risks may not be known or predicted at the launch of the pilot. Clearly, there are some ethical issues here, which means a need to take a closer look at how to explicitly manage risk inherent in experimenting.

Experimentation has to involve the BoP, but it can't be done at the expense of the BoP. They simply don't have the resources to absorb any undesirable outcomes generated by the experiment. In developing a pilot, the enterprise leaders must seek to assess the full risk profile. This includes assessing what types of risks may be generated, who owns them, how big they could be, and how likely they are to occur. The entire risk profile, including what value is likely to be created and who will own what risk should be presented to all partners, especially those from the BoP, to ensure full transparency. This kind of dialogue can also surface previously unrecognized risks. This risk profile should then be managed so that the burden of any failure falls to the enterprise or a partner, not to the BoP. This includes taking ownership of any unexpected negative outcomes that may occur.[22]

If local partners or communities are required to take substantial risks in support of the pilot, which by its very nature is a risky proposition, the enterprise must consider what type of safety net to provide in the case of failure. Encouraging local entrepreneurs to take out a loan or asking local leaders to invest their social capital can have substantial negative local impacts if the pilot proves unsuccessful. Enterprise leaders must be able to articulate how they plan to manage or minimize these types of risks. If, for example, loans are required, there could well be a covenant in the loan agreement stating that if the enterprise fails or withdraws, the local entrepreneur's responsibility for paying off that loan is limited.

Oxfam America and its partners in Ethiopia faced a challenge like this while piloting a microinsurance initiative for local farmers. The initiative sought to help farmers deal with climate-related risk by combining risk-reduction activities (e.g., irrigation) with risk transfer (through microinsurance) and prudent risk taking (through the provision of credit).[23]

In the initial pilot, uptake rates were strong, suggesting that the index-based crop insurance program could be a viable approach. Yet when a crop loss on the part of one group of farmers failed to trigger the relevant index, meaning no payments would be forthcoming to the affected farmers by the partner insurance companies, the entire enterprise faced a critical decision point. Because the design of the index was still in an experimental stage, Oxfam America decided to make a one-time voluntary donation to the affected farmers. In other words, it rewarded the farmers for taking prudent risks and then held them harmless when an unexpected negative outcome in the model surfaced.

In another example, Procter & Gamble (P&G) ran a series of pilot programs in Guatemala, the Philippines, and Pakistan to test a water purification system called PUR, often in partnership with the U.S. Centers for Disease Control and Prevention (CDC). As it developed the PUR venture, P&G carefully considered the implications of ending the trial at each phase of the piloting process. In particular, the company worked with its partners to set initial expectations among all stakeholders and ensured that each pilot concluded in an orderly and well-considered manner. The CDC, highly sensitive to generating any negative local impacts, continued to partner with P&G only because the company was so careful in accessing and managing risk.

Over time, it became clear that the business couldn't be made to stand on its own legs. Despite substantial investments in marketing and a demonstrably effective product, repurchase rates weren't high enough to justify further investments in trying to build a commercial enterprise. At that point, P&G's leaders made a consensus choice. They explicitly recognized the remaining challenges they faced in creating a sustainable, scalable impact enterprise and decided to transition from running pilots to managing a project. And of course, there is nothing inherently wrong with adopting a donation-based model focused on providing clean water to children in the developing world. Renamed the Children's Safe Drinking Water program, the project works with seventy partners in fifty countries to improve health and quality of life of the BoP.[24]

Addressing Market Creation

Most enterprises seeking to serve BoP markets won't find a fortune waiting to be unearthed.[25] Instead, these enterprises will most likely have to play an active role in fortune creating, which requires enterprise leaders to look beyond the enterprise and learn how to build the market opportunity.

In other words, to succeed, enterprises engaging in innovation must expand their focus beyond designing products, providing services, and developing business models. Their pilots must also address the issue of market creation, which can require innovative approaches to increasing consumer demand, reducing transactions costs with suppliers, and facilitating development of and access to public goods. Success in BoP markets requires not only building a viable enterprise but also understanding the need to improve the market environment that surrounds the enterprise. The enterprise leadership must consider a broader portfolio of investment requirements and, in so doing, explore prospects for accessing some of these resources from a diverse set of partners.

It has been argued that enterprises pursuing new market opportunities can adopt a finding perspective or a creating perspective.[26] The difference has substantial implications for how entrepreneurial ventures proceed, including (as discussed in Chapter 2) the resources, structures, metrics, and problem-solving approaches that they embrace. In adopting a finding perspective, an enterprise's leadership team assumes that while the market exists, a particular opportunity within that market may remain undiscovered. Once an observant entrepreneur or firm identifies the opportunity, the key is to develop the missing technology or the desired product. Next, the focus shifts from innovation to execution. From there, standard business development approaches apply. A guiding assumption is that the opportunity exists independent of the actions of the team or the enterprise.

Market creation requires a very different perspective. In adopting this view, the BoP impact enterprise team sees itself as needing to actively participate not only in providing the technology, product, or service but also in bringing forth the market for this new offering. How do you equip yourself to innovate from the perspective of market creation? The answer is to put on new lenses and think about piloting more creatively. The challenge lies in looking beyond the enterprise and seeing what other investments are needed. Market creation requires more than just innovation within the enterprise. The enterprise must also consider how to build a more enterprise-friendly market environment.

In BoP markets, the difference between adopting a finding or a creating perspective is particularly stark. The first core activity seems obvious—understanding who the competition is—but impact enterprise leaders often perform this poorly in the pilot stage. In BoP markets, the competition may not always be other enterprises; the competition may be the status quo. If an enterprise team claims to have no competitors, my first reaction is skepticism. At the very least, enterprises will have to change existing behaviors and consumption patterns. For example, an enterprise offering clean water to a local community might claim no other firms are making this same offering and thus there are no competitors. That could be true, but community members may well consider their existing water supply as sufficient or perhaps are boiling it to clean it. The enterprise must create awareness of the benefits of their offering as compared to the competition, which in this case is the status quo. Otherwise, the chances for success are minimal.

Once competition is identified, assessing the need for market creation is the next crucial step. As illustrated in the example of clean water, the market for a technology, product, or service doesn't necessarily exist in any organized form. Just because the enterprise teams identify a need—at least from their perspective—doesn't necessarily mean that a corresponding market exists.[27] In many cases, market awareness and demand may not yet be sufficiently developed for the BoP to consider transacting with the enterprise.

Even if awareness exists, the BoP may not have sufficient disposable income to create adequate demand for the product. While the BoP may need little education about the dangers of malaria, they still may lack the resources to afford the mosquito bed net or indoor residual spraying that can reduce transmission.

Impact enterprises seeking to serve BoP producers also can face market creation issues.[28] BoP producers can be unaware of or unable to take advantage of new channels to sell their goods. Without an investment in information sharing, for instance, local farmers may not realize that alternative markets exist and may not understand what they need to do to meet buyer expectations in terms of quality and quantity. Even if farmers are interested in participating in a new channel, a failure to address local infrastructure constraints may prevent these BoP producers from capitalizing on the perceived opportunity.

When these kinds of opportunities for market creation present themselves, BoP impact enterprises must consider both the short- and long-term implications. The short term is about exploring different approaches to market creation. The long term requires careful consideration about how to scale the proposed solutions. Optimally the enterprise has budgeted sufficient resources to invest in these innovations, but that often does not occur. Furthermore, the leadership must understand the cost structure of taking these piloted market creation efforts to scale.

A crucial challenge here is that most investments in market creation become common goods that other enterprises can leverage. For example, if potential customers do not understand the link between dirty water and disease, a water purification enterprise must invest in creating awareness. Even if this investment is focused on building a brand, the enterprise may well struggle to build a loyal customer following in BoP markets, where the switching costs are low.[29]

For all these reasons and more, enabling innovation in market creation generally requires finding one or more partners that are already on the ground, have local expertise, and are open to providing support and access to resources. In many cases, these potential partners do exist and may well be interested in working with a BoP impact enterprise.[30] There may be local nonprofits or community-based organizations looking for new ways to support the individuals with whom they are working, or international development community actors interested in exploring market-based approaches to alleviating poverty.

Seeking field-based partners, particularly from the development sector, to support the pilot's market-creation efforts offers at least three benefits. The first is that costs can be shared, making piloting efforts more efficient. Second, these partners may know quite a bit about developing effective awareness and behavior change campaigns that can result in more effective experimentation. And finally, the enterprise leadership should gain a better understanding of the development community's willingness to support awareness efforts and their skills to do.

Kenya-based honey producer Honey Care Africa recognized early the need for market creation and leveraged several partnerships to address this challenge.[31] The company first focused on understanding why beekeeping was not a thriving local business, and what it and its partners could do about this. Recognizing both a lack of demand and ineffective access to production inputs, Honey Care's market creation efforts targeted the BoP as both producers and consumers. To encourage production of honey, the company's pilot business model was to create a guaranteed market for local beekeepers. It established a "money for honey" program, whereby it committed to buying all the locally produced honey from company-supplied hives at a fixed minimum price. Honey Care was able to initiate this program thanks to support from several development sector collaborators. Collecting honey directly from the producers in convenient locations and also paying on the spot helped catalyze local interest in supplying honey to the enterprise.

At the same time, the enterprise introduced the Langstroth hive into the region, a ground-level hive design that makes beekeeping easier and more accessible to women and helped local farmers learn how to use it.[32] Given that this "new" hive and associated technologies were more expensive than existing hives (which were made out of logs, baskets, clay pots, and similar materials), Honey Care developed partnerships with local nonprofit organizations to provide the financing, awareness, and training. These partners were asked to provide microfinancing to prospective beekeepers, subsidize training courses—which were a prerequisite to receiving the financing—and monitor local honey production. Such efforts helped ensure that the local beekeepers could provide the quality and quantity of honey needed to meet market expectations.

In short, Honey Care reinvigorated a market opportunity for a neglected product that had existed for a long time. The results included doubling the income of BoP farmers, providing a far higher-quality honey to the Kenyan market, and demonstrating that innovation focused on market creation could create a model that rewarded both local farmers and partner institutions for their investments in Honey Care.

A second example of market creation in the pilot stage involved Movirtu, a start-up that developed and patented "cloud phone" software to serve the BoP.[33] Movirtu saw the opportunity to offer a mobile identity that operated independent of a particular mobile device or SIM card.[34] Using the idea of being able to access e-mail from different computers, the company's cloud phone service provided users with a phone number that could be accessed from any handset in the network. With this technology, people could share cell phones and SIM cards and still have full and private access to their own data and services.[35]

The business model and associated market creation efforts drew in a number of partners from both the private and development sectors. Working with mobile network operators (MNOs), mobile telephone networks (MTNs), and village phone operators (VPOs) that collaborated to provide service to mobile subscribers, Movirtu envisioned a revenue-sharing system that benefited all parties. If the costumer paid ten cents per call, the VPO kept three cents, the MNO kept five cents, and Movirtu kept the remaining two cents. In addition, revenue could be made from NGOs or companies wishing to reach the company's customers. Movirtu anticipated, for example, that NGOs or for-profit firms might use its system to deliver critical information to subscribers, which would help subsidize the price of Movirtu's products. Ultimately this model was designed to earn Movirtu approximately twenty cents for every dollar the customer spent.

The key market creation challenge was to introduce the concept of "owning" a phone number without owning any sort of physical device or card. This was where Movirtu initially struggled in its piloting efforts. In Madagascar, for example, while the VPOs were introduced to selling cards with cloud phone numbers, those phone operators didn't fully understand the model or the subscriber benefits. Customers also failed to understand this new market opportunity. They were buying a new number, but then throwing them away—rather than topping them up—when the initial minutes ran out. They were viewing the cloud phone numbers as disposable rather than permanent, meaning that they did not realize many of the benefits associated with the service. As a result, sales were not as robust as had been hoped.

In hindsight, the company realized that greater awareness creation was required. They invested more in marketing, an investment that included introducing a plastic scratch card to replace the initial handwritten paper card, offering more training to VPOs, and developing an outreach campaign that used radio and posters. The company also placed increased emphasis on business users by making it possible for them to add a second number to their existing mobile account. As a result, business users were able to separate their private and business calls without having to invest in more equipment.[36]

Movirtu made much of this additional investment with limited partner support, which had implications for the longer-term costs and benefits of scaling. Indeed, a lack of emphasis on partner support for BoP market creation may have been a key contributing factor to Movirtu's transition to a focus on markets higher up the economic pyramid, a move reflected in Black-Berry's purchase of the company in September 2014.[37]

EMBED: EXPANDING THROUGH INTEGRATION

We now arrive at the third strategy in the C-I-E scaling cycle: embedding. Whereas co-creating and innovating are particularly valuable during the process of envisioning and piloting, respectively, embedding is especially crucial for the BoP impact enterprise as it seeks sustainability and scalability. The concept of embeddedness recognizes that business transactions occur not in isolation but within a broader context of social relations. Economic activities that seem rational may well fail if they do not consider social connections and constraints within the market environment.[38]

In BoP markets, most economic activity occurs in informal markets where transactions are largely guided by social norms, values, and tradition rather than by formal rules and legal requirements.[39] As a result, the ability to understand and respond to how economic activities are embedded in the social context is particularly important.[40] Embedding requires becoming connected to, and integrated with, knowledge, resources, individuals, and organizations found in BoP markets.

Generating integration-based competitive advantage through leveraging the resources of and co-mingling assets with a variety of partners provides a way to embed through relationships. Building social embeddedness, which enables the efficient accessing of critical market information and the effective interpretation of these data to gain a deep sense of the market opportunity, provides a way to embed through capability development. This capability enables the enterprise to move more rapidly through the process of envisioning, piloting, and scaling as it expands within existing markets, or into new markets.

Taken together, these two key elements, integration-based competitive advantage and a social embeddedness capability, provide a strong foundation for achieving an embedded strategy. Using Figure 3.4 as our starting point, we look at each in more detail.

Generating Integration-Based Competitive Advantage

As an enterprise moves through the co-creation and innovation strategies, its leadership team also must begin to consider sustainability and scalability. This becomes the enterprise's focus in the embedded strategy. Specifically, for an enterprise to survive and thrive in a specific market, it must outperform the competition. That requires establishing a competitive advantage, which depends on creating a value proposition that "competitors"—which I put in quotes because it includes the status quo—are unable to replicate.[41] This may sound all too obvious, and yet many BoP impact enterprises are uncomfortable explicitly articulating a reality of marketplace competition: that business has to win in the marketplace, which means besting the competition.

This brings us to the first core component of an embedded strategy: BoP impact enterprises must create integration-based competitive advantage. As we learn in Business 101, competitive advantage in top-of-the-pyramid markets generally requires developing and protecting internal assets. In these markets, competitive advantage is typically achieved by developing organizational strengths—in marketing, manufacturing prowess, logistics, access to resources, and so on—and then creating barriers to protect corporate assets and attributes. These barriers can be erected through legal mechanisms such as patents, copyrights, and contracts; market power; or other advantages. The system thrives on higher walls and deeper moats.

Achieving competitive advantage in BoP markets turns this logic on its head. In most BoP contexts, enterprises can't be sure that their investments will be protected by normal legal processes. They have to accept that property rights, contracts, and copyrights may be hard to enforce through legal

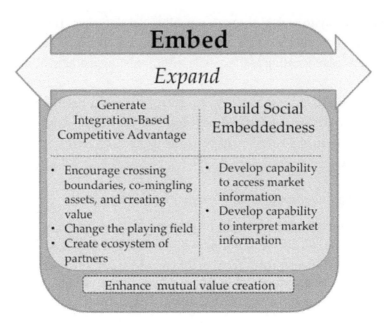

FIGURE 3.4 Embed: scaling strategies

mechanisms. Furthermore, creating and controlling assets is expensive, and it can be difficult to recoup these kinds of sunk costs. As a result, enterprises in BoP markets must understand how to build competitive advantage around assets and platforms that exist outside firm boundaries. Indeed, crucial to creating integration-based competitive advantage in BoP markets is a focus on crossing boundaries, co-mingling assets, and creating value, as opposed to creating barriers, protecting assets, and extracting value.

To build this type of competitive advantage, BoP impact enterprise leaders should seek to change the playing field rather than try to extract value out of an existing one. This means the enterprise wins in the marketplace by creating new sources of value and capturing a piece of that new value. Remember the discussion in Chapters 1 and 2 about the differences between a strategy based on fortune finding, which emphasizes a rationale of identifying and exploiting existing sources of value, and fortune creating, which stresses the importance of creating new value that can be shared between enterprise and its partners.

A fortune-finding approach to competitive advantage primarily depends on extracting value already present in these markets, which may well be limited and not available in sufficient quantities to enable scaling by the enterprise.[42] It also emphasizes the advantages of monopolizing a portion of the existing playing field, a strategy that may antagonize local partners and stakeholders seeking a more, not less, equitable playing field.

In fortune creating, the objective is to develop a new playing field, where new sources of value are created and competed for, that favors both the enterprise and its partners. Integration of assets is critical to creating and capturing this new playing field. And at its heart, this places high values on embeddedness: the opportunity to identify, leverage, and enhance platforms that already exist in the BoP marketplace.

Stated differently, after you discover what is in place and working in the BoP market environment, you must find ways to access, adapt, nurture, and enhance it for your own purposes, without necessarily trying to gain control of that platform for your exclusive use. These platforms could include network infrastructure, such as existing distribution systems and local self-help groups; social infrastructure, such as relationship capital and informal leadership; and physical infrastructure, such as underused business assets and existing resources that were previously used for nonbusiness purposes.

Many of the most attractive existing platforms have been created and are managed by development sector organizations. Most likely, those partners provide platform access only if you are willing to make investments—such as providing training to network members or making physical improvements to physical assets—that are outside your enterprise's usual boundaries and difficult to recover in the long run. Ultimately you will probably need to find a way to co-mingle some of your assets and resources with those of your development sector partners.

This is almost always a disconcerting process for enterprise leaders familiar with the competitive advantage-based building of barriers. They are being asked to voluntarily cede some degree of control over resources that businesses normally guard zealously. You run the risk of your investments being shared with others or your partner withdrawing with limited notice. But in many cases, understanding and managing these risks is what's required.

To do so, enterprise leaders must understand that they are integrating its activities with partners that most likely value social performance more than financial performance and see value creation as more than the creation of economic wealth. To establish and maintain these relationships, the BoP impact enterprise must incorporate, and continually enhance, its social impact value proposition (a topic discussed in much greater detail in Chapter 4).

Ultimately the enterprise must establish collaborations with a broad set of partners to achieve sustainability at scale in the marketplace. This means that enterprise leaders must embrace the idea that expansion in BoP markets requires integrating their activities with a diverse ecosystem of partners (a topic discussed in much greater detail in Chapters 5 and 6).

The Honey Care example illustrates some of the opportunities and challenges inherent in integration-based competitive advantage. As we've seen, there are opportunities not commonly found at the top of the pyramid—for example, circumstances in which partnerships with nonprofits and other development community organizations can help create markets and facilitate enterprise success. When executing an embedded strategy, the BoP impact enterprise seeks ways to leverage and enhance the resources of these unconventional partners, even if it means they have to invest in organizations that tend to have a different perspective when it comes to the concept of value, in most cases favoring social return over profits.

Consider the case of Unilever's Shakti initiative, aimed at developing the potentially vast Indian market for Unilever's retail goods. To reach the rural population in India, Unilever understood that it needed a better distribution network than the geographically limited structure that it had in place there. Rather than building a new network from scratch, which across the vastness of India would have been prohibitively expensive, the company decided to try to leverage an existing resource: a large network of self-help groups already at work in many communities in rural areas. Over several years, Shakti invested in partnerships with more than 350 nonprofits and development organizations. In almost all cases, these were organizations that placed a premium on poverty alleviation and improving the human condition, not necessarily the most obvious partner for a profit-oriented multinational like Unilever. Nevertheless, these partnership efforts have proved fruitful, in large part because Shakti sought to understand and deliver on their partners' value proposition—while also using its embedded position to leverage resources critical to building scalable enterprise. Since its inception in 2001, Shakti has expanded its network to cover eighty thousand villages in twelve of India's states, relying on the skills and energies of some twenty-five thousand entrepreneurs, most of whom are part of existing self-help groups.

Building Social Embeddedness

Creating a new playing field through integration-based competitive advantage offers the opportunity to establish a sustainable enterprise in a particular market environment. In some respects, achieving competitive advantage is the fruition of all the investments in co-creation and innovation that enabled successful envisioning and piloting. You may well be asking, How is it possible to achieve an even broader level of scale? Can an enterprise gain skills and expertise that facilitate moving through the C-I-E scaling cycle as it seeks to enter new markets?

The answer is yes. The enterprise must still envision and experiment, as well as establish competitive advantage, but the process can become more efficient and effective. This is where capability development comes in, as it allows the transfer of newly developed skills from one market to another. From the perspective of an enterprise, a capability is the venture's capacity to deploy its resources. While resources—such as talent, equipment, and raw materials—can generally be purchased, rented, or leased, capabilities must be built.[43]

Social embeddedness, the capacity to gain a deep understanding of and integration with the local environment, is one such capability.[44] As it builds its social embeddedness, the enterprise can reduce the time and investments required to envision and experiment in new market environments, as well as achieve integration-based competitive advantage that enables sustainability at scale. Developing a capability in social embeddedness involves two key factors. The first is the enterprise's capacity to access critical, market-specific information; the second focuses on developing the skills to interpret that information.

Gaining access to important and relevant information greatly benefits from a capacity to develop deep and mutually beneficial connections with a diversity of local stakeholders. These relationships yield a wealth of market intelligence, help in identifying and connecting to established networks, and provide key insights into how things really work in specific environments. The goal here is engagement with a wide range of local individuals and organizations and a robust process of information sharing. These relationships can provide key inputs into other scaling strategies, such as unearthing previously unrecognized market assets, identifying socially based customs and rules that can influence market development, and initiating the collaborations necessary for generating competitive advantage.

In building a diversity of contacts, the enterprise team must also understand whom they have not yet talked to. These connections may be hard to find, very busy, or shy. As a result, they are often unlikely to seek out the enterprise team. Interestingly, from my work in Malawi and Indonesia, I have found these types of sources are often particularly thoughtful and insightful. They usually don't have an agenda, and they deeply understand the local market environment.

The enterprise team must also gain an appropriate perspective in order to effectively interpret the information collected. The quality of the information is more important than the quantity. By engaging with a wide number of partners with varying perspectives about a particular market environment, the enterprise team may become overwhelmed by a mountain of data, many of them qualitative. The team must be able to sift through this information based on a deep understanding of who provided it and what they provided.

One natural tendency is to rely more heavily on charismatic sources who are comfortable in the native language of the team (e.g., English, French, Spanish) and are familiar with dealing with foreigners. This kind of information is often easily accessible and digestible for the team, but it presents clear risks. Enterprise leaders should be able to understand and appropriately weigh the motivations and potential biases of different sources of the information. Some sources may seek future partnerships with the enterprise and be exceedingly optimistic. Others may distrust enterprises and present an exceedingly pessimistic outlook. Both perspectives can provide valuable information. The enterprise must have the capacity to interpret and integrate this information to gain a full picture of the opportunity space.

When successfully developed, social embeddedness enables the leadership team to efficiently assemble critical knowledge about BoP markets and effectively use this information while moving through the enterprise development process. If you lack this capability, everything is new each time you launch a pilot or consider a new business opportunity, and that's not an attractive approach for achieving economically viable scale across multiple market environments. For all these reasons and more, developing the capacity to establish high-functioning relationships based on two-way sharing with a diverse set of partners is a critical skill for BoP impact enterprises. To enhance expansion efforts, the enterprise leadership team must ensure that its capability in social embeddedness is recognized, nurtured, and transferred across contexts.

Social embeddedness, achieved successfully, can also be a powerful source for future competitive advantage as more enterprises seek to enter BoP markets. You need to know who to talk to and how to gather and interpret the information you need—and more quickly and effectively than your competitors. To win, you have to move through the C-I-E scale cycle more quickly than your potential competitors do.

Let's look at the case of ITC, the Indian multinational that has successfully served the BoP for more than a decade.[45] As one of India's largest companies, ITC operates in a variety of top-of-the-pyramid markets, including tobacco, paperboard, retail, and hospitality. Its name used to be India Tobacco Company until 1974, but it has deemphasized tobacco in recent years, and has invested heavily in developing and selling packaged consumer goods that use agricultural products as raw material.

The situation when ITC began investigating BoP agricultural opportunities was weighted heavily against small farmers. Imagine their situation: They'd load up their carts, spend as many as four hours getting to the market, where they would often be offered a low price for their goods by the local intermediaries, who might be colluding to keep prices down. If the farmers protested, the intermediaries would shrug and say, "Fine. Come back here tomorrow or try another market." But if you've already transported a perishable crop over long distances in the hot sun, that is unlikely to be a realistic option. So the farmers were forced to be price takers and were taken advantage of on a consistent and widespread basis.

Seeing opportunity in changing this playing field, ITC's International Business Division launched its eChoupal initiative. (*Choupal* is the Hindi word for meeting place.) The eChoupal leadership team spent considerable time gaining a deep understanding of the opportunities and constraints faced by local growers, starting with soybean farmers. Perceiving the need to create a new market channel, the team piloted various models based on deploying personal computers at the local village level—computers that were intended to provide information on the price of soybean transactions in distant auction markets. At the same time that it was creating price transparency, ITC used computer kiosks to announce its own guaranteed forward price for next-day procurement of the commodity. Farmers were in no way compelled to accept ITC's offered price, but for the first time, they could see their options, and when ITC was offering the most, which it often did, the farmers gladly sold their soybeans to ITC.

After a systematic process of iterating between design and a series of pilots, ITC felt it had developed a potentially viable and scalable business model. It invested in providing computers and training to carefully selected farmers to create a network of eChoupal kiosks. These specially trained farmers (called *sanchalaks,* the Hindi word for coordinators or directors) enjoyed the prestige and recognition associated with serving as the official intermediaries between the soybean farmers and ITC. By providing a guaranteed price, lower transaction costs, and prices that were aligned with product quality, ITC generated greater returns and—significantly—shared some of this surplus with the local farmers.

The eChoupal venture scaled up a new model in which the key stakeholders—the company, the local farmers, and the sanchalaks—were all satisfied with the returns they received. That model, as we've seen, depended heavily on an integration-based competitive advantage and led to a growing capability in social embeddedness.

Success for eChoupal, however, envisioned further scaling, and the enterprise leaders wanted to both buy other agricultural product markets from local farmers and provide inputs to these farmers. Toward the former end, eChoupal explored the opportunity to procure other commodities, such as wheat and coffee grown in other regions of the country. These efforts moved forward more quickly than the initial foray into soybeans. The leadership team leveraged its burgeoning capacity to establish strong local relationships, as well as its growing skill at interpreting the information generated. This enabled the enterprise to rapidly envision, experiment, and expand its business model for these different crops.

In subsequent years, ITC used the capabilities it had developed to build deeper relationships with the farmers.[46] For example, e-Choupal 2.0 envisioned how the existing interface could become a two-way channel for connecting farmers to markets. Recognizing that the productivity of the local farmers suffered due to low-quality inputs, ITC used its procurement platform not only to source products from BoP producers but also to provide a channel that local farmers could use to purchase high-quality seeds, fertilizers, and pesticides. When this new business model reached scale, eChoupal and farmer success became further intertwined. The farmers purchased better inputs from ITC and produced better yields, while ITC received a more consistent and stable source of supply and provided greater returns to the farmers.

The enterprise then further leveraged its social embeddedness to gain an even deeper understanding of how to enhance the quality and reliability of the produce from local farmers in its existing markets. For example, ITC made available the advice of agriculture scientists through its network—expanding the information farmers could find though interacting with the eChoupal initiative—and offered agricultural productivity improvement training. Significantly, this information was offered free of charge to any villager who wanted it. The enterprise also began providing soil testing services at nominal cost so farmers could apply the most appropriate fertilizers.

And from there, ITC saw an opportunity to further personalize its relationships with the farmers. Learnings from individual farmers and sanchalaks—specifically focused on the co-creation of new anchor businesses, diversification solutions for farmers, and microentrepreneurship opportunities—were systematically developed, creating a richer ecosystem linking the farmers and the company. In each of these new endeavors, leveraging and transferring social embeddedness proved critical to the efficiency and effectiveness of these efforts and others.[47]

Currently e-Choupal serves forty thousand villages and 4 million farmers across ten states. There are more than sixty-five hundred eChoupals throughout India.[48] Each eChoupal serves ten villages in a five-kilometer radius to reach an average of six hundred farmers.[49] In 2012, ITC released a new version, 3.0, for e-Choupal that it hopes catalyzes on existing networks to reach over 10 million farmers.

ITC has annual revenues around $7 billion. Although the company does not provide specific financial results for the eChoupal model, the chief executive for ITC's Agri Business, S. Sivakumar, says it is "significant."[50] The eChoupals serve as an important sales and distribution channel for the company. ITC has also partnered with more than 160 companies—including Bayer, BASF, State Bank of India, Bharat Petroleum, Nokia, TVS Motors, Maruti Suzuki India, and Tata Motors—to offer access to the eChoupal platform.[51]

As the eChoupal story demonstrates, sustaining and scaling a BoP impact enterprise in BoP markets is possible. What has been missing to date is a set of principles that can guide enterprise leaders in their enterprise development efforts. The C-I-E scaling strategies, set out in Figure 3.5, offer such a framework, which—if successfully executed—can increase the likelihood of enterprise sustainability and scalability.

Chapters 2 and 3 have focused on presenting guiding principles for enterprise development. In its discussion of scaling strategies, the C-I-E- framework also recognized the critical need for mutual value creation in each stage of enterprise development, the topic addressed in chapter 4. Enterprise leaders need to truly understand and strengthen their poverty alleviation impacts and the associated potential for value creation. To help meet those challenges, I introduce the BoP Impact Assessment Framework, a robust tool that enterprise leaders can use to better understand and improve their value proposition.

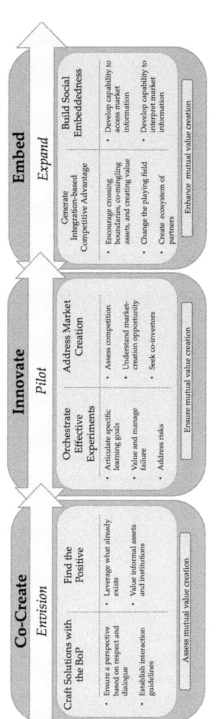

FIGURE 3.5 Summarizing C-I-E scaling strategies

4 MUTUAL VALUE CREATION

In this chapter, I underscore and dig more deeply into the second cornerstone of this book: that understanding and enhancing poverty alleviation impacts must become second nature in efforts to build viable, scalable enterprises with impact. Of course, alleviating poverty is a key part of the social performance goals of a BoP impact enterprise. But it is much more than that. Creating mutual value, which must include alleviating poverty, is imperative to enterprise success.[1] Yet I have seen many enterprises, and their investors and partners, fail to embrace this perspective, thereby substantially constraining the opportunity to build a viable business.

Alleviating poverty in many cases is the most crucial aspect of the enterprise's value proposition.[2] Indeed, reducing poverty is not a threshold or state of grace that you reach, commemorate, and celebrate. It is not just a requirement to satisfy funders and other partners with social goals. Rather, it's a key performance indicator that reflects the enterprise's viability. Why? Because creating value for those it seeks to serve—selling to consumers, buying from producers, or partnering with local entrepreneurs—is a central tenet of well-designed businesses.

The importance of mutual value creation has also been underscored in some more recent and captivating approaches to using the power of business to address social issues, such as shared value and impact investing. Both of these approaches recognize the interdependence between creating social impact and generating economic returns.[3]

Finally, a deep understanding of the opportunity to enhance mutual value must be at the heart of an enterprise's efforts to scale. As discussed in Chapter 3, it is a key component in each of the strategic imperatives in the co-creating, innovating, and embedding (C-I-E) scaling framework. After all, the more value that business creates for the BoP, the greater the opportunity for the enterprise to capture more value for itself.

There is a cost to creating value for the BoP. The enterprise must understand the relationship between the costs associated with different value creation opportunities and the amount of that value it can capture from these investments. But in a very real sense, the enterprise's long-term financial performance is tied to its ability to create net positive changes in poverty alleviation.

I should make one important clarification of terminology at this stage. In discussing the results of poverty alleviation efforts, I use the terms *impact* and *outcome*. There is a distinction between them based on the length and depth of the change. *Outcomes* are more near term, while *impacts* focus on the changes that are longer term and have a broader scale. The differences can be important, but they can also be difficult to interpret.[4] Thus, for simplicity, I generally use the terms interchangeably, although I do recognize that an impact assessment will result a more holistic understanding of change.

Fortunately, assessing and enhancing poverty alleviation impacts aren't as complicated, expensive, or time-consuming as most enterprise leaders tend to think. In this chapter, I introduce the BoP Impact Assessment Framework, a relatively straightforward—but still powerful—tool that enterprise leaders can use to understand and enhance their poverty alleviation impacts and the associated potential for additional value creation. It can also be used in different ways depending on the skills, needs, and resources available to an enterprise. I then present case studies, on VisionSpring and Sanergy, that show how two businesses, working in very different contexts and offering very different products, put the framework to good use in their efforts to understand how to boost their value proposition.

To start, though, I first discuss several risky shortcuts that I have seen too many enterprise leaders use in place of a more robust assessment of impacts, and explore why those shortcuts need to be avoided.

HUBRIS AND AN OVERRELIANCE ON ANECDOTES AND OUTPUTS

I use a simple test to tell whether an enterprise leader or an aspiring entrepreneur has a realistic perspective on their potential value proposition. Early in our conversation, I ask for a summary of the actual or expected impacts for their enterprise. I want to learn if they have a holistic sense of performance along two key dimensions: who is affected and how. Do the enterprise leaders recognize the multidimensional nature of both poverty impacts and the local stakeholders who are affected?

Second, I listen carefully to see if they have identified any negative impacts. If I don't hear anything negative, I am skeptical that they have a representative or holistic appreciation of their actual impacts. It is exceedingly rare to make a meaningful intervention that doesn't have any negative outcomes. Microcredit, for example, is an effective way to provide access to capital through loans, but it also means the borrower is taking on debt, a negative outcome. On balance, microcredit can be a good intervention, although the negatives should not be ignored. Too much debt, for example, can lead to serious problems.[5] That is why a BoP impact enterprise is defined as having a net positive impact rather than simply a positive impact.

When I hear people describe an enterprise with no negative impacts, I generally don't doubt their sincerity. Most enterprise leaders say that they're committed to poverty alleviation and other positive impacts, and most of them are. But when you ask them to identify the specific value they are creating, many struggle to provide answers with sufficient depth. Their responses are usually overly optimistic and often fall within one or more predictable categories. For example, they may resort to individual anecdotes: "Take the example of this farmer who has increased his crop yields," or, "Let's talk about this woman who has established herself as an entrepreneur." What then follows is an inspiring story of resilience, achievement, and impact. The change wrought by the enterprise on this person's life is truly inspiring.

Of course, these stories have their uses. They can be an effective way to show prospective donors, partners, and others the potential for good outcomes. But at best they represent what is possible. They are wholly inadequate as a representation of actual impact and value creation because each is based on a sample size of one—and a carefully selected sample at that. No special statistical skills are needed to understand the inherent limitations of relying on a biased sample of one. Compounding the problem, the story that is presented is rarely complete. There is usually no reference to negative twists and turns along the way or alternative explanations for the changes seen.

And what if some funders or other partners are persuaded that a compelling "sample of one" is representative of the expected social performance of the enterprise? Surely this leads to expectations that can't possibly be met. In the process of talking itself up, the enterprise is also setting itself up to over-promise and underdeliver on social impact. This can then create incentives to continue to rely on approaches that overrepresent the impact.

Inherent in this tactic is an important, and surprisingly often ignored, moral aspect. Those who rely on anecdotes and stories as a replacement for more robust approach to assessing impact are in my estimation knowingly "cooking the social books." What happens to business leaders who are caught misrepresenting their financial performance? At the very least, they are con-demned in the court of public opinion and may also face stiff legal penalties for knowingly overstating performance. Some might say that when it comes to social performance, this calculated misrepresentation is somehow okay. After all, some would say, these enterprises are only trying to do good; we can cut them some slack if it will help them garner more support. And besides—you may hear, if you listen carefully—they *know* they are doing good. Of course their enterprise is alleviating poverty. Who would question that?

I fundamentally disagree. Some might argue that by overrepresenting social performance, an enterprise may raise more money, generate favorable news coverage, acquire new partners, encourage staff, and build a following for the enterprise and its leadership team. But in embracing this approach, enterprises are also setting themselves up to fail the very stakeholders these enterprises are designed to serve: the BoP. Overpromising and underdelivering, combined with an implicit bias against recognizing mixed or disappointing outcomes and the associated need for additional learning and improvement, are all impedi-ments to achieving substantial social impact and they increase the likelihood of enterprise failure. It may sound strange to our developed world ears, but it's true: Humility and transparency must be our constant companions.

On a more positive note, a growing number of enterprise leaders are acknowledging that anecdotes alone aren't sufficient. A considerable percent-age of this group, however, then falls into another crucial misjudgment: They assert that the benefits of a deep understanding of their impacts can't be cost justified. Collecting this type of performance data, they claim, is simply too difficult or too expensive in the BoP context. The market (following this line of argument) is too fragmented, too remote, or too unfamiliar, and therefore it's too costly and time-consuming for an enterprise to invest in gaining a rich and holistic assessment of impact and value creation.

These enterprise leaders instead take what might be considered a middle road. They focus on output measures as a proxy for impact: "We distributed X bed nets last month," "We sold Y hybrid seeds," or, "We generated X gallons of clean water." Of course, output measures have their legitimate business uses, but until rigorously tested, they remain at best uncertain proxies for the core business issue of value creation. Distribution of bed nets does not mean use of bed nets or, more important, reduction in the incidence of malaria. Some people don't use the nets every night; others turn them into fishing nets. Providing clean water is different from drinking clean water because of the many ways that clean water is recontaminated. People don't want better seeds; they want better crop yields. What's important are the ends (the enterprise's impacts) rather than the means (the enterprise's outputs). And if we don't deeply understand the true relationships between the means and the ends—which we still generally don't in BoP markets—we can't claim great confidence in our understanding of poverty alleviation and value creation.

BoP impact enterprise leaders can't forget or ignore the fact that local value creation is about impacts, not outputs. From my more than twenty-five years of experience in this field, I can comfortably say that a failure to focus on impacts has been the death knell for too many enterprises. Enterprise leaders must understand the types of value that are being generated by their ventures, how much value of each type is being created, and how this value is allocated among the stakeholders involved with the enterprise. And they must also understand how to create more value. Yes, it may require an investment of time and money, but it is an investment they can't afford not to make.

THE MULTIDIMENSIONAL NATURE OF POVERTY

You can't create value if you don't understand the value you are trying to create. So as a first step in developing a richer perspective on this key issue, we need to arrive at a shared perspective on a well-used word that can evoke a complex range of connotations: *poverty.* Too often, I hear the statement, "I know poverty alleviation when I see it." But poverty is much more than what can be seen. Others will say that poverty is about income, and poverty alleviation is measured by changes in income. Yes, income is important, but it is only part of the picture. We need to be much more thoughtful and thorough.

Poverty represents a lack of well-being, and well-being is multidimensional.[6] Alleviating poverty results from improving local well-being, and improving well-being creates value for the BoP—and this value creation is the basis for the enterprise's value proposition.[7] While income or expenditures are often used as the key proxy for measuring levels of poverty, relying solely on measures of economic well-being is inadequate.[8] Poverty is more than simply the absence of money.[9] In 2001, the World Bank broadened its definition of *poverty* to include not only material deprivation but also risk, vulnerability, and powerlessness.[10] As Amartya Sen has highlighted, individuals and communities also must have the skills, health, and confidence to help themselves and influence the world around them.[11] Capability well-being captures this agency-oriented aspect of poverty. Relationship well-being recognizes the influence of geographic, social, and other types of isolation and the role that the quality of the physical and natural environment can have in impoverishing individuals and communities. For example, social or geographic exclusion due to a lack of respect or awareness from fellow community members, economic actors, government, and other institutions leads to impoverishment.[12]

Framed holistically, these dimensions can be summarized as a lack of three types of well-being: *economic, capability,* and *relationship.* These are often are found in combination, but substantial deficits in any of them alone can have devastating impacts on the lives of the BoP.

The influence of poverty also varies across stakeholders. Enterprises focused on providing products or services, for example, often rely on local distributors (sellers) to reach local consumers (buyers). In enterprises that buy products, local agents (buyers) purchase the output of local producers (sellers). In some enterprises, such as the case of ITC, the company may both sell to and buy from the BoP. The enterprise can affect the broader community in which the local buyers and sellers live. A specific enterprise therefore has potential impacts on three groups of local stakeholders: sellers, buyers, and the local communities in which the venture operates.

BOP IMPACT ASSESSMENT FRAMEWORK: AN INTRODUCTION

The BoP Impact Assessment Framework (BoP IAF) is a tool that harnesses and responds to this multidimensional perspective on the how and who of alleviating poverty and creating local value. I designed the BoP IAF with the intent of helping enterprise leaders assess and enhance their value proposition.[13] While it can also help organizations meet their requirements to evaluate and report their impact, this framework's specific focus is on learning and improving—the opportunity to assess and enhance local value creation.

There are other terrific tools that do other things. For example, IRIS can be valuable for donors who seek to compare the outputs of alternative solutions.[14] Similarly, the Social Progress Index taps broader measures of poverty alleviation at a macrolevel, but it is not as useful as a tool for assessing and strengthening value propositions in local contexts.[15] Another helpful tool, the Grameen Foundation's Progress out of Poverty Index, is designed to tell whether a person has moved above—or fallen back below—a predetermined poverty line.[16]

Comparatively, BoP IAF is especially well suited to efforts that seek a higher level of stakeholder engagement and co-creation of a value proposition.[17] It focuses on identifying how a person's poverty—that is, well-being—has or can be changed. I've found that this tool works well for providing enterprise leaders what they need to know to understand and enhance their value proposition in terms of measurable changes, positive and negative, in local poverty levels. It also has been identified by independent third-party evaluators as a particularly useful tool for business leaders interested in improving their socioeconomic impacts.[18] But my main point here is that you need a proven tool—mine or someone else's—to assess and enhance your value proposition.

Developed to be a managerially friendly tool, the BoP IAF identifies how the enterprise is creating value and how that value proposition can be enhanced, and it presents a holistic picture of impacts across the full set of local stakeholders. It achieves these ends through incorporating four attributes:

Holistic: The BoP IAF provides a complete view of social and economic value created across three areas of well-being: economic, capability, and relationship. This includes capturing both positive and negative impacts and assessing these impacts across a variety of BoP stakeholders.

Interactive: The framework is highly collaborative as key stakeholders help inform which impacts are tracked. Through a participatory process, the BoP impact enterprise staff, a variety of partners, and the BoP can work together to identify and prioritize the set of key impacts resulting from the enterprise's activities. If the co-creation process is well done, these qualitative impacts offer a rich perspective on the enterprise's value proposition. A survey instrument and associated data collection process can then be co-created to quantitatively capture the venture's impact over time, which provides an even richer assessment of what is actually happening.

Actionable: Using the results from this framework to implement improvements in the business model and then track their changes in impact over time, enterprises create a powerful process for continually enhancing their value proposition and better meeting the needs of those they seek to serve. This also ensures that the enterprise has a platform for learning and dialogue with key local stakeholders.

Flexible: The framework is designed to respond to the budget, skills, and data management capabilities of different enterprises. Even early-stage start-ups can use this tool. (In fact, a partner organization asked that enterprises seeking their support complete the BoP IAF as part of their business plan.) The framework can incorporate qualitative and quantitative data, or both. It can collect information that summarizes the voices of the BoP and their partners, or it can yield scientifically rigorous results that demonstrate whether changes are statistically significant. It can accommodate randomization and other types of approaches that seek to control for any impacts not associated with the enterprise's activities.[19]

The BoP IAF is depicted in Figure 4.1.[20] This figure includes only a subset of possible impacts that could be incorporated within each of the cells:

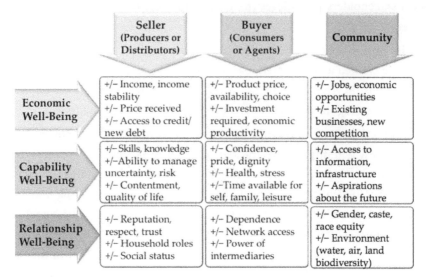

FIGURE 4.1 BoP Impact Assessment Framework

The vertical axis poses the question, "How are your constituencies being affected?" Alleviating poverty is not only about economic survival, but also prospering as a human being, including having the capabilities to influence the course of your life. It also has to do with the network of interactions that begin in the family and the household and move outward into the larger community—interactions that help ensure that through relationships, your voice is being heard. An enterprise that seeks to alleviate poverty must consider the value creation opportunity across economic well-being, capability well-being, and relationship well-being.

The first of these, economic well-being, encompasses changes in income, income stability, assets, liabilities, consumer surplus, and economic productivity resulting from the enterprise's activities. It has to do with the flow and stock of economic capital. The second, capability well-being, incorporates changes in physical (e.g., health, ability to perform specific activities), intellectual (e.g., skills, knowledge, capabilities), and psychological (e.g., self-esteem, dignity) well-being resulting from the enterprise's activities. Broadly, this is about the ability to influence one's own situation or, as some have phrased it, the opportunity to flourish.[21] The third, relationship well-being, captures changes in roles, status and values (e.g., within family, community), access to support (relationships with individuals, groups, and partners), levels of dependence on and responsiveness of those in positions of power (e.g., suppliers, intermediaries, government), and quality of the local physical infrastructure and environment (e.g., land use, waste generated) resulting from the enterprise's activities. It is about respect, having your voice heard, and connections to individuals, institutions, and the surrounding context.

The horizontal axis poses the question, "Who is being affected?" Here, I consider the basic constituencies of an enterprise: seller, buyer, and community. These constituencies can vary depending on the nature of the business. Sellers may be the producers of the goods or services, or they may be the distributors that offer goods and services to local consumers. Buyers can be local consumers of goods and services or the intermediaries that connect the sellers with your enterprise. In some cases, there may be more than one group of buyers or sellers. In other cases, there may be no local buyers or sellers (if, for example, the enterprise takes on that role). The number and labeling of these columns can be adjusted accordingly. The community column ensures that other impacts that occur locally are captured—things like jobs created or lost, impacts on other local enterprises, changes in access to information or views about gender and caste, gains or losses in geographic and social isolation, and increases or decreases in water quality, land, and local biodiversity.

The information yielded from the BoP IAF is designed to provide more than a snapshot of current social performance or milestones achieved. It offers an active, forward-looking picture, focused on both the who and the how of a value proposition. It invites a granular investigation of gains and losses in local value and the opportunity for enhancing value creation through business activities. Remember that value creation requires recognizing that the goal is to generate net-positive changes. Certainly a local buyer or seller may do well by investing his or her limited capital in your business, but this person may also be taking on unaccustomed risk. And a new enterprise may result in more choices, lower prices, and better access to a good or a service; that success may also mean that indigenous competitors are facing greater competition that they likely don't appreciate. Empowering women as buyers or sellers may greatly improve the economics of their families, but it may also change the structure and stability of those relationships.

Identifying both positive and negative impacts, and understanding how to enhance the former and mitigate the latter, are crucial in enhancing value creation and the associated opportunity for enhanced enterprise financial performance. The BoP IAF provides insights and can help guide actions toward strategies the enterprise can implement that respond to value creation opportunities and make sense from a cost-benefit perspective.

DIGGING DEEPER

One important aspect of the BoP IAF framework is that it offers flexibility, so different enterprises can use it in different ways. There are in fact two broad approaches to data collection and analysis: the strategic impact assessment and the performance impact assessment. Enterprises can use one or both of these, choosing the more appropriate option for assessing and enhancing value creation based on their current situation.

Implementing the BoP IAF as shown in Figure 4.2 can be conceived of as a one- or two-stage process that allows varying degrees of investment and rigor to match an enterprise's resources and capabilities. Ongoing enterprises, as well as those still in the design phase, can use the framework to make a strategic analysis of their poverty alleviation impacts. While this emphasizes qualitative data, it can still be quite rigorous. Second, BoP impact enterprises can conduct a performance analysis, based on developing a set of measurable indicators to track poverty alleviation outcomes over time, a process that tends to be more quantitative in nature. These approaches can also work in tandem, with all options designed to yield important information that can enhance the enterprise's business model.

In this section, we look at each of these approaches, the strategic analysis and the performance analysis, in greater depth.

Strategic Analysis: Understanding Value Creation

Implementing a strategic analysis of impact requires rich discussions with key stakeholders, does not necessarily require quantitative data collection, and can vary in terms of the depth of commitment in terms of time and resource investment. This leads to one important implication: no enterprise should claim that it doesn't have the time, resources, or capabilities to assess

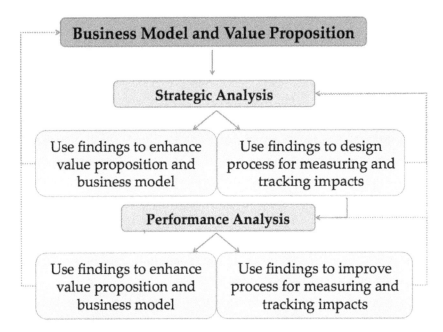

FIGURE 4.2 Using the BoP IAF

its impact and understand its value proposition better. With that in mind, the venture's assessment team must still commit to adopting a rigorous and carefully considered approach to completing the framework.

First, the data collection team must commit to receiving feedback, positive and negative, in an unbiased way. Ideally, this team consists of individuals both inside and outside the enterprise. The reason for including outsiders is that they are more likely to be seen by the local stakeholders as impartial and more likely to accept negative reactions. Regardless, everyone on the team should embrace two key skills: the ability to listen and a willingness to learn. Surfacing the team's embedded assumptions and establishing interaction guidelines, as discussed in Chapter 3, are key strategies that can contribute to the quality of the interactions with stakeholders.

After the team has been trained, it should seek to generate a preliminary sense of the expected impacts of the enterprise, both positive and negative, on local stakeholders. A good initial step is to review existing research on the enterprise's intervention, followed by conversations with experts experienced in this type of intervention. For example, researchers have examined impacts of improved sanitation, including changes in the health of community members and the quality of the local environment. This information can then be matched to the enterprise's business model to develop a first cut at filling in the BoP IAF.

Next, the team should develop an interview protocol that includes a series of questions that explore the initial impacts identified as well as probes for other potential outcomes. These questions can vary somewhat depending on the interviewees' relationship to the enterprise. Indeed, incorporating a wide diversity of perspectives in their data collection—including the views of field staff, partners who are opening local doors or providing funding, local intermediaries and competitors (if possible), government officials and development professionals, and, above all, local community members—is crucial to developing a robust impact assessment.

As depicted in Figure 4.3, hearing the voices of the local community requires particular care to ensure capturing a wide diversity of perspectives.[22] This means valuing what actual and potential buyers and sellers have to say.[23] It also means seeking feedback from those who may be a little more distant from the enterprise's typical perspective. Where possible, the team should also interview unsuccessful sellers, disgruntled buyers, those who have decided to not participate in the enterprise's activities, and individuals who don't appreciate the enterprise's presence in the community.

In other words, listening to and engaging with a variety of stakeholders, especially within the BoP, is the central component of this process. Using multiple methods and collecting various types of data helps ensure a more complete assessment and allows triangulation of findings. Potential approaches include structured and semistructured interviews, in-depth conversations on a particular topic or issue, and participatory group-based designs.

This information then needs to be carefully reviewed and integrated using the BoP IAF as a template for completing this process. In reviewing their data, the team may find some discrepancies across respondents, which may require more fieldwork to resolve these issues. Once they have developed a holistic understanding of the enterprise's positive and negative impacts on the economic, capacity, and relationship well-being of the local buyers, sell-

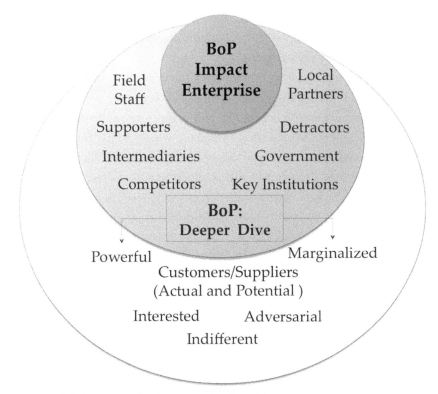

FIGURE **4.3** Mapping the diversity of stakeholders

ers, and communities, the team then needs to evaluate each of these along two dimensions: expected magnitude and relative likelihood of occurring. This evaluation should be part of the data collection process. Here, local perspective is crucial, and the analysis of the relative importance of various impacts should again incorporate the views of those who face poverty on a daily basis.

High-impact and high-likelihood outcomes are clearly the most important, and low-impact and low-likelihood outcomes deserve the least amount of attention. In general, it also makes sense to focus on any outcome that potentially could have a substantial poverty alleviation outcome even if its likelihood is relatively small. Ultimately the enterprise team may decide to include major and some or all of the minor impacts in their IAF. This is an effective way to be on the lookout for weak signals, which helps to keep minor impacts from being neglected, and it avoids the possibility that minor impacts will turn into major ones. That said, the team must find the right balance in identifying key impacts: comprehensive enough to be valid and selective enough to be manageable.

Once the strategic analysis is completed, the assessment team has enough information to pinpoint opportunities for enhancing positive and mitigating negative poverty alleviation impacts. Weighing the costs and benefits, the team can then make more informed decisions about potential changes to the business model and the associated opportunity for enhanced mutual value creation. Remember that this is a dynamic process rather than a one-time event, so each time the business model changes substantially, the team needs to update its impact analysis and consider the options for continued improvement.

Performance Analysis: Measuring Value Creation

To gain an even deeper and richer understanding of the enterprise's impacts, the team can undertake a quantitative performance analysis. The objective is to generate a set of targeted short- and long-term performance metrics that track and quantify changes in the most salient local impacts. An effective approach is to begin with a strategic analysis. Then the team determines its data collection strategy by identifying a representative sample of the population affected by the venture and, if possible, a comparable unaffected group to better account for the counterfactual, or what would have happened in the absence of the intervention.[24] The choice of whether to collect data from a comparable group should be based on a clear understanding of the benefits and costs associated with different research designs. For example, while collecting data from a comparison group is costly, this additional information can offer a more valid assessment of the enterprise's actual impacts. In making this decision, the enterprise leaders must clarify their expectations about the type of information that will be generated through this performance analysis.

Measuring impact, of course, requires assessing change over time. Collecting initial baseline data on buyers, sellers, and the community prior to any local enterprise activities is clearly the most straightforward and robust approach for facilitating a comparison of well-being before and after the intervention. The timing for follow-up data should be based on the realities of the local situation. For example, is any seasonality involved? How long should it take for the intervention to have an impact? This type of before-and-after design can also be valuable when the BoP impact enterprise makes a substantial change to its business model or launches a major new initiative.

Designing the data collection instruments is the next step. This includes developing indicators for the most salient impacts. Depending on the impact under consideration, these indicators may come from existing surveys or involve creating new measures. If possible, using existing measures is preferable because reliability and validity are usually already established. Prior to full-scale launch, pretesting and piloting allow for final refinements of the indicators and the associated data collection process. I stress that both the content (the survey instrument) and the process (the approach to conducting the survey) require careful consideration. A well-developed survey that is ineffectively administered will rarely generate much useful information.

Analyzing pre- and postintervention data and comparing the affected group with a control group requires experience in statistical analysis. If that skill is not part of the enterprise's portfolio, then outside help may be needed. Depending on budget and skills, the enterprise team may decide to hire an outsider or work with a partner to conduct the data collection and analysis process.

By conducting regular strategic or performance analyses, the venture establishes an ongoing process for truly hearing the voices of the enterprise's buyers, sellers, and other members of the local community in which it operates. This information can then be used to maximize the value creation opportunity for the enterprise and its stakeholders. Enterprise leaders must recognize that understanding impact—whether through a strategic analysis, a performance analysis, or both—is not a cost of doing business in BoP markets. Rather, it is an investment in enhancing the value proposition—an investment they can't afford not to make.

While the strategic analysis and the performance analysis can be conducted independently, they can also be seen as a holistic approach to impact assessment. As shown in Figure 4.4, the results of the strategic analysis can be used to identify and develop the most appropriate set of measurable performance indicators, a systematic and cost-effective way to track impacts over time and understand how changes in the business model or the environment may be affecting value creation through poverty-alleviation outcomes.

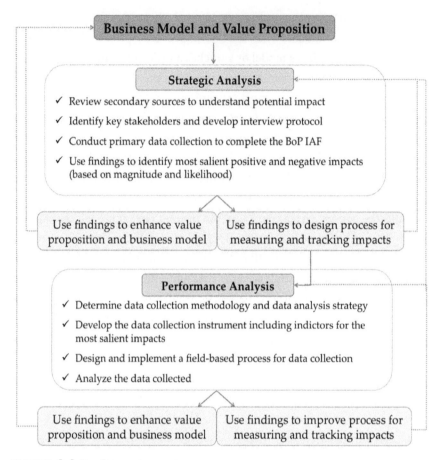

FIGURE 4.4 Implementing an impact assessment

APPLYING THE FRAMEWORK: VISIONSPRING'S IMPACT IN RURAL INDIA

Perhaps the most useful way to illustrate how the BoP IAF works is to show it in action in the context of a real-world case study. I use VisionSpring, an enterprise aimed at providing affordable eyeglasses to the BoP, as that case study.[25] The organization has worked hard to ask and answer the kinds of mutual value creation questions posed in this chapter. In partnership with my colleagues and me, VisionSpring used the BoP IAF to create more value for sellers, buyers, and the community—and, in the process, for itself.

VisionSpring's roots date back to 1998, when two friends, optometrist Jordan Kassalow and entrepreneur Scott Berrie, traveled to India together. Kassalow had spent a year after graduating from optometry school volunteering at the Aravind Eye Hospital in India, one of the more successful and creative examples of health care for the BoP.[26] Berrie was looking for a way to combine his entrepreneurial skills with his passion for public service. On that trip, they discovered what they thought was a substantially underdeveloped market: reading glasses for the poor. Specifically, they thought they could build a business-based approach to address the challenge of presbyopia (diminished ability to focus on near objects) in the developing world.

Presbyopia, a result of the eye's natural aging process, makes it difficult to see up close. On first blush, this might seem to be a problem mainly for readers, which might seem to rule out business solutions for areas in which large numbers of people are illiterate. In fact, people in almost all economic circumstances and walks of life need the ability to see things up close. Tailors need to be able to see their work, shopkeepers need to be able to quickly and accurately distinguish among bills and coins as they make change for their customers, and farmers need to be able to see the seeds they are using and the soil they're planting in. Helping those tailors, shopkeepers, farmers, and many more see better can improve multiple dimensions of well-being.

In some cases, presbyopia can only be addressed through a complex intervention. But for most people, a simple pair of glasses can effectively address the problem. So in 2001, VisionSpring, initially funded by George Soros's Open Society Institute, was launched in India.[27] India's population was then approaching 1 billion people, of whom more than 90 million were afflicted by some degree of presbyopia. There was an average of one eye care professional for every 30,200 Indians, and most of those service providers were located in urban areas.[28] And since many had no idea that their vision could be improved with relative ease, most of this population simply did without.

VisionSpring's initial business model was relatively straightforward: select local community members, almost all women, to become vision entrepreneurs (VEs). These individuals were trained in giving eye screenings for presbyopia and were provided with a "Business in a Bag," which contained all the materials, stock, and information they needed to launch their business, including an initial inventory of forty pairs of reading glasses. If this sounds like the door-to-door salesman of old, it was: The VEs approached local homes, administered a vision test to these prospective customers, and assuming the diagnosis was presbyopia worked with that individual to determine which of the five supplied strengths of glasses was most helpful to him or her. Then the VE confirmed the utility of the selected glasses by having the customer attempt some livelihood-related activity, such as threading a needle or reading.

Recognizing the limitations of a door-to-door approach, VisionSpring soon began running vision camps in local communities. After getting the word out that anyone with near-vision problems should come in for a consultation, the local VE then set up a table and screening area in the middle of town on a particular day.

In the majority of cases in which a sale is made, a pair of glasses costing around 165 Indian rupees (approximately $3.40) solves the problem on the spot. Although more affordable than alternative options, this still represents a substantial investment for the individuals being treated—more than a day's pay for many of them. So they expect to receive a fair value proposition in return for their money.

VisionSpring enlisted my help in using the BoP IAF to more deeply understand its poverty alleviation impacts and seek out new opportunities for enhanced value creation. We conducted both a strategic analysis (a simplified version is presented in Figure 4.5) and a performance analysis.

The analysis of our findings across both stages of the impact assessment offered useful insights. For example, VisionSpring was frustrated by the fact that some of the venture's most successful female entrepreneurs were dropping out just as they seemed to be gaining momentum. A probing of the circumstances revealed that the very success of these women was creating tension within the family structure, which tended to be dominated by the male of the household. VisionSpring realized that if the VEs' husbands could be recruited into the enterprise, formally or informally, at an early stage, the business was more likely to hold on to some of its most successful entrepreneurs. This solution helped manage VE turnover, which is critical in developing a viable enterprise that uses this type of distribution model.

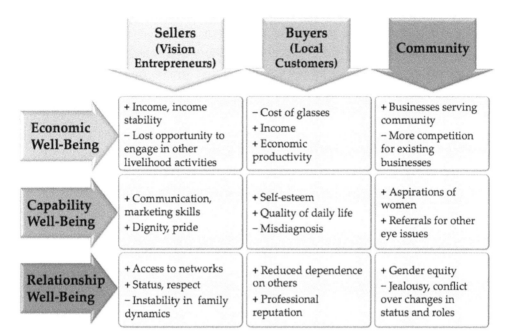

	Sellers (Vision Entrepreneurs)	Buyers (Local Customers)	Community
Economic Well-Being	+ Income, income stability – Lost opportunity to engage in other livelihood activities	– Cost of glasses + Income + Economic productivity	+ Businesses serving community – More competition for existing businesses
Capability Well-Being	+ Communication, marketing skills + Dignity, pride	+ Self-esteem + Quality of daily life – Misdiagnosis	+ Aspirations of women + Referrals for other eye issues
Relationship Well-Being	+ Access to networks + Status, respect – Instability in family dynamics	+ Reduced dependence on others + Professional reputation	+ Gender equity – Jealousy, conflict over changes in status and roles

FIGURE 4.5 VisionSpring's BoP IAF

Our performance analysis focused on assessing VisionSpring's impacts on its customers, the buyers in the BoP IAF. Toward that end, we collected survey data from more than five hundred individuals, all of whom had been diagnosed by VisionSpring as nearsighted and suitable candidates for vision correction with glasses.[29] This sample was almost evenly divided between those who elected to purchase VisionSpring's low-cost glasses (our treatment group) and those who did not (our comparison group). We were interested in two things: How did an individual's poverty influence his or her likelihood of purchase, and what were the impacts on individuals who purchased their glasses? The former involves an examination of buyers and the comparison group at baseline data, while the other incorporates both baseline and end-line data for the two groups.

As might be expected, income levels did influence the purchase decision—but so did the presence or absence of capability and relationship factors. For example, social support (including family and community), social status in the local community, and gender all also influenced purchasing decisions.[30]

VisionSpring can use this information to enhance its value proposition by better understanding, for instance, what is limiting purchase by women. Do gender norms influence purchasing, or is it that women thought the models of glasses were unattractive?

In terms of impact, the productivity gains to buyers, who included local craftspeople, retailers, and farmers, seemed to outpace increases in income. Although they reported increased income, these gains were not necessarily equivalent to the increases in productivity. There are at least two explanations. The first is that there isn't a large enough market to absorb increased productivity. For example, a tailor may be able to sell only four shirts per week, even if he or she could produce more. The other is that increased productivity translated into more time to do other things. Sometimes we have to remind ourselves that the BoP are not necessarily seeking to work more: they are pleased to spend less time earning the same amount of money.[31] Eyeglass purchasers also reported that their quality of life had improved—again, validation of the VisionSpring value proposition and a signpost toward improved marketing in the future. These and other findings (preliminary as of this writing) can help VisionSpring refine its business model and its market message about local value creation.

VisionSpring is constantly seeking ways to improve its value proposition to its customers and its distributors. For example, it has branched out into a partnership model to tap into the existing distribution network that these organizations had created, including an extensive partnership with BRAC, a large and well-respected Bangladeshi development organization, which was designed to train seventy thousand health care workers to sell reading glasses.[32] It also has now developed a hub-and-spoke model that allows it to provide access to an ophthalmologist and thereby sell prescription glasses for treating myopia (diminished ability to see distant objects). Since its inception, VisionSpring has sold nearly 2 million pairs of glasses.[33]

By capturing multidimensional impacts on well-being across its key constituencies, VisionSpring learned a great deal about the value it was creating and potential paths forward. Rather than depending on an impressionistic, anecdote-based view or on measures of outputs, the enterprise's leadership team now had a holistic and fact-based picture of its impacts (good and less good) and its value proposition. This new self-awareness made finding and pursuing new opportunities easier. At the same time, developing a more accurate and robust self-portrait offered a new way for VisionSpring to demonstrate to potential partners the value of investing in the organization.[34]

THE FRAMEWORK IN A SECOND CONTEXT: SANERGY

In this second example of the BoP IAF at work, which illustrates how an enterprise can choose to pursue only the strategic analysis and still derive benefit from the BoP IAF, the framework was applied in the context of addressing sanitation in urban Kenya. The focus is Sanergy, a for-profit enterprise launched in Kenya in 2009.[35] It was built around an integrated business model that addresses the challenges of open defecation, waste disposal, and poor hygiene practices in the urban slums of Nairobi—and ultimately energy generation using the collected wastes.

In the developing world, and especially in densely populated urban areas, sanitation, defined by the World Health Organization as the safe disposal of human waste, as well as the maintenance of hygienic conditions, is a major challenge.[36] Central to that challenge are reducing open defecation and enhancing water quality.

Young children are particularly vulnerable to poor sanitation, in part because they tend to experience greater exposure to hazards—for example, by playing in vacant lots contaminated by feces—and in part because their bodies' defenses are weaker.[37] Children who live in an environment characterized by poor sanitation can be affected in a range a ways, including lower-than-average height, diminished cognitive capability, sickness, and even death.[38] It is estimated that diarrhea kills 1.5 million people annually in developing countries, 90 percent of them children under the age of five.[39]

For all these reasons and more, reducing open defecation is critically important. So too are sanitary practices like hand washing, which by itself can reduce the occurrence of diarrhea cases by 35 to 45 percent. Finally, preventing the contamination of drinking water through runoff from rain, transmission by flies and other animals, and human activity is also critical since diarrhea morbidity can be reduced by 6 to 25 percent through improvements to the water supply.

Because these risks are fairly well understood, there have been repeated attempts to address them in the urban neighborhoods of developing countries. These initiatives have tended to be either top down (government-led interventions) or bottom up (community-based solutions). Neither approach has proven consistently effective.[40] Top-down efforts often fail to obtain the funds needed to install a comprehensive sanitation infrastructure. Bottom-up initiatives, which tend to rely on local community ownership of resources, struggle with the transitory and heterogeneous nature of urban populations, which limits coherence, commitment, and adherence to the solutions that are implemented.[41]

Sanergy seeks to build a scalable enterprise that also addresses the urgent social needs associated with poor sanitation. Drawing lessons from both of the models, it combines top-down central management with bottom-up ownership, and its business model seeks both economic and social performance. At the heart of the Sanergy system are modular sanitation facilities called fresh life toilets (FLTs), which are set up on a pay-per-use basis. These modular units, which combine toilets and sinks, are small enough to be deployed in crowded urban settings.

To facilitate expansion, Sanergy adopted a franchise model, which helps ensure that a set of operating procedures is applied across all FLTs, and local franchisees are responsible for ensuring the cleanliness of their facilities and the proper collection and disposal of waste. Toward that end, franchisees receive training in the proper maintenance of their FLTs. As part of their franchise agreement, they agree to strongly encourage all of their customers to practice good sanitary hygiene, especially the washing of hands with soap (supplied) after each use of a toilet.

An FLT costs about $588, an investment that in many cases can be facilitated by local microfinance groups. Annual waste removal, handled by Sanergy, tends to run just over $100 per year, with the first year being free. The franchisees charge between 3 and 5 Kenyan shillings (about $0.04 to 0.06) per use, which is competitive with other local and generally inferior commercial alternatives (typically a structure with a hole in the ground lined with plastic sheeting). As of June 2015, Sanergy had 701 communal FLTs generating twenty-seven thousand daily uses from community members.[42] With 10 million people living in Kenya's slums, Sanergy sees an annual market potential of $72 million.

With financial assistance from the Bernard van Leer Foundation and the support of the Sanergy leadership team, my colleagues and I applied the BoP IAF to the company's business model with a particular focus on the impacts on young children in the communities being served by Sanergy franchisees.[43] In June 2012, we initiated field-based data collection. Sanergy welcomed the opportunity for this kind of effort to be done by people outside the company—in part because it wouldn't burden existing staff, and also because the findings were more likely to be objective. The Sanergy team had developed a strong model and was interested in understanding opportunities for potential improvements. Our research began with a review of existing secondary information, as well as phone interviews with the venture's founders and other leaders in the sanitation field. Based on this information, we developed a structured interview format, which we planned to use not only to elicit specific information from various stakeholder groups but also as a way of initiating more open-ended discussions. We adopted the model depicted in Figure 4.1, focusing on three areas of well-being—capability, economics, and relationships—and three key constituent groups: franchisees, customers, and community members, who were nonusers.

We began with interviews of key members of the company's management and operations team. Next, we interviewed twenty local stakeholders across our three constituent groups and interviewed representatives of locally based partners, including schools, clinics, governmental agencies, and NGOs. Because we were not able to conduct before-and-after interviews in this situation, we asked our respondents to make comparisons, such as the current well-being of children as compared to their status before the Sanergy intervention. We also asked respondents whose children used the FLTs to compare the well-being of their children to the well-being of children in nonusing families. We asked about all three dimensions of well-being, and encouraged them to tell us both positive and negative aspects within each one. It's worth noting that to the extent that Sanergy's efforts were effective, all community members, including nonusers, probably derived some benefit from those efforts—but nonusers were the best comparison group available given the scope of the study.

We assessed the collected data on an ongoing basis, which enabled us to probe more deeply into the key impacts that our research was turning up. This developed detailed summaries of each interview, with codes attached to identify and compare impacts, which helped us incorporate the lessons of the raw data in our BoP IAF. With these resources in hand, we conducted within-group analyses for each stakeholder group and, subsequently, cross-group comparisons. A summary of the strategic analysis is presented in Figure 4.6. [44]

Our focus was the impact of Sanergy's business model on young children. Most important, our findings showed how impacts varied within and across different groups of stakeholder children and provided a platform for understanding the implications of these differences. In terms of capability well-being, we found that the business model did indeed have important positive impacts on health. Children across all three of the studied stakeholder groups benefited from greater use of Sanergy's FLTs in the community, with children of franchise owners, who had the greatest access to the FLTs, seeing the greatest impact. The environment also was cleaner, especially the area immediately surrounding the FLTs. Because of this, the youngest children, including those who crawled on the ground and put things in their mouths, tended to benefit more than older children.

As might be expected, the assessment of economic well-being led to a more complex variation in impacts. There were both important positive and negative impacts, and these varied by both stakeholder group and time frame. The most substantial potential negative impacts—mainly short term—were on the children of franchisees, who either saw the family draw down their limited assets or incur debt, or both, to secure a franchise. This reduced the family's resilience in the face of any financial shocks, such as an unanticipated health event. Sanergy estimates that something like seven months are required for the typical franchisee to repay his or her loan, a relatively fast repayment time frame. If, however, during that interval, loan repayment costs exceeded FLT-generated revenues, the family could come under further financial stress. And because running an FLT required a regular on-site presence, franchisees were restricted in opportunities for generating income by other means, which again could reduce their children's economic well-being.

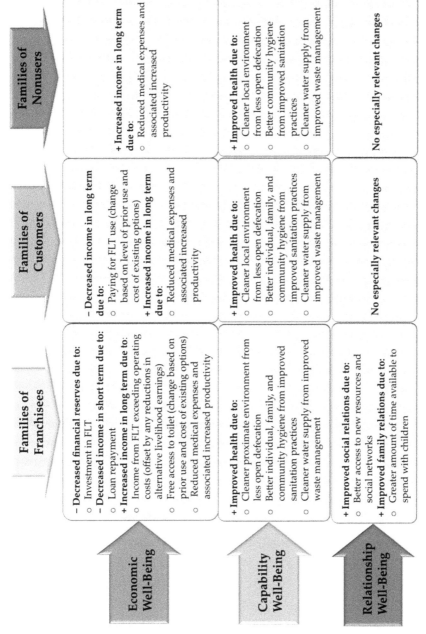

FIGURE 4.6 Sanergy's BoP IAF

The long-term benefits, however, were much more positive. If the franchise operated successfully, the family would have a steady source of additional income. The positive unit economics and short loan payment period for each FLT, and the fact that a number of franchisees have purchased a second FLT, offer support for the viability of the model.

The children of users could also suffer short-term economic consequences, depending on how their families had previously dealt with waste disposal and sanitation. (There were less expensive, and far less sanitary, alternatives available, such as so-called flying toilets, whereby waste is deposited into a plastic bag that is then tossed into the local environment.) And while there appeared to be long-term economic benefits for user families, such as decreased medical expenses and fewer sick days, there were clear shorter-term trade-offs to be dealt with in terms of disposable income. Children of nonusers generally only saw positive changes to economic well-being. With a cleaner local environment, they and their families were generally less sick. This came at no additional cost, as they were not using the FLTs.

Our exploration of relationship well-being underscored the complexities inherent in impacts and impact assessment. A franchisee's child might well be negatively affected in economic terms by the fact that his or her parent was tightly tied to the operation of the FLT and thereby was prevented from picking up part-time or seasonal work. The flip side of that coin was that the franchisee was closer to home on a more consistent basis and was therefore a more accessible caregiver. (Most research into child development shows that parental stimulation in the first three years of life is particularly important; franchisees were better positioned to provide that stimulation.[45]) Similarly, although families that incurred debt were more at risk of financial woes, especially when emergencies arose, those same families were now generally incorporated into the microcredit universe, which implied good things for their longer-term opportunities through expanded resources and networks.

Obviously, this is only a sample of the interesting findings that grew out of the application of the BoP IAF to Sanergy's operation in Nairobi.[46] The primary goal of the BoP IAF is business related, so the question then became, How can Sanergy create more value by better understanding the poverty alleviation opportunity? Although there were many positive impacts to amplify,

Sanergy also sought to mitigate the negative ones. For example, Sanergy's current business model produces financial burdens on users that can have a negative effect on the well-being of their children. These impacts on economic well-being may also discourage nonusers from converting to users or limit FLT use by current users. Our findings complemented Sanergy's understanding of these impacts and reinforced the leadership team's efforts to seek out donors or other external funders who would be willing to invest in providing vouchers, or similar mechanisms for minimizing negative financial impacts, to targeted existing customers and nonusers.

Similarly, the current business model imposes a financial burden on franchisees, on whom the entire operation hinges. If those franchisees don't experience an overall improvement of their economic well-being, they may abandon the effort. Again, this reinforced Sanergy's efforts to explore ways to provide low-cost financing or reduce the cost to the franchisee of an FLT.[47] Addressing these and other poverty alleviation (and value creation) opportunities will allow the business to grow faster with more a robust value proposition that addresses opportunities along multiple dimensions of poverty.

WHAT'S REQUIRED: COURAGE AND COMMITMENT

Successful businesses understand their value proposition and are always looking for ways to enhance it. For enterprises operating in BoP markets, creating value means alleviating poverty. BoP impact enterprises will succeed only if they have a deep understanding of how to access and enhance their poverty alleviation impacts. The BoP IAF offers a holistic, interactive, flexible, and actionable tool for doing just that.

The focus on mutual value creation, and the BoP IAF as a tool to facilitate this effort, complements other approaches that center on greater investment in impact enterprises. Shared value, for example, highlights the economic benefits of business strategies based on addressing social issues. Champions of impact investing use investment capital to achieve social good. Measurement tools such as the Progress out of Poverty Index and the Social Progress Index track individual and broader society outcomes with regard to changes in specific measures of poverty.[48] None, however, are specifically designed to access and strengthen value propositions in a local context. The BoP IAF is especially well suited to efforts that seek a high level of stakeholder engagement and co-creation.[49]

Yet there are forces that work against conducting a robust impact assessment. Some emerge internally—for example, from the leadership team. Hubris and a tendency toward overconfidence in the local value creation potential of the enterprise's business model also can play a role here. The thinking goes something like this: "We are trying to make a difference, and of course we *are*—so therefore, we really don't need to measure impact, and we can rely instead on anecdotes and output measures."

We have noted that anecdotes capture the imagination and can be very useful in conveying purpose and vision. They also have the advantage of being carefully selected. But they have important limitations as a representation of impact. Output-based assessments are also relatively easy to manage and control, yet these too are limited because their actual relationship to impact is unclear.

Even if the BoP impact enterprise's management is committed to understanding impact, there is still one more countervailing force against conducting the type of impact assessment necessarily to truly understand and unlock that enterprise's value proposition. This force is external, emerging from the enterprise's partners and supporters. In interacting with these organizations and individuals, the incentives to report anything other than success are generally weak or entirely absent. In fact, the presence of development community partners—although generally a highly positive outcome, given their capacity to support an enterprise's development—can create pressure for the leadership team to paint a relentlessly positive self-portrait. Development agencies, foundations, and nonprofit organizations have to satisfy their own constituents, who want to see success stories coming from the organizations that they have supported directly and indirectly. At the same time, enterprises receiving financial and other types of support from development community partners often receive those resources in tranches. This means that demonstrating success, especially in terms of social impact, may be crucial to liberating the next round of funding or when seeking financial or other types of support from a new partner.

For all these reasons, using the BoP IAF or a similar framework requires both the courage to learn and a commitment to improve—attributes that both VisionSpring and Sanergy demonstrated. Impact assessments are likely to generate mixed results—in other words, exactly what you need in order to see opportunities to create more value, but not necessarily what enterprise leaders want to share with their partners and funders, or even with themselves.

There are bound to be unexpected or negative impacts. Everyone who works in a complex human community has encountered the law of unintended, unexpected, or unanticipated consequences—both good and bad. Especially in the BoP context, the possibility that any enterprise that has a positive impact will also do no wrong is fairly remote. The goal, again, is to have a net positive impact and to understand how to enhance the positives and mitigate the negatives to build a more robust value proposition.

Enterprises have to develop a holistic picture of their value proposition and the opportunity for further value creation. The sometimes conflicting tugs and pulls don't change that requirement. BoP impact enterprise success is premised on understanding and enhancing their poverty alleviation impacts. A deeper understanding of impact generates a more robust value proposition and leads to opportunities to enhance mutual value creation.

Partnerships with the development community can present challenges that BoP impact enterprise leaders must be prepared to address. Indeed, close collaborations with a network of partners will likely prove indispensable in efforts to create a sustainable and scalable enterprise. In the next two chapters, I focus on that universe of potential partners, exploring both with whom to partner and how to build viable collaborative relationships with them.

5 CREATING A PARTNERSHIP ECOSYSTEM

So far, we have considered two of the three foundations described in the Preface to this book: leveraging customizable tools, frameworks, and strategies to enhance enterprise development, and creating value with the BoP by truly understanding the poverty alleviation opportunity. This chapter and the following explore the third foundation: establishing an ecosystem of partners to help sustain those ventures. In particular, BoP impact enterprise leaders must find ways to integrate their business development efforts with outside investments and other kinds of support, available from an ecosystem of potential partners that I call "scaling facilitators": the set of organizations, primarily from the development community, that are willing to invest their expertise and resources to support BoP impact enterprises in achieving sustainability and scalability.

These scaling facilitators are a diverse set of potential partners, including nonprofit organizations that can provide information, distribution support, and advocacy; investment funds that offer financial and other resources; development institutions that can deliver market strengthening and advisory services; and in some cases, government bodies that seek to encourage market-based approaches to poverty alleviation. In short, the landscape of scaling facilitators is complex and diverse.

There has been a proliferation of scaling facilitators and a growing recognition of their importance in supporting BoP impact enterprises.[1] The challenge is that enterprise leaders still lack the kinds of actionable tools that would help them better understand the potential partnership landscape and develop a proactive and effective partnership strategy. In this chapter, I address that deficit by focusing on the who of creating a partnership ecosystem. I address the how in Chapter 6.

In exploring the who, I begin with the premise that BoP impact enterprises struggle if they try to get to scale alone. This is true of enterprises operating across a wide variety of contexts, of course, but the challenges inherent in underdeveloped BoP markets make this partnering requirement particularly important.

Most enterprises that attempt to serve BoP markets have to play an active role in fortune creating, and this almost surely requires the support and resources of an ecosystem of partners. In the developed world, if an enterprise team comes up with a great product or service, markets are likely to be in place or they can invest in market awareness with confidence that the needed infrastructure and institutions will be there to support these efforts and that their investments in awareness can be tied to their brand. Consumers are generally educated and accessible, distribution channels (ranging from the web to the retail sector to commercial delivery systems) are in place, and regulations are typically commerce friendly and enforceable. And even in the developed world, alliances, partnerships, and bridge-spanning roles such as community relations, government affairs, and corporate liaisons to particular organizations and institutions are common.[2]

In BoP markets, by contrast, these key building blocks of a business environment may not exist or may operate in very different ways.[3] BoP impact enterprises focused on achieving scale almost always find that they must locate partners willing to provide support across a wide range of functions—for example, helping to facilitate operational activities, providing access to needed financial and other resources, influencing supply or demand (or both), or otherwise enhancing the context in which the enterprise operates.

In other words, to achieve sustainability and scalability, enterprise leaders need to carefully construct the appropriate network of supporting organizations that I call the partnership ecosystem. They must ask and answer the questions, "What kinds of partners and partner resources will be needed for success, and how should this ecosystem of partners evolve over time?"

While the idea of collaborating with a set of partners is not a new concept, the ability to do so effectively in BoP markets is. The challenge for most enterprise leaders in understanding the "who" is twofold: organizing the landscape of potential partners into a managerially friendly framework and then using this framework to identify the appropriate portfolio of scaling facilitators that can enhance organizational performance. Toward these two ends, I introduce a key tool that I call the Partnership Ecosystem Framework (PEF).[4]

LANDSCAPE OF SCALING FACILITATORS

Countries across the globe have spent billions of dollars in development and foreign aid since World War II toward the goal of alleviating poverty and improving well-being in developing nations. These efforts have met with only modest success, leading to greater interest in exploring new approaches.[5] The U.S. Agency for International Development, the U.K.'s Department for International Development, the Japan International Cooperation Agency, the International Finance Corporation, the Inter-American Development Bank, and many other bi- and multilateral development institutions have developed, for example, a variety of programs aimed at supporting impact enterprises. As Oxfam America has noted, "Market-based approaches...have become an increasingly vital area for anti-poverty development work, spurring a wide range of new actors, partnerships, and initiatives."[6]

One result is the emergence of scaling facilitators, organizations that provide expertise and resources to support BoP impact enterprises in their efforts to achieve impact, sustainability, and scale. Primarily coming from the development sector, they can target this support at both the venture level and the industry or market-environment level and generally work with multiple enterprises concurrently.

Scaling facilitators employ a wide variety of implementation models—accelerators, incubators, impact investing, challenge funds, last-mile distribution and sourcing support, strengthening market systems, advisory services, network building, advocacy support, and many others—to provide their mix of services. Table 5.1 provides examples of some of the variation in services within and across implementations models used by scaling facilitators.

A scaling facilitator may use one or more implementation models, each of which may provide multiple kinds of support. In other words, understanding the landscape requires identifying the scaling facilitators in your context, recognizing which implementation models they are using, and determining what portfolio of services is offered within each implementation model.

TABLE 5.1 Scaling facilitators: Landscape of implementation models

Implementation Model	Description	Scaling Facilitators Using This Model
Incubator	Provides services to early-stage enterprises, including in-kind resources, coaching and mentoring, and access to capital and potential collaborators. Incubators often facilitate the ideation process as a first step.	Echoing Green Impact Hub
Accelerator	Building capacity of enterprises to increase their investment readiness, prepare for scale, and connect to potential funders. Accelerators can take equity positions in the ventures they support.	Unreasonable Institute Global Social Benefit Institute
Impact investing	Investing debt or equity in ventures that intentionally achieve both positive social and financial returns. These investments may be provided by private investors, managed funds, or program-related investments by foundations or nonprofits.	Acumen Root Capital Grassroots Business Fund
Challenge fund	Financing mechanism targeting a specific purpose (such as health care delivery in a particular market) that uses competition among organizations. Funds, typically grants with no expectation of return of capital, are awarded based on which enterprises best meet the objectives and criteria specified by the fund.	Africa Enterprise Challenge Fund USAID Development Innovation Ventures Saving Lives at Birth
Last-mile distribution and sourcing	Addresses the challenge of reaching local consumers or producers. This can be through providing access to local platforms, supporting local institutions such as cooperatives, or engaging a distribution network.	CARE Living Goods Solar Sister Clinton Giustra
Strengthening market systems	Building the business capacity of local BoP entrepreneurs, including providing training and access to credit. Also facilitates connection and linkage among market participants, including value chain development.	BRAC TechnoServe Accion Abt Associates
Advisory services	Provides consulting, technical assistance, or broader knowledge creation that builds the capacity of enterprises or promotes development of a sector.	William Davidson Institute Poverty Action Lab
Network building	Provides a platform to exchange ideas, promote collective action, and lend legitimacy to enterprises and the broader domain. May also support certification or similar compliance-oriented efforts.	Business Call to Action BoP Global Network Inclusive Business Action Network
Advocacy	Advocates for particular issues or communities. Often seeks changes in regulations, policy, and/or levels of enforcement.	Oxfam Global Health Advocates

The growth in resources available to BoP impact enterprise through these scaling facilitators and their associated implementation models is extraordinary. A decade or so ago, development organizations remained leery about supporting any enterprises that were not owned or operated by the BoP.[7] While the exact amount of support available today is difficult to calculate, looking at the evolution of just one of the implementation models, impact investing, provides a powerful data point for extrapolation.

Impact investing captures a growing category of financial investments that are intended to have a positive impact beyond the purely financial.[8] Impact investors provide capital and at times other resources to businesses in the expectation that they will earn a return on their investment—generally at below market rates—while also generating positive social returns. Their investments can take the form of traditional equity or debt instruments or more innovative forms, such as bonds whose rate of return is linked to the success of the enterprise being funded.[9]

By most measures, it's a potentially huge market segment. In J. P. Morgan's 2014 survey of the Global Impact Investing Network, members reported $46 billion of assets under management.[10] In another report, J. P. Morgan estimated that in five core sectors alone (housing, water, health, education, and financial services), the investment potential may approach $1 trillion over the next decade, with potential returns to investors of between $183 billion and $667 billion.[11]

As might be expected with this level of growth, the number of impact investors has also increased substantially. Each generally works with multiple businesses concurrently and offers a different mix of support to the enterprises in their portfolio. The same is true for other implementation models. As a result, as illustrated in Figure 5.1, there is both a diverse set of implementation models and a wide range of services provided within each type of implementation model.

Even these noncomprehensive lists and graphics suggest that this is a complicated ecosystem, with a growing number of scaling facilitators, each offering different combinations of support across a wide variety of implementation models. This support can be targeted toward enterprises in different stages of growth, ranging from start-up entrepreneurs to established enterprises seeking

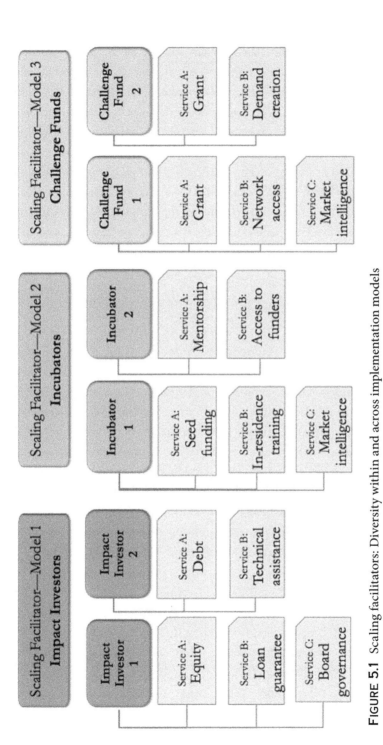

FIGURE 5.1 Scaling facilitators: Diversity within and across implementation models

resources to facilitate further scale. Furthermore, scaling facilitators can focus on supporting specific enterprises or provide resources targeted to the broader market environment in which enterprises operate. Clearly it can be a complex challenge to understand and sort through the wide range of available options, a challenge that the BoP impact enterprise must accept and overcome if it hopes to maximize the value from building a partnership ecosystem.

Some concrete examples of how scaling facilitators operate is useful at this point. With that in mind, we next look at two implementation models—impact investors and last-mile distribution support—used by two scaling facilitators that have established themselves as effective partners, and consider an example of their interactions with a specific BoP impact enterprise.

IMPACT INVESTING: ACUMEN AND WATER HEALTH INTERNATIONAL

One of the earliest players among today's impact investors is Acumen (formerly known as Acumen Fund), which seeks to prove that small amounts of patient capital, combined with large doses of business acumen, can help build thriving enterprises that serve vast numbers of the BoP.[12] Acumen was founded in 2001 with seed money from the Rockefeller Foundation, Cisco Systems Foundation, and a number of private donors. After four years of operations and proof of concept, it received further institutional support from Google.org and the Bill and Melinda Gates Foundation in the amounts of $5 million and $3.9 million, respectively.

Acumen, which originally provided grants, now focuses on making equity or debt investments in the range of $300,000 to $2 million to enterprises in areas of health, water, housing, agriculture, energy, and education. By 2015, it had approved more than $88 million in investments in Ghana, India, Kenya, Nigeria, Pakistan, Rwanda, Tanzania, Uganda, and Ethiopia. It has invested in eighty-two enterprises since its founding in 2001, which by its own estimates translates into creating some sixty thousand jobs and otherwise helping more than 100 million people.[13]

Acumen primarily supports ventures by providing financing, using a variety of financial vehicles, to develop sustainable and scalable ventures. It also offers management support, ranging from having a seat on the board of directors to providing expertise through the short-term placement of staff, consultants, or fellows with investees.[14]

Acumen generally takes only a minority stake, typically between 10 and 33 percent of the capitalization. Its investments target a "reasonable but often below-market financial return on capital invested." Expected payback period is in the range of five to seven years, but could extend longer if needed. Debt investments are exited through principal and interest payments over the term of the loan. Equity stakes have three liquidation options: in order of likelihood, sale to strategic investors, management buyback, or initial public offering. During an investment cycle or after an exit, Acumen can make a new investment depending on the stage of the enterprise. If an enterprise is able to access more traditional private capital after an exit, Acumen views its role as finished. Capital is not returned to the investors in Acumen, who receive tax deductions for their contributions as philanthropic donors to a 501(c)(3); rather, any returns are reinvested into other enterprises.

For an example of Acumen at work, we look at WaterHealth International (WHI), an international for-profit water company, founded in 1995 and based in the United States, which manufactures and markets water purification systems in developing countries using a proprietary water technology system, UV Waterworks.[15] Its mission is to "achieve unprecedented scale in providing affordable, safe, potable water to underserved populations worldwide, to save lives and enhance economic development."

WHI initially sold its water filtration systems to entrepreneurs, community organizations, nongovernmental organizations, and local governments serving both rural and urban communities. These water systems could provide a community of two thousand to seven thousand people with up to twenty liters of safe drinking water per person per day. In addition to selling the water systems, WHI offered support in financing, maintenance, site selection, systems operations, marketing, and advertising support.

In 2004, in an effort to scale its operations into India and expand in the Philippines, WHI opened a $2.55 million Series B equity round of financing. Acumen invested $600,000 in preferred B shares (8 percent noncumulative dividend) in the company, joining the International Finance Corporation and a private entrepreneur as co-investors. Acumen considered its equity stake as a high-risk, low-return investment. Since finance theory suggests that a high-risk investment demands a probability of a high return, the equity investments by Acumen and the other investors should be considered a form of subsidized equity.

After making the investment, Acumen provided significant management and technical assistance free of charge to WHI to support its operations. For example, it funded a redesign of the water purification system, assisted in recruiting efforts for senior management, and advised in decisions on operations, marketing strategy, and board and governance work, all focused on building enterprise capabilities.

In 2006, Acumen entered into another financial arrangement with WHI, guaranteeing a WHI credit facility with ICICI Bank in India to finance the growth of water system sales in India. Under the agreement, Acumen provided a 30 percent first-loss guarantee on a loan of $1 million, which would support approximately thirty-five water systems in the state of Andhra Pradesh. Acumen did this primarily to protect and enhance its equity investment and did not charge WHI for providing this guarantee. ICICI would not have extended the credit to WHI without the support of an outside guarantor because the economics of the water systems were not yet proven.

In 2008, Acumen provided a second loan guarantee on an $8 million credit facility with IFMR Trust, a private financial services affiliate of ICICI Bank; the credit facility would be used to further scale water systems throughout India. This time, Acumen provided IFMR Trust with a 15 percent first-loss guarantee, compared to 30 percent in the first guarantee in 2006, an indicator of WHI's progress in proving its business model. In addition, unlike the terms of the first guarantee, Acumen received warrants in the agreement—securities allowing Acumen to purchase stock of WHI at a specified price. Though closer to commercial market terms than the first guarantee, this second loan guarantee still had elements of subsidy support, as Acumen could have received greater compensation by undertaking a similar risk position in the capital markets.

Acumen thus supported WHI as a scaling facilitator in a number of key ways. Not only did it provide access to subsidized capital through several different approaches, it also offered free-of-charge management and technical assistance to support WHI's operations: funding a redesign of the water purification system, assisting in the recruitment of senior management, and advising in key decisions on operations, marketing strategy, and board and other governance work.

Acumen was not the only source of support for WHI. In 2006–2007, for example, WHI began to realize the benefit of leveraging public funds in India to roll out its systems. Each year, the national government and state municipalities allocated funding in their budgets to support water infrastructure and the distribution of potable water to citizens. Accordingly, WHI started applying for public funds to build out its water systems. One benefit of doing this was that by partnering with the government, WHI could sell water systems in larger orders rather than system by system. It also relied on the village-level governments, *panchayats*, to support the rollout of its WaterHealth Centers. The panchayats ensured that there was a suitable piece of land, a water source, and access to electricity to establish the water systems in their communities.

WHI is a work in progress; it is still working toward the goal of being sustainable at scale. Toward that end, it continues to explore new partnership opportunities. Recently, for example, the Coca-Cola Company announced it has taken a minority equity ownership in WHI and is supporting the company through its Replenish Africa Initiative (RAIN), a $30 million corporate commitment that aims to help give 2 million Africans access to clean water.[16]

LAST-MILE DISTRIBUTION: CARE AND HINDUSTAN UNILEVER LIMITED

Another type of implementation model that generally offers a different combination of support from impact investing is what is known as last-mile distribution support: addressing the challenges found at the end point in the distribution system, when the good or service finally reaches the intended consumer. I illustrate this model this by reintroducing CARE, an organization we met in Chapter 3 in the context of a seed project aimed at helping India's farmers.

Headquartered in Geneva, Switzerland, CARE is an international, humanitarian nongovernmental organization (NGO) composed of twelve member countries that manage field operations in over eighty-seven countries around the world, running some nine hundred poverty-fighting development and humanitarian aid projects that reach more than 50 million poor people.[17] It attempts to find long-term solutions to overcome poverty and to "seek a world of hope, tolerance and social justice, where poverty has been overcome and people live in dignity and security."

CARE has worked in India since 1949, focusing its poverty-fighting efforts on the most vulnerable sections of society, especially underprivileged women and girls. CARE India runs programs in the areas of nutrition, health, HIV/AIDS, and economic development. It is far from a simple assignment. India's nearly 639,000 rural villages comprise over 128 million households and have a population of 742 million, nearly three times the population of urban India (285 million). The Indian rural population is substantially poorer, with a per capita annual income below Rs 10,000 ($227), compared to the national average of approximately Rs 21,000 ($477).

To understand how an organization like CARE India can work as a scaling facilitator, we consider at some length a serious business challenge that one of India's largest and most ubiquitous companies faces in serving BoP markets, and examine how CARE India's support in last-mile distribution contributed to the solution of that challenge.

Hindustan Lever Limited began operating in India in 1888 with the distribution of its "Made in England" Sunlight detergent.[18] In 1931, when India was still a British colony, Hindustan Vanaspati Limited was formed as a 100 percent subsidiary of Unilever in India. It primarily sold soaps, detergents, and other household products to a select group of affluent consumers, such as British government employees and the Indian elite. Until the 1960s, the company remained a medium-sized player, choosing to market high-end brands to wealthier Indian consumers. In the years that followed, it continued to launch new brands in the fast-moving consumer goods (FMCG) segment, including the highly successful Lifebuoy and Liril bath soaps, Surf detergent powder, Fair and Lovely Fairness cream, and Close-Up toothpaste. In 2007, the company name was formally changed to Hindustan Unilever Limited (HUL).

After seeing revenues grow at a fast pace throughout the 1990s, the company hit a growth plateau. Early in the decade, sales had surged fivefold to

Rs 101.42 billion ($2.305 billion). By 1999, however, sales had flattened out, and at the April 2000 shareholders' meeting, the chairman, K. B. Dadiseth, unveiled its Millennium Plan, a strategic blueprint for the years ahead. One important component of this plan was a new approach for reaching rural India, a market that HUL had barely penetrated.

Roughly three-quarters of India's population lives in rural villages. Due to the sheer size of the population, rural India is potentially a lucrative market for any consumer products company. In fact, its consumption has also been growing steadily since the 1980s and is now bigger than the urban market for FMCGs (53 percent share of the total market). More than half of HUL's products were bought by rural consumers. Yet when HUL considered that its products were available in less than 15 percent of the villages, it recognized the vast untapped potential of rural India.

With a seed capital of Rs 100 million ($2.3 million) and a new management structure, a new initiative, Shakti, was born. Shakti (which means "strength" or "empowerment" in many of the local Indian languages) is different from HUL's other rural expansion efforts, as well as those of other consumer product companies in India, in that it sought to leverage an extensive network of self-help groups that had been created and support by local partners and the federal and state governments. These self-help groups were development initiatives targeted at enhancing local savings and industry (such as handicrafts and other hand-made products) and creating a stronger social system within rural villages.

A typical self-help group consists of eight to twenty members, and its activities include learning new vocational skills, airing grievances, and resolving local disputes. Self-help groups also act as savings cooperatives. Regular contributions by the members are invested in a joint account and then loaned internally to members according to their needs. Based on savings, these groups also can gain access to microcredit institutions, many of them supported by the government or local or international nonprofits.

Shakti's strategy for entering rural India and addressing the generally thorny issue of last-mile distribution was to harness the skills, energy, and contacts of the members of existing self-help groups. Typically HUL invited one woman (or sometimes more, depending on the size of the area to be served) from a self-help group in a targeted village to become a Shakti entre-preneur to promote and distribute HUL products within a cluster of four to six neighboring communities.

As the Shakti initiative was being launched, CARE India had access to a network of more than seventy thousand self-help groups across four states. Negotiations between HUL and CARE India got underway, in large part due to CARE's Credit and Savings for Household Enterprise (CASHE) program. CASHE, originally funded by the British government's Department for International Development for a seven-year period, was designed to increase the incomes of rural women in India and enhance their limited control over that income. It supports the development of microfinance organizations and enables its participants to gain access to capacity-building services. CASHE activities include facilitating the development of self-help groups, providing financial and technical assistance to microfinance institutions, encouraging the flow of financing from formal financial institutions to borrowers in low-income markets, and influencing government policy at the state and national levels.

Clearly HUL benefited from its partnership with CARE, including greater access to rural markets through the CASHE-supported network of self-help groups and enhanced local credibility through its affiliation with CARE India. It is also fair and important to ask what was in it for CARE India. How would CARE India achieve its mission by partnering with a for-profit company?

One answer is the economic gains generated through Shakti and enjoyed by CARE India's constituents. HUL provided the members of self-help groups with a potentially profitable microenterprise opportunity that was complementary to the limited menu of entrepreneurial activities then available through the self-help groups. In addition, Shakti invested in creating local awareness in areas particularly relevant to CARE's mission such as health and child care.[19] Moreover, by focusing on women, Shakti helped improve the status of women in a primarily male-dominated rural society, a key goal of CARE and CASHE.

The success of Shakti also advanced CARE India's broader efforts to facilitate wider use of private sector mechanisms to address development issues and encouraged other nonprofits to evaluate how the corporate sector might play a role in their own poverty alleviation activities. CARE India, for instance, has partnered with DuPont in a program involving distribution of agricultural inputs and with the ICICI Bank in microfinance initiatives in the rural sector.

CARE India was not HUL's only such partner. In fact, the company has entered into relationships with more than 350 nonprofits in India, many of which have helped it through facilitating access to local markets, knowledge, and resources. But CARE India, by virtue of its last-mile distribution support, served as a key scaling facilitator in the Shakti initiative's growth strategy.

MANAGING A PARTNERSHIP ECOSYSTEM

Acumen and CARE India are representative of the large and growing number of scaling facilitators that use one or more implementation models to support BoP impact enterprises. BoP impact enterprise leaders need to understand and manage that complexity and build their own holistic ecosystem of partners.

I have developed the Partnership Ecosystem Framework (PEF) to help with the challenge of determining who should be in this ecosystem. As illustrated in Table 5.2, the PEF is a managerially friendly tool that helps BoP impact enterprises understand the different roles that partners can play, assess where partnership support is most crucial, plot their existing ecosystem of partners and the support they are currently providing—in the case of start-up enterprises, this existing set of partners may be quite limited—and identify key gaps that remain.

Specifically, the PEF provides a strategic perspective that allows enterprise leaders to organize and categorize their current partnership ecosystem and compare that to their partnership needs. Assessing these needs requires understanding the enterprise's existing resources and capabilities and identifying gaps in this portfolio that are best filled through partnerships. After plotting their current partners and determining remaining gaps, enterprise leaders can then use the PEF to efficiently and effectively scan the overall landscape of potential partners to prioritize opportunities for building a more robust partnership ecosystem. An enterprise doesn't necessarily need equal partnership representation within each quadrant, and may not even need a partner in every quadrant. But successful BoP impact enterprises have a clear understanding of the role that partners are currently playing and the prioritized set of relationships they seek to build, now or in the future that best enables sustainable, scalable enterprise development.

The PEF also helps the broader development community understand the landscape of scaling facilitators within a particular context (e.g., geography, sector, stage of growth), assess the types of support currently available to enterprises, and determine where additional investments in support might have the greatest impact.

The PEF organizes support from scaling facilitators and their associated implementation models based on the focus (horizontal axis) and type (vertical axis) of that support. This generates four quadrants that capture the landscape of support that can be provided by potential partners. The result is a diagnostic tool that enterprise leaders can use to develop and manage their partnership portfolio.

The horizontal axis (the who) is divided into two categories that reflect an important distinction in partnership support: one targeting enterprise development, which provides support directly to a specific enterprise, and the other targeting market creation, which focuses on creating a better market environment to benefit the entire set of enterprises serving that market. Partner support can also be divided by the type of support provided (the what), as presented on the vertical axis. A useful analogy can be to consider these two types of support in terms of stock and flow. Support directed at action enabling enhances the flow, or the total number and/or value of transactions, by facilitating enterprise activities and market transactions. Support directed at capacity building increases the stock, or the value of assets, including an enterprise's capital or a market's infrastructure.

In each of the four quadrants of the PEF in Table 5.2, a subset of possible support from or investments by scaling facilitators is presented.[20] The terms in the left-hand column of the PEF are familiar to anyone who creates ventures in the developed world. In the BoP context, though, they take on new meaning. The right-hand column is not something most developed world entrepreneurs need to address. In BoP contexts, though, enterprise leaders must ensure they explicitly consider opportunities for market-creation support. With that in mind, we explore each of the four quadrants.

TABLE 5.2 Partnership Ecosystem Framework

	Enterprise Development	Market Creation
	Facilitate Enterprise Activities	**Facilitate Market Transactions**
Action Enabling	*Market Intelligence* • Cultural context, competitive landscape • Consumer demand, supplier preferences *Market Access* • Connection to distributors, other platforms • Implementation support *Value Creation* • Assess poverty impacts	*Demand Creation* • Awareness raising, behavior change • Microcredit, other sources of financing • Vouchers/subsidies *Supply Enhancement* • Advisory services for producers • Improved inputs • Aggregation of outputs
	Enhance Enterprise Resources	**Enhance Market Environment**
Capacity Building	*Financial Capital* • Grants, equity, debt, loan guarantee *Human Capital* • Talent development, technical assistance *Knowledge Capital* • Processes , tools, and frameworks *Social Capital* • Legitimacy, access to networks	*Value Chain Infrastructure* • Physical infrastructure development • Quality assurance and certification • Market transparency *Legal Infrastructure* • Policy changes and regulation enforcement *Institutional Infrastructure* • Banking, legal, property sector enhancement

Facilitate Enterprise Activities

Action enabling support for enterprise development, the upper-left quadrant in Table 5.2, facilitates the enterprise's operational activities in the field. This includes providing intelligence on the market that the venture is targeting. This could be information about local customs and key players, consumer preferences and constraints, or supplier gaps and challenges. This type of support reduces barriers to the development of enterprise strategies and business models for entering new markets or scaling existing market opportunities.

Support for market access occurs when the scaling facilitator acts as a catalyst in building relationships between the enterprise and a wider distribution network to which that enterprise may not have access, as in the example of CARE's support for HUL's Shakti initiative, or acts as an distributor for the enterprise. An example is Living Good's microfranchising model, where its network of agents carries a diverse basket of goods.[21]

Understanding local value creation, including the opportunities for enhancing social impacts, remains a challenge for many BoP impact enterprises. Organizations including the Abdul Latif Jameel Poverty Action Lab (J-PAL), the William Davidson Institute, Grameen Foundation, and the Global Impact Investing Network's IRIS Initiative provide tools and data collection approaches that can help these enterprises access and enhance how they create value in BoP markets, including their poverty alleviation impacts.[22] A number of other organizations have also created tools and models of support to help enterprises in this area.[23]

Enhance Enterprise Resources

Capacity building at the enterprise-level enhances the enterprise's stock of resources (the lower-left quadrant in Table 5.2). A scaling facilitator can build financial capital by providing a variety of types of financial support, including grants, loans, lines of credit, convertible debt, leasing, equity, first-loss coverage, and loan guarantees at or below market rates. The Acumen example provides one scaling facilitator's approach to this.

Another way scaling facilitators enhance enterprises' resources is through building human capital. Here, the scaling facilitator could provide training to the enterprise team in business skills, product development, or other types of technical skills. Other examples might include financial training or sharing best practices, successes, and failures from the field. The scaling facilitator can also provide direct access to talent. In this model, the facilitator can offer access to or placement of experienced executives who can complement the venture's existing management team.

Scaling facilitators can also build knowledge and social capital, respectively, by sharing best practices through the transfer of processes, tools, or strategies and providing increased legitimacy or access to new or more robust networks.

Facilitate Market Transactions

Most BoP impact enterprises likely need to participate in or benefit from market creation activities that seek to facilitate the flow of transactions in the marketplace (the upper-right quadrant in Figure 5.2). Such pump-priming activities are challenging and costly undertakings for an enterprise and require investments that may benefit future competitors, thus discouraging individual action.[24]

When scaling facilitators engage in behavior change to increase awareness of a particular product or service category, they help build demand for the products or services within a certain industry by educating consumers on the value propositions of products or services being sold in a particular market. Examples include conducting marketing campaigns or holding public seminars about the benefits of hand washing to protect against disease or the dangers of chronic exposure to smoke from many traditional cooking practices.[25]

Buyer incentives can be useful in markets where consumers may not have the will or the resources to buy certain goods or services that are deemed beneficial to their health, social well-being, or the surrounding environment.[26] In these markets, a scaling facilitator may try to close this value gap in order to create demand by making it easier for consumers to purchase products—for example, by facilitating access to credit or providing consumption subsidies in the form of vouchers.

Scaling facilitators can contribute to supply enhancement by identifying and communicating market needs and providing advisory services that help increase the volume, quality, and consistency of producer yields. They can also partner with input providers to identify and offer context-appropriate inputs—such as seeds, fertilizer, and equipment—that improve harvests. By facilitating aggregation, local producers are then able to become more reliable and desirable suppliers. In addition, these producers can see increases in the price they receive for their products.

BoP impact enterprises that fail to consider the need to facilitate market transactions run the risk of delivering goods and services for which adequate demand does not exist or sourcing products that are not available in sufficient quality or quantity.

Enhance Market Environment

Capacity building focused on market creation involves enhancing the assets in the market environment in which the enterprise operates (the lower-right quadrant in Table 5.2). This includes support for value chain infrastructure, which enhances competitiveness and performance at the industry level.[27] Here, scaling facilitators may invest, for example, in building a more robust physical infrastructure encouraging certification, or improving transparency across the players in the value chain.

Support for enhancing legal infrastructure often focuses on policies that regulate and control the market. This can involve providing information or supporting actions that contribute to a change in the approach that government agencies use to design policies, create regulations, and enforce rules. Examples include encouraging the development of policies and regulations that create a more business-friendly market environment or advocating for greater public investment in certain sectors or geographic locations.

In order to ensure the persistence of the market and its legitimacy, investments can also be made in structures that support it, such as the banking, legal, and property institutions. This can be particularly important in formalizing the informal markets.

USING THE PEF: BUILDING A PARTNERSHIP ECOSYSTEM

To reiterate, the PEF is a diagnostic tool that can help any BoP impact enterprise systematically assess and enhance its partnership portfolio. Enterprise leaders can do this by first evaluating where their existing partnerships (if any) plot onto the PEF and comparing that to where they need partnership support. This requires a careful assessment of the enterprise's capabilities and its business strategy, as well as the strength (or weakness) of the market environment that surrounds the enterprise. The BoP impact enterprise must have a clear understanding of ways in which the enterprise itself can enable action and build capacity, and a good sense of where there are critical gaps. They should then consider what the broader landscape of potential partners looks like and where the best opportunities are to generate additional support from scaling facilitators. These identified gaps and opportunities become the priorities for seeking new partners.

As the enterprise grows and evolves, it may also find that some earlier partners are no longer valuable contributors to its partnership ecosystem. The enterprise's partnership portfolio is dynamic and evolving, and the PEF can help identify not only which new partnerships are needed to facilitate growth but also which current partnerships could be pruned.

The portfolio of partners will vary according to the sector, strategy, and strengths of the specific BoP impact enterprise. Furthermore, the relative salience of partnerships within each the four quadrants of the PEF will likely evolve as the enterprise moves through various stages of development as presented in the co-create, innovate, and embed (C-I-E) framework from Chapter 3. In the co-creating stage, enterprise leaders most likely want to emphasize partnering to understand customer needs. At this stage, invention is paramount, and seeking access to market intelligence and understanding expectations with regard to support for business model implementation and value creation is critical. Thus the enterprise may find its PEF is mainly populated with partners in the upper-left quadrant.

As the enterprise enters the innovation stage, additional partners may be needed to facilitate enterprise activities in the field. For example, the enterprise may need partner support to conduct market trials, evaluate technologies, and assess value creation. The enterprise also may be seeking support for its financial, human, and other resources. One risk to be guarded against at this point is that the leadership team will develop a partnership ecosystem that is overly weighted toward the left-hand column of the PEF.

Indeed, at the innovation stage the BoP impact enterprise should ensure that its partnership strategy moves beyond a focus on financial and other organizational capital. The enterprise should be piloting both its field operations and its strategy for creating demand or enhancing supply. The goal is to innovate across all aspects of its business model, an effort that will benefit from identifying partners that can support initial efforts to facilitate market transactions.

As the enterprise moves to the embedded stage and seeks to expand, greater support is required across all four quadrants. It will likely need access to substantial growth capital and other resources, as well as a growing commitment by existing and new partners in facilitating field activities at a much larger scale, although enterprise leaders should not neglect the growing importance of support for market creation. The enterprise will want to explore, for example, partnerships focused on demand creation, upstream and downstream supply chain development, market infrastructure and governance, and industry standards that can yield a market environment more conducive to its growth goals.

One conclusion is evitable: Creating a robust ecosystem of partners is a challenging undertaking, but it is certainly manageable, especially if the enterprise uses a tool like the PEF. BoP impact enterprises need to consider more partners for more roles than they would if they were operating in developed-world markets. And a good number of these partners will be scaling facilitators that come from the development sector. As the next example shows, the benefits of creating a robust partnership ecosystem almost always outweigh the challenges.

CREATING A PARTNERSHIP ECOSYSTEM: OXFAM AMERICA IN ACTION

This example of an organization in action looks at the development of a partnership ecosystem from the perspective of an NGO because it is not unusual to find cases where the NGO is the organization leading the efforts to build the BoP impact enterprise.[28] We explore how Oxfam America engaged Swiss Re and others in building a BoP impact enterprise that provided microinsurance and other critical resources to low-income farmers in Ethiopia. The person overseeing the development of this initiative, David Satterthwaite, Oxfam America's senior global microinsurance officer, did not use the PEF, which I created subsequent to the story that I'm about to relate.[29] But Satterthwaite's and Oxfam America's experience well illustrates the need for developing a robust partnership ecosystem and how the PEF can help this process.[30]

Founded in 1970, Oxfam America is an independent international relief and development organization that focuses on the needs of people in developing countries. Its mission is "to create lasting solutions to poverty, hunger, and social injustice," and it is one of the affiliates within the confederation Oxfam International, which was founded in 1942 as a famine relief committee for World War II refugees. Oxfam International's seventeen affiliates work together to serve local populations in more than ninety countries.

With eight offices around the world and total revenues of nearly $70 million in 2013, Oxfam America saves lives by offering humanitarian aid, campaigns for social justice, and develops programs that help people overcome poverty.[31] More specifically, its activities include building local organizational capacity, fostering new and innovative ideas, and supporting initiatives in communities working their own ways out of poverty.

In fall 2007, after assessing its own capabilities, Oxfam America brought together more than a dozen organizations—nonprofits, for-profits, and governmental agencies—into an ambitious partnership aimed at helping Ethiopian farmers deal with climate-related risk and food security. The initiative was initially dubbed HARITA (Horn of Africa Risk Transfer for Adaptation) and later transitioned to the R4 Rural Resilience Initiative as part of a strategic partnership with the World Food Programme. The result was a novel and holistic risk management solution that packaged risk transfer (through microinsurance) with risk-reduction activities (e.g., composting and water harvesting), prudent risk taking (through the provision of credit), and risk reserves (through individual and group savings).[32]

Since the initiative's inception in 2007, Oxfam America had convened an impressive ecosystem of more than a dozen scaling facilitators—including Columbia University's International Research Institute for Climate and Society; the Relief Society of Tigray, the largest NGO in Ethiopia; private Ethiopian insurer Nyala Insurance; Dedebit, Credit, & Saving Institution, the second-largest microfinance institution in Ethiopia; local farmer associations; and various agencies of the Ethiopian government—to develop a pilot initiative that helped farmers deal with drought and other challenges associated with climate change. Although many of these partners had been involved in the envisioning stage of this model, Oxfam America was especially pleased that Swiss Reinsurance Company, a leading global reinsurer, had become part of the partnership ecosystem as the enterprises moved into the innovation stage.

Swiss Re operates through offices in more than twenty countries and has approximately twelve thousand employees. Founded in Zurich, Switzerland, in 1863, it offers financial services products that enable risk taking that is essential to enterprise. The company's traditional reinsurance products, related services for property and casualty insurance, and life and health insurance businesses are complemented by insurance-based corporate finance solutions and supplementary services for comprehensive risk management. In 2013, it generated some $29 billion in premiums earned and fee income. The company's mission is "to be the leading player in the wholesale reinsurance industry," as well as to be known as an innovator and thought leader.[33]

This cross-sectoral partnership with Swiss Re marked a new milestone in Oxfam America's growing effort to partner with the private sector on poverty reduction initiatives in BoP markets. In fact, over the previous decade, the organization's relationship with the business community had evolved dramatically. Prior to that time, Oxfam America viewed corporations either as adversaries or potential donors. In 2005, however, it established a private sector department to encourage new attitudes and policies toward the corporate sector and find ways to collaborate more effectively with business.

For its part, Swiss Re had adopted a corporate responsibility framework that it considered a key part of its strategy for creating sustainable long-term value for the company. This framework asserted that working with local stakeholders and being a good corporate citizen would not only help generate business opportunities but would establish the company as an employer of choice. Climate change and the associated issue of food security soon emerged as key areas of focus in its corporate responsibility efforts, which led in turn to an interest in innovative solutions for sustainable development.

On the business side, Swiss Re was interested in exploring new opportunities in Ethiopia, among other countries in the developing world. In 2009, Ethiopian insurance companies served only around 300,000 of the country's

80 million residents, almost all of them wealthy individuals and families in urban areas. Was there a way to put together a cross-sectoral partnership that could help the rest of Ethiopia—mostly poor, mostly rural—get access to insurance? Could crop microinsurance be one answer? Could it be done in a financially sustainable way?

Oxfam America's initiative spoke specifically to that interest. In that spirit, Swiss Re in 2008 joined the HARITA initiative, providing financial and technical assistance that filled key gaps in the enterprise's partnership portfolio.[34] Gradually the two organizations got to know each other. Swiss Re began to see Oxfam's potential as an invaluable resource in the pursuit of its climate change strategy, especially in parts of the world where Swiss Re had few contacts or experience. At the same time, Oxfam America wanted to engage a corporate partner with the technical expertise to build financial tools around the world and was eager to demonstrate its own value and dependability.

The initiative's first pilot, as noted, was in Ethiopia. Of that country's 80 million residents in 2009, some 14 million were deemed to be "food insecure." With 85 percent of the population dependent on agriculture for their livelihood and 98 percent of crops dependent on seasonal rains, droughts can have tremendous impacts on Ethiopia's economy and the well-being of its citizens. Because droughts can be so devastating, Ethiopia's farmers have traditionally been unwilling to invest their limited savings and other resources to experiment with new agricultural tools, techniques, or seeds. Climate change threatens to hit Ethiopian's farmers particularly hard.

The initiative initially set up operations in the small Ethiopian village of Adi Ha. Oxfam brought together all the necessary parties, designed the pilot, and undertook much of the detailed, on-the-ground efforts working closely with its partners.[35] Swiss Re served as technical advisor and funder, supplying $250,000 in support. The partnership agreement ensured that Oxfam would retain its independence as an advocate and that all intellectual property generated through the collaboration would be made publicly available, key considerations for the nonprofit. Interestingly, although the ultimate goal of the initiative was market building, Swiss Re decided to provide funds through its corporate citizenship unit. At that time, the venture was considered risky, long term, and not well suited for Swiss Re's business units to shoulder.

Building partnerships with Swiss Re and other organizations was crucial in the development of this initiative. David Satterthwaite's boss, Chris Jochnick, Oxfam's director of private sector development, explains why:

> Looking back on it, I think this was a very fortuitous partnership....What this project has really required is the kind of things from the Oxfam side that we do really well. And the kind of things we don't really have experience in—the technical side—we were able to find partners that could cover that. So we brought in the local insurers, and we brought in Swiss Re, and we brought in Columbia University, and we brought in the local credit and savings. And they could help us figure out the technical sides of insurance and insurance for work and other parts of this project.
>
> But what the project also needed was those long-term, trust-filled relationships that we had on the ground with the farmers. It required an understanding of how to work with those farmers effectively, and farmer cooperatives, and that can always be tricky.
>
> And it required an understanding of how to work with local NGOs on the ground....So we needed to bridge the communication gaps between a large, northern multinational and an impoverished farmer on the ground. So this project really needed a bridge, a convener, for all that. And that is one role I think Oxfam plays really well—that really plays to its strengths. And finally, it required a certain nimbleness and agility to overcome little problems.[36]

Although much of the hard work of product development had been done elsewhere in the world, including technical specifications for microinsurance products for local crops, what had not been accomplished elsewhere was satisfactory uptake on the part of the farmers. Demand for these products remained too low to be viable. To address the challenge of demand creation, the Adi Ha Design Team recruited a focus group of twenty-one local farmers and conducted a community-wide market assessment. These parallel efforts led to valuable insights in designing a product that would appeal and be affordable to local farmers. For example, on the advice of the farmers, the initiative devised a way to accept labor, rather than scarce and precious cash, as payment for insurance premiums for the lowest-income farmers. Over time, it was anticipated these farmers would experience greater financial returns and would gradually shift to paying their premiums in cash.

The initiative officially launched in 2009. A two-day kickoff in Adi Ha attracted some six hundred farmers, and approximately two hundred people (representing 20 percent of the village's households) signed up for crop insurance—roughly twice HARITA's initial enrollment goal. Swiss Re, encouraged by this response, agreed to continue its annual support, which helped enable the initiative to expand its piloting activities to four more Ethiopian villages in 2010. In these villages, as in Adi Ha, enrollments were unexpectedly high (and in fact were 9 percent higher, on average, than in Adi Ha), with close to 40 percent of the represented households headed by females.

By 2011, thirteen thousand households in forty-three villages were enrolled, and the initiative was looking to expand further through new partnerships. Around that time, the United Nations World Food Programme joined the initiative and provided support to facilitate scale within Ethiopia. By 2013, the initiative had reached twenty thousand farmers in eighty villages in Ethiopia. In the same year, the initiative was ready to enter a new country. To do so, Oxfam America secured a $450,000 grant from the Rockefeller Foundation to help enable expansion into Senegal.[37]

"It is wonderful to see this pilot working for farmers," commented Oxfam America's David Satterthwaite. "This is a great moment that comes on the heels of the announcement that we, with additional collaborators and support, will scale up the pilot over the next five years and expand into Senegal."[38]

While this abbreviated account of the initiative and its associated portfolio of partners understates the complexity of a multiparty, cross-sectoral relationship—in this telling, for example, I have underplayed the key role played by the Ethiopian government and other official players—it does illustrate the importance of actively managing an evolving partnership ecosystem As a BoP impact enterprise develops, it often needs to add some scaling facilitators that can provide new types of support. As Oxfam America sought to expand the initiative, the leadership team recognized the need for additional financial capital and more support for demand creation. These were provided by the Rockefeller Foundation and the World Food Programme, respectively. In addition, some existing ones may need to be phased out.

TABLE 5.3 PEF for Oxfam America's R4 Rural Resilience Initiative

	Enterprise Development	*Market Creation*
	Facilitate Enterprise Activities	**Facilitate Market Transactions**
Action Enabling	*Market Intelligence* • Tigray Regional Food Security • Ethiopian Farmers' Associations *Market Access* • Relief Society of Tigray: Coordination Productive Safety Net Program • Tigray Cooperative Promotion Office	*Demand Creation* • Ethiopian Government • Dedebit Credit and Savings Institution • World Food Programme *Supply Enhancement* • Africa Insurance Co. • Nyala Insurance Co.
	Enhance Enterprise Resources	**Enhance Market Environment**
Capacity Building	*Financial Capital* • Swiss Re • Rockefeller Foundation *Knowledge Capital* • Ethiopian National Meteorological Agency • Institute for Sustainable Development • International Research Institute for Climate and Society • Mekelle University	*Value Chain Infrastructure* • Relief Society of Tigray

Although Oxfam American did have someone dedicated to understanding the organization's capabilities and the associated gaps in the initiative that required building a partnership ecosystem, a tool such as the PEF could have greatly facilitated this effort. While Table 5.3 summarizes key partnerships as the initiative prepared to enter Senegal, it doesn't fully reflect the dynamic nature of the partnership ecosystem over time. That said, I hope it underscores the main point: the BoP impact enterprise increases its chances for success if it develops and maintains a robust partnership ecosystem, based on an ongoing strategic assessment of the enterprise's capabilities, its current set of scaling facilitators, and the gaps that need filling.

This example also illustrates another key point: that an organization's partnership ecosystem need not be limited to the development sector universe, but also can include private sector organizations, such as the local insurance companies, and government agencies. Understanding the value of all potential partners is crucial. That said, it is in the area of scaling facilitators from the development sector where many BoP impact enterprises continue to stumble. .

The PEF addresses the who of developing and executing an effective partnership strategy. But BoP impact enterprise must also understand the how of creating an ecosystem of partners to support its journey to scalability at scale. This is the topic of the next chapter, which focuses on a partnership perspective that I call collaborative interdependence and relies on the skills, energy, and talent of an individual whom I call the chief ecosystem director.

6 COLLABORATIVE INTERDEPENDENCE

BoP impact enterprise leaders must integrate their business development efforts with investments and support from a variety of partners, especially those from the development community I have referred to as scaling facilitators. Properly conceived and executed, this ecosystem of partners can support enterprise development and bring forth a more robust market environment. Without this type of external support, the leadership team will struggle to build an enterprise that can achieve sustainability at scale.

These kinds of collaborations don't happen on their own. An ecosystem of partners has to be identified, developed, and managed over time. Toward that end, I propose a new role for top management teams: a chief ecosystem director (CED) who is responsible for a critical, but often neglected, role that is essential to the success of the BoP impact enterprise. Optimally this role is taken on by a particular individual, potentially with support from a broader team as the enterprise scales. At the very least, this role should be built into an expanded set of expectations for an existing member of the leadership team. The latter option is probably most viable for a start-up, in which the leadership teams may already have hybrid roles. In any case, achieving the necessary state of cross-organizational collaboration is far more likely to happen with the active involvement of someone in the CED role.

The use of the term *ecosystem director*, as opposed to *partnership director*, is intentional.[1] The goal of this position is not simply to establish one collaboration or a handful of them. Rather, the objective is to build and maintain the appropriate ecosystem of partners: an integrated and evolving portfolio of relationships that holistically responds to key challenges in the enterprise's journey to sustainability and scalability.

In addition to having the right person, creating an effective partnership ecosystem also calls for adopting a particular collaboration mind-set. The CED in a BoP impact enterprise works in a unique market context and must establish collaborations with partners that can often seem like strange bedfellows. In other words, traditional developed world approaches to partnering will likely not be sufficient. In that spirit, I explain the concept of collaborative interdependence,[2] a strategic perspective on partnering in BoP markets, and argue that CEDs should adopt this perspective to advance their work effectively.

Embracing collaborative interdependence helps CEDs tackle three potential roadblocks that can constrain the opportunity for a BoP impact enterprise to develop a sufficiently robust partnership ecosystem: overcoming biases about subsidized support, dealing with internal resistance to cross-sector collaborations, and responding to cross-organizational tensions. I address these important issues, explain how they can have a powerful bearing on building successful collaborations, and suggest how a CED adopting a collaborative interdependence approach can deal with them. An effective CED recognizes these issues and has the tools and knowledge needed to overcome them and create a robust set of scaling facilitators.

ADDING A CHIEF ECOSYSTEM DIRECTOR
TO THE LEADERSHIP TEAM

Just as in the natural world, a broader ecosystem of partners exists with or without the enterprise. The challenge is to organize a subset of these partners into an ecosystem that works with and for the enterprise.

Identifying and understanding the partnership opportunity is a complicated and challenging role. A BoP impact enterprise is almost certain to encounter a substantial and growing number of potential scaling facilitators, and it's unrealistic to think that this complex ecosystem will simply align itself with the enterprise in optimal manner. What's needed is an individual who expressly owns the role of building a dynamic web of partnerships that responds to the enterprise's strategy as it evolves.

This CED proposal grows directly out of my observations of enterprises managing cross-sectoral collaborations in a wide range of contexts over the years.[3] All too often, the collaboration process is managed as a secondary aspect of what is often viewed as the "real" job of directing an enterprise. As a result, the partnership model can become reactive, focusing on those who reach out to the enterprise, and then tends to be executed without a clear overarching strategy. This means that the quality, quantity, and timing of partnerships are often out of sync with the enterprise's current needs and the outcome rarely results in an optimal portfolio of scaling facilitators.

The solution is to identify a specific senior member of the leadership team as responsible for assembling and integrating key partnerships into an effective whole. By locating this crucial activity within senior leadership, the business puts appropriate emphasis on it. The CED takes responsibility for strategizing how to extend the enterprise's partnership model, using tools and frameworks such as the PEF, and guides the efforts to generate the appropriate level of external support, at the right time, for both enterprise development and market creation.

Think back to the Oxfam America example. David Satterthwaite, Oxfam America's senior global microinsurance officer, filled that role. Although Satterthwaite did not hold the specific title of CED, he did perform that portfolio-building role within the R4 Rural Resilience Initiative.[4] Satterthwaite's and Oxfam America's experience with this initiative underscores the importance of that role within a BoP impact enterprise.

Satterthwaite was responsible for identifying the potential partnership opportunities that were available in that content, prioritizing which relationships were most crucial, establishing the full ecosystem of partnerships, and then managing the ongoing complexities and challenges.[5] This last point can't be overemphasized. Oxfam America's director of private sector development, Chris Jochnick, had this to say:

> When I was looking back over the four or five years of history, it just struck me how many times this project was ready to go off the rails. We look at it now, and it has been three beautiful years of piloting. But in the day to day, there were all kinds of problems, and all kinds of small and large crises. And it really required an ability to go with the flow and react quickly to different challenges—economic, political, cultural, and otherwise.[6]

The Oxfam America example also provides some insights into the skills and capabilities a CED should have. Perhaps the most important attribute is that this person be multilingual in the specific way that I use that word. It's not simply fluency in multiple languages used across different countries, although that can be a valuable skill. Rather, I mean being able to communicate and act as a translator across different sectors. The CED must be fluent in the language of the business community, including understanding what drives business performance and how these enterprises measure success. He or she must also be fluent in the language of the development community, including understanding the incentives and stakeholders who influence decision making and the metrics used to assess performance. Language fluency in still other communities—for example, those of government officials, policymakers, and academic researchers—may also prove invaluable.

The CED must also have the capability to act as a strategic bridge, enabling key players on both sides of the relationship to effectively communicate. Rather than being the hub that conversation flows through, the CED is the bridge that communication flows across. This is where the role of translator becomes so important. The CED must be able to understand and explain how the goals, objectives, and strategies of cross-sector partners are more aligned than players on either side might initially realize. A key part of the translation role is to find points of connection and areas of commonality.

Clearly the CED must also be familiar with the BoP market context and recognize the critical importance of mutual value creation with the BoP. Other useful skills of a CED include internal influence, external respect, negotiation experience, and an ability to deal with conflict and ambiguity. These skills highlight that the CED's role includes not only building relationships but also maintaining them and maximizing their value over time.

CASE IN POINT: PATRIMONIO HOY
LOOKS FOR PARTNERS

We return to the CEMEX Patrimonio Hoy initiative, the BoP impact enterprise introduced in Chapter 2. You'll recall that this initiative began as a way to supply more materials to lower-income communities in Mexico and evolved into a holistic approach to home building.

By the end of the first decade of the twenty-first century, CEMEX had reason to be proud of Patrimonio Hoy's accomplishments.[7] Its leaders had created a new and profitable business model. In 2011, the initiative had enjoyed its best year yet, generating a profit of $3.5 million on $45 million in revenues. The initiative was also contributing toward alleviating the critical and chronic housing shortage in Mexico, then affecting nearly 20 million people.

At the same time, there were reasons for concern. It appeared that the initiative had reached a plateau in its growth trajectory unless it received a major infusion of new resources. But 2011 was a difficult time for the leadership team to approach CEMEX for additional money. The construction industry was in a downturn, and CEMEX's top managers were focused on managing costs and raising capital.

As Israel Moreno, Patrimonio Hoy's general manager, commented at that time:

> In the last three years, we've been growing about 35,000 families per year. But we have not opened new facilities and new offices, because of CEMEX's [contribution] for this initiative. Things are getting better in Patrimonio Hoy in a very hard period for CEMEX. This past three years has been the best era for our program. We've been selling even more each year. But we have a set of big challenges to face in CEMEX in order to take it to the next step.[8]

One possible answer was to look outside the company for partners who could provide new kinds of funding and other support. And in fact, there was some indication that this could be a good model for the enterprise. One of Patrimonio Hoy's more recent partnerships was with the Mexican government's Comision Nacional de Vivienda (CONAVI, or National Council for Housing) and its subsidy program, Esta Es Tu Casa (This Is Your House). Under this partnership, the government offered home-building subsidies, with the aim of accelerating the building process. Subsidies were awarded to qualifying clients who already had saved at least 5 percent of their project cost in order to evaluate commitment and avoid overreliance on subsidies. The conditions and approval of subsidies were the government's responsibility.[9]

Because the Mexican government's investment in this program could vary from year to year, this type of market creation investment was not necessarily a stable source of support for Patrimonio Hoy. Patrimonio Hoy had also partnered with Accion International, a private, nonprofit organization providing microloans, business training, and other financial services to low-income families. From 2007 through 2009, Accion International and Patrimonio Hoy created new microfinance products, such as variable credit amounts, immediate access to microloans for building materials, and pure microloans, to address the needs of Patrimonio Hoy clients. After the pilot program ended in 2009, Patrimonio Hoy continued to provide microfinancing services to low-income Mexican families, but Accion was no longer actively participating.

Another partnership, this time focused on enterprise development, was with Gesellschaft für Technische Zusammenarbeit (GTZ), a German government enterprise supporting sustainable development.[10] In 2009 and 2010, GTZ Mexico partnered with Patrimonio Hoy in a pilot program to introduce environmentally friendly products (e.g., energy-efficient homes, efficient light fixtures) in order to sensitize clients to global warming and climate change issues, with the overall objective of improving living standards. This partnership too ended after the pilot program was completed.

In an effort to streamline operations in Mexico and facilitate expanding the business model elsewhere, Patrimonio Hoy hired a consultancy to analyze the gaps in its program. Subsequently the Inter-American Development Bank (IDB), a scaling facilitator focused on Latin and South America, provided a grant to support standardization of operations across locations. Next, the IDB provided a partial credit guarantee to support new credit offers in Mexico, as well as in Colombia, Costa Rica, Nicaragua, and the Dominican Republic.

In 2014, Patrimonio Hoy reengaged with CONAVI on a new subsidy program. While anticipating growth in clients through the Mexican government's renewed participation, Patrimonio Hoy remained concerned about the instability and burdensome bureaucracy inherent in this type of government-supported program.

It's fair to say that Patrimonio Hoy sees substantial opportunities for scale. Its team estimated, for example, that Mexico's major cities could support a maximum of one thousand offices, or "cells," each with a staff of three people, or four thousand cells with one employee per cell. This did not include the possibility of covering rural areas. While the initiative had reached fifty-six cities across Mexico by 2014, there was certainly room to grow in both the number of cities and the number of cells within a city. Mexico City, for example, could add more than two hundred cells, and Monterrey and Tijuana could still grow by twenty or more cells each.

Patrimonio Hoy also saw enormous opportunities for international expansion. The initiative had a handful of cells across several countries in Latin America. It wanted to expand these efforts, as well as roll out the initiative into other countries with large, low-income populations that had a tradition of self-building. Israel Moreno said, "Right now we are also running the program in Colombia, Costa Rica, Dominican Republic, Nicaragua. But this program can operate also right now in Philippines or Egypt or Bangladesh. The potential client and the kind of solutions that we are offering—the program is ready for operating in a lot of countries and CEMEX is [already] present over there....I know that we have a good business model. We have...a lot of potential clients, so this is ready for huge expansion." [11]

It is also fair to say that its partnership approach has been more opportunistic than strategic, and these collaborations have generated only modest success. In my view, the initiative would have benefited from more focused attention to the partnership opportunity, including having someone on the leadership team committed to and focused on filling the role of CED. This position, combined with access to a tool like the PEF, could have helped the organization better understand the universe of potential scaling partners and more strategically build a robust ecosystem of partners.

That person could have also played a key role in addressing some internal tensions that hampered the opportunity for partnership development. Internally the company was not yet comfortable with pursuing a more robust partnership ecosystem. Israel Moreno commented, "CEMEX sees Patrimonio Hoy as a father sees his youngest daughter at her Quinceañera.[12] Just like a proud father, the CEMEX leadership team wants everyone to look at her, but feels that no one can dance with her except him."

Given the constraints Patrimonio Hoy faces in accessing additional internal capital and other resources, achieving further scale in a significant way will likely depend on the initiative's ability to build and sustain an ecosystem of partnerships. To do so, it not only needs the kind of strategic vision that can be brought forward through the role of the CED but also an approach to overcoming internal and external barriers to building these collaborations.

NEW PARTNERSHIP PERSPECTIVE: COLLABORATIVE INTERDEPENDENCE

As the Patrimonio Hoy example shows, creating partnerships in BoP markets is challenging, and those that are initiated may not develop into effective collaborations. One reason these collaborations may generate only limited returns is that for-profit enterprises and development sector organizations value different results and measure success in different ways. These differences, though, are not as daunting as many people initially think. At the same time, these differences mean that each side has unique strengths and particular perspectives. The challenge, and the opportunity, is to be aware of these differences, leverage them as much as possible, accommodate them when necessary, and ensure that both partners keep a shared long-term vision in sight.

What is crucial in achieving these collaborations, especially in BoP markets, is how these collaborations are framed. The scaling of BoP impact enterprises requires co-creating, innovating, and embedding. From a collaboration perspective, this means embracing a more symbiotic mind-set—which I refer to as collaborative interdependence—grounded in the potential to generate mutual value across sectors. This collaboration mind-set applies whether enterprise leaders approach BoP markets from the perspective of impact enterprise, shared value, or sustainable development.[13]

Collaborative interdependence is a partnership in which each party has to recognize on a fundamental level that the organizations' economic and social performance goals are not mutually exclusive and, in fact, can overlap with and reinforce each other; that working together can create new strategies and capabilities that generate value that neither party could create alone; and that achieving this mutual value creation will require sharing and integrating skills, knowledge, values, and perspectives.

In framing these cross-sectoral collaborations, the central question is "How can we help each other?" This perspective is particularly valuable for BoP impact enterprises seeking scale. Relationships based on dependence or independence, alternatively, are framed, by "How can you help me?" or "How can I help you?" Dependence or independence can work for time-bound engagements where the plan of execution and the individual roles are clearly spelled out, such as in a short-term pilot. In going from pilot to scale, however, much changes. Cross-sector relationships grow more complex, the investment in and risk from engagement is greater, the future is harder to predict, and success is a moving target. Here, interdependence can become the glue that helps keep the partners together.

The developed world offers few relevant models for how BoP impact enterprise leaders and development community professionals can work together productively. In that world, sector-spanning roles are often handled by individuals in community relations, government affairs, and corporate social responsibility.[14] These partnering efforts differ substantially from what I mean by collaborative interdependence. Companies in developed world markets often, for example, look to cross-sectoral partners as sources of legitimacy, opportunities for advocacy and policy change, or resources for reputation building or protecting. As a result, these sector spanners generally emphasize stakeholder management as their prime goal. The objective in most of these cross-sectoral connections is to retain independence.

In these types of collaborations, interactions across partners often occur at the public policy and public relations levels rather than at the enterprise level. The skills, knowledge, and other resources and capabilities that each cross-sectoral partner controls remain largely separate rather than being co-mingled.[15] This is somewhat less true in corporate social responsibility initiatives, which may involve some co-mingling of resources, but in this context, the co-mingling remains limited, and the initiative is usually designed to further the social agenda of one of the partners, often with the objective of creating small-scale demonstration pilots. As a result, the interactions with these external stakeholders remain at the periphery of the "business" strategy.[16]

This model of maintaining independence and emphasizing short-term impact has limited appeal in the BoP market context. The informal and relatively impoverished nature of the market environment requires a much closer coordination among these potential partners.[17] In the BoP marketplace, business leaders and development professionals must break free of their mind-sets of independent metrics and responsibilities and of interaction strategies based on predetermined roles and short-term deliverables. Instead, they must embrace cross-sectoral partnerships as an opportunity to link metrics and goals and co-create something that may not exist already.

THE LOGIC OF COLLABORATIVE INTERDEPENDENCE

Central to building and sustaining collaborative interdependence is the opportunity for mutual value creation: Both parties need to create value that satisfies their key stakeholders. To grow and prosper, the enterprise needs to generate sufficient financial returns. Development sector partners—aid agencies, nongovernment organizations, impact investors, local community organizations—emphasize a different type of value: social returns. This means the CED must have a clear understanding of the link between enterprise strategy and social performance. In this case, social impact can be measured by poverty alleviation, the value that the enterprise is creating for the BoP. The key is creating a joint perception of the opportunity to collaboratively create more value than currently exists.

One way to achieve this joint perception for new value creation is to recognize that investments in BoP impact enterprises by the private and development sector have different but complementary floors (what will happen at a minimum) and ceilings (the potential upside). As illustrated in Table 6.1, investments by the private sector have a low floor (not much may happen, as a proposed enterprise may not launch or may shut down earlier than expected), but a potentially high ceiling (if things work out, it can really scale).[18] In contrast, development community investments have a high floor (something will happen, given that the project plan will likely be executed) but a relatively low ceiling (investments are bounded in terms of time and money).

Here is where the CED—and potentially his or her counterpart from the development sector—can bring together two disparate but potentially highly complementary worldviews. This is rarely a simple proposition. Each party has to reconsider existing (and probably outdated) institutional mind-sets about roles, capabilities, metrics, and investments. For example, the development community needs to understand, and find ways to overcome, the inherent challenges in trying to encourage innovation through fixed-term projects with fixed time

TABLE **6.1** Comparing floors and ceilings of investments by different sectors

	Development Community Investments	Business Investments
Floor	**Relatively High**	**Relatively Low**
	• Funds are dedicated to project	• Limited or no dedicated funds
	• Committed to implementation	• Committed only to testing
	• Something will happen	• Nothing may happen
Ceiling	**Relatively Low**	**Relatively High**
	• Investment capped	• Investments can escalate
	• Exit planned	• Plan is to not exit
	• Scale not part of strategy	• Scale is key to strategy

lines, planned spending, and predetermined deliverables. Instead of an execution orientation, they may need to identify opportunities to embrace an innovation orientation, such as a time horizon that extend out five years or longer, flexibility in spending, and actions based on ongoing results, and allow expected outcomes to be initially presented in broad form rather than specific details.

The BoP impact enterprise, for its part, has to see the value in incorporating development sector measures of social performance, including assessing and enhancing the opportunity to improve lives of those who are poor and vulnerable. The goal is to find ways to truly combine and leverage the high floor of development community investments with the high ceiling that comes from for-profit involvement. The opportunity to leverage complementary resources and capability underpins the emergence of collaborative interdependence.[19] The development community can help make things happen that wouldn't otherwise occur, and the enterprise sector can take these efforts to scale in a way that the development community can't. In many cases, this means accessing some type of subsidized support from these development sector partners. Overcoming biases over subsidized support, however, is one of the obstacles the BoP impact enterprise faces in achieving collaborative interdependence. Indeed, establishing collaborative interdependence—a challenge that should never be underestimated—requires addressing three major issues that can prove challenging:

- Overcoming biases about seeking subsidized support
- Dealing with internal resistance
- Responding to cross-organizational tensions

Let's look at each in turn, and explore how a CED can address them.

OVERCOMING BIASES ABOUT SEEKING SUBSIDIZED SUPPORT

Does subsidized support mean that the enterprise isn't viable? In theory at least, most enterprise managers subscribe to the idea of seeking subsidized support to facilitate growth. Yet in practice, an unfortunate bias that often seems to cloud judgment and decision making centers on the word *subsidy* and the associated connotations it conjures up with regard to business viability.

Although definitions of *subsidy* abound, most agree that subsidies are targeted to "make activities happen that otherwise would not take place."[20] Beneath that umbrella definition, subdefinitions differ on a variety of criteria, such as providers, recipients, beneficiaries, instruments, and intention.

The Organization for Economic Co-operation and Development (OECD), which brings together thirty governments and is committed to supporting economic growth and world trade, defines a subsidy as "a measure that keeps prices for consumers below market levels, or keeps prices for producers above market level or that reduces costs for both producers and consumers by giving direct or indirect support." This definition seems to apply mainly to governments, but attributing subsidies only to governments is too limiting, given that foundations and NGOs frequently make financial or in-kind transfers to benefit the same or similar target audiences as governments. For example, NGOs and private foundations often transfer resources from their network of members or high-wealth individuals to people or institutions in need of support (e.g., the Bill and Melinda Gates Foundation, the World Wildlife Fund).

Subsidies can have an impact on key strategic decisions, such as market entry, target consumers, production levels, pricing decisions, resource allocations, and financial forecasts. Many economists believe that subsidies are helpful when they are used appropriately, because they can encourage market development and a more equitable distribution of benefits and resources in society. Others disagree, believing that subsidies create more problems than they solve by distorting markets, creating inefficiencies, and misallocating capital. This can be particularly relevant when governments or others use subsidies for political goals as opposed to legitimate policy ends.

I use the phrase *subsidized support* to refer to a broader base of potential partners beyond government that includes scaling facilitators from the development sector. Furthermore, I'll underscore that the following discussion is not intended to be a comprehensive explanation of subsidies—a subject that is debated hotly and continually by legions of economists, policymakers, and business strategists—but rather, a primer for enterprise leaders who want to explore this sometimes complicated landscape.

Many BoP impact enterprise leaders have an instinctive negative bias against seeking any sort of subsidized support. They believe that such support tends to make a business unsustainable and that it demonstrates that the business concept can't stand on its own two feet.[21] This is a mistaken—and, in my view, risky—perspective to adopt. In supporting an enterprise, most scaling facilitators likely provide resources and other types of support at a below-market rate.[22] This is not an embarrassment but a boon. Look at this from another perspective: If all that's needed to pursue this opportunity is a savvy entrepreneur with a great new technology and business model, it's likely that some business would already be serving this market. In most cases, there are pieces in the market environment that are either missing or poorly developed. BoP impact enterprise leaders need to seek out and secure this kind of support to address the market challenges they inevitably face. They may also need subsidized access to financial and other resources to enhance enterprise development.

Too many enterprise leaders still seem to be debating the wrong question: Is subsidized support good or bad for my business? Rather, the question that these leaders should be asking is: How can I better access subsidized support? The goal is to encourage others to partner with and invest in the enterprise, and if these investments are below market rate, that's all the better.

SUBSIDIZED SUPPORT IN THE DEVELOPED WORLD

When I encounter a bias against subsidized support, I point out that global subsidies are estimated by some authorities to amount to more than $1 trillion a year, or roughly 4 percent of world GDP.[23] There's a whole world of support out there, much of it going to businesses. Subsidized support generally falls into one of three major categories: transfers of financial resources, transfers of goods or services, or supportive regulation.

Transfers of financial resources can take the form of cash subsidies, which tend to be one-time events. These are highly flexible, highly desirable, and, perhaps not surprising, highly unusual, since they require someone to put down cash. More common are unit subsidies, in which governments or other institutions purchase goods or services from producers at market prices and then sell to buyers at below market price. These are often used in the agricultural sector but can be applied to other sectors as well. Other approaches, such as loan guarantees and direct credit support, are not an immediate commitment of financial resources. In addition, supporting institutions sometimes subsidize businesses by purchasing shareholder equity and becoming either a minority or majority owner, which is considered a subsidy if the equity injection is made under terms or conditions that would not be acceptable to a typical investor. This was true of the Troubled Asset Relief Program, launched in 2008 by the U.S federal government to help distressed financial institutions.

Transfers of goods and services also take several forms. For example, in-kind transfers are the direct transfer of goods or services from one entity to another. This can comprise infrastructure built for a specific company's use (as opposed to public infrastructure), access to government-owned or -controlled resources, or the provision of specific services. They can also take the form of vouchers: coupons that enable consumers to receive specific goods or services at below-market prices.

Finally, supportive regulation can be implemented by local governing bodies. For example, they can enact import quotas, thereby protecting favored enterprises by keeping the price of competitive imports artificially high. Tariffs, which impose a tax on imported goods or services, similarly keep domestic prices high by artificially inflating the price of imports.

The United States is generally held out as the purest example of unfettered and, perhaps some would say, unsubsidized capitalism. The fact is, however, that the U.S. government regularly makes investments to promote market activities that otherwise would not take place, again a pretty good definition of a subsidy. For example, it has provided the agricultural sector with around $13 billion annually to support production and supported the airframe industry with a $23 billion investment in Boeing.[24]

Sometimes subsidized support is put in place in response to perceived economic emergencies. For example, the U.S. government has provided subsidies in recent years to the insurance and automotive sectors, in addition to banks. The economic disaster of the Great Recession, which according to the U.S. National Bureau of Economic Research began in December 2007 and ended in June 2009, also led to specific types of indirect subsidies, such as the cash-for-clunkers program (intended ultimately to breathe life into the auto and financing industries), infrastructural investments to sustain the construction industry, money for the housing sector, and others.

Government funds can also be used to subsidize basic research and investments in new technologies and innovations in cases where private capital is either unwilling to accept the risks for the investments or unable to provide sufficient capital to bring an innovation to production.[25] Today the federal government still plays a large role in funding basic research, often for defense, biotechnology, or communication, which has then led to commercial start-ups.[26] Larry Page and Sergey Brin started Google while conducting research for grants funded by the National Science Foundation.[27]

Subsidized support doesn't target only specific enterprises. It can also play a role in supporting the market environment in which enterprises operate. To explore this in some depth, we examine how a federally sponsored subsidy program, the Supplemental Nutrition Assistance Program (SNAP), provides vital support not only to lower-income consumers but also to build the market opportunity for businesses at the heart of the American "free enterprise" system.

SNAP is a federal government program administered by the U.S. Department of Agriculture under the Food and Nutrition Service.[28] In fiscal year 2013, 47.6 million people were participating in SNAP nationwide. The average benefit per person was $133, and the average benefit per household was $274. The total cost for the program in 2013 was more than $79 billion, triple the cost of the program just one decade earlier.[29]

SNAP replaces what was formerly known as food stamps, food coupons worth a certain dollar amount.[30] SNAP now uses electronic benefits transfer (EBT) cards by which participants receive a balance every month and can use the card at stores that have specialized equipment and approval to accept the cards.[31]

As part of the American Recovery and Reinvestment Act of 2009, the federal government authorized an increase in funding for SNAP. As a result, benefits increased from $125 per person in 2009 to just over $133 per person from 2009 to 2013.[32] Those increased benefits expired in 2013, however.[33] In addition to the reduction in benefits, legislation signed in February 2014 cut SNAP benefits by another $8.7 billion over ten years. These cuts would affect roughly 850,000 households by reducing their benefits by up to $90 a month.[34]

These cuts to SNAP highlight the market-creation role that the program plays. SNAP beneficiaries are of particular importance to retailers such as Walmart that serve low-income customers. In Walmart's annual report for 2013, the company disclosed several factors that could affect stock prices in the coming year, including changes to SNAP and other public benefits pro-grams. [35] Although Walmart does not disclose what percentage of its sales come from SNAP, it receives more revenue from food stamps than any other company (18 percent of all food stamp revenue, according to the *Wall Street Journal*),[36] and more than half of its sales overall come from groceries.[37]

According to a news release by Walmart on January 31, 2014, "the sales impact from the reduction in SNAP (the U.S. government Supplemental Nutrition Assistance Program) benefits that went into effect Nov. 1 is greater than we expected."[38] During the fourth quarter, in fact, the company's earn-ings were down 21 percent.[39] Walmart confirmed on February 20 that fourth-quarter earnings were below those expected and gave a full-year forecast that included a possible decrease in sales due to food stamps.[40] That morning, the company's share price on the New York Stock Exchange fell by 2.2 percent. Of course, multiple factors contributed to poor sales and revenue for Walmart, including exceptionally cold winter weather, but SNAP reductions appear to have been an important factor.[41] *Time* reported Walmart as claiming that "in the absence of a reduction of government SNAP benefits...we believe the quarter would have been flat."[42]

Two conclusions seem inevitable. The first is that subsidized support from the government enables companies to make profits from serving the low-income individuals. SNAP recipients use the private sector, not some government warehouse, to purchase their goods. And the companies charge these customers the same prices as they charge everyone else. The second conclusion is that Walmart (and other similar retailers) has no particular concerns about whether subsidized support is good or bad for its business. Indeed, it is mainly interested in maximizing the benefits of these programs to its business. This kind of subsidized support allows companies to scale by facilitating their ability to serve lower-income segments.

If these kinds of subsidized support are needed to achieve social goals in the developed world, where the market ecosystem is fairly robust, they are even more vital in the developing world context, where these investments can have a substantial impact in developing enterprises and industries.[43] If we are comfortable with companies that serve developed world consumers making a profit through these programs, why should we have a bias against subsidized support for the private sector in the developing world context?

SUBSIDIZED SUPPORT: UNDERSTANDING THE ASK

Scaling facilitators can provide numerous and varied types of support, much of it subsidized. Given that concerns about subsidized support are numerous and varied, often with good reason the CED has to be very clear about what the organization is asking for when seeking this type of support. Specifically, this means that the CED plays a major role in addressing three issues that that will be top of mind for any potential partner considering providing this type of support: How much? For what? and For how long? To generalize, most discussions of subsidized support benefit from using a high level of granularity on cost, impact, and commitment—this specific amount of support is being requested for this specific purpose for this stated amount of time—and the CED must help achieve that degree of granularity.

We'll start with the first question: "How much subsidized support is useful for your business and acceptable to your local partner?" Like almost any other investor, the NGO or development agency hopes to minimize its investment while getting the maximum return. The BoP impact enterprise therefore must have a clear understanding of the investment gaps it faces and the levels of resources needed to address specific issues. The CED may well find that using the PEF or a similar tool can be helpful in determining specific needs from a particular scaling facilitator. In addition, using the PEF can be helpful in building these relationships, because it demonstrates that the scaling facilitator is part of a broader ecosystem of partners, and there are likely synergies among partner efforts that will amplify the impact of each partner's individual support.

Exploring the "For what?" question is perhaps the most contentious issue, as it requires carefully considering positive and potential negative outcomes and contemplating intended and unintended outcomes. It's sensible and reasonable to begin by identifying the impacts of the subsidized support on an enterprise's development, but it's neither sensible nor reasonable to stop there. It's time to start thinking not only in terms of the company but other potential stakeholders and positive and negative impacts on them. Who exactly is going to be affected, and how? (Again, the CED has to become comfortable with making these kinds of arguments to both internal and external audiences.) The BoP Impact Assessment Framework introduced in Chapter 4 can be helpful in this regard.

While it is crucial to articulate the full set of intended beneficiaries and the value proposition for them, the CED must also explore potential unintended impacts, including spillover and downstream effects. Are there economic or environmental externalities that have to be taken into account? Will we be distorting markets in the short or long term, and what are the implications resulting from the infusion of resources in this particular place or industry?[44] Addressing the "How long?" question requires answering another issue, which is of particular concern to many scaling facilitators: Is the subsidy something the enterprise will continually require to survive, or it is more catalytic in nature and therefore able to be phased out over time? While the latter is generally more palatable to those who are considering providing subsidized support, the CED must be honest in assessing long-term needs. Some subsidies are planned to extend for a long period of time.

For three years, I ran the Small Business Development Center (SBDC) in Loudoun County, Virginia, an independent nonprofit organization located just outside Washington, DC.[45] Supported by the Small Business Administration (SBA), municipal funds, and private donors, we provided free-of-charge advisory services to local small- and medium-scale entrepreneurs. We also helped these entrepreneurs access other subsidized resources, such as loan guarantees offered by the SBA. In other words, the U.S. government, through the SBA and other agencies and programs, has offered a variety of different types of ongoing subsidized support to business across the country.

The same can occur in BoP markets. While I was in Malawi, Africa, where my motorcycle encounter with the swarming bees, described in the Preface, took place, I was engaged in DEMATT (Development of Malawian Traders Trust), a program that was similar to the SBDC: It provided business advisory services to local small- and medium-scale entrepreneurs.[46] We charged them a small fee to participate, mainly to ensure that they were committed to the consulting process.[47] On balance, I felt that we had a positive impact on the businesses we supported and that, just like the case in the United States, this type of support was needed for an extended time.[48] But it could also be argued in both cases that we were distorting the market for firms seeking to sell their consultancy services.

By offering a clear rationale for how much is needed, what impacts this support will generate, and how long these resources will be needed, the CED can address concerns about providing subsidized support. This will help ensure that the foundation for creating collaborative interdependence is in place and allow the partners to focus their attention on how to forge a productive collaboration. Our attention now turns to the biases that many BoP impact enterprises seem to carry against the very entities that offer that support: the universe of scaling facilitators, mostly found within the development sector.

DEALING WITH INTERNAL RESISTANCE

In both research and practice, I have encountered significant misunderstandings about nontraditional partners that can create unnecessary internal barriers to cross-sectoral collaborations. Here the multilingual skills of the CED are especially important. In particular, the CED must devote adequate time and energy to building a deeper understanding within his or her organization about these new kinds of partners. He or she will have to dispel myths—and most likely will have to continue those clarifying efforts over time.

The first myth that many business leaders hold is that NGOs and the broader development community aren't very entrepreneurial or innovative and that, more broadly, their culture and values are generally antithetical to supporting market-based approaches. The second is the idea that all the organizations in a subset of the sector (e.g., the NGO community or aid agencies) are more or less the same. In other words, many business managers and entrepreneurs, in discussing the sector, implicitly lump together all the players within it and then say something like, "Well, you know, NGOs are hard to work with," or, "I've heard about Company X's problems with an aid agency, and we certainly don't want to engage with that sector." In countering these misapprehensions, I focus on the NGO sector, where the most prevalent misunderstandings occur, though these misapprehensions, and the associated remedies, apply equally well to other subsectors of the broader development community.

The first thing the CED has to do is to cut through prevalent stereotypes about the type of individuals who work for different sectors. For example, across the many graduate students and executives I have taught—nearly all with some practical business experience—there's a fairly prevalent myth that people who work for nonprofits are caring, passionate, and committed to helping humanity. They are "warm and fuzzy," as the saying goes. In contrast, many in the nonprofit community frame businesspeople in quite different terms: competitive, single-minded, and materialistic. What's the opposite of warm and fuzzy? Perhaps "cold and cranky."

If you think that way, stop right there! These generalizations are silly. In fact, some of the most unethical people I have ever met during my career hail from the nonprofit sector, and some of the most generous people come from the for-profit sector. In general, both sectors are filled with terrific people, with a few unsavory types thrown in on each side. The CED needs to help both sides of a potential partnership overcome these damaging stereotypes. The goal is to find and work with good people and good organizations regardless of sector.

Furthermore, individuals in the nonprofit sector are also more entrepreneurial than many businesspeople assume. One study indicated that within the sector, more than three-quarters (77 percent) see themselves as entrepreneurial. Almost 90 percent of nonprofits that have revenue-generating ventures say that those ventures relate strongly to the mission of their organization.[49] The case that the CED should be prepared to make is that people in the business and nonprofit sectors are more alike than many think.

A second myth that seems to surround the nonprofit sector is that it is monolithic. In fact, not only do nonprofits consist of a diversity of people—some good, some not so good; some who believe that business is part of the problem, and some who consider themselves entrepreneurs—the sector itself consists of a diversity of organizations. While few in the business world would say that all businesses are the same, many still have an overly simplistic and undifferentiated view of the nonprofit sector. In fact, the size and diversity of the sector is quite extraordinary.

To help the CED untangle this myth, let's take a step back. What's a nonprofit? In the United States, it's an organization on which is conferred a special tax status by the Internal Revenue Service. The most common nonprofit tax status is the 501c(3), which is reserved for organizations serving a charitable purpose, including (among others) universities, hospitals, social service groups, and—most important for our purposes—nonprofits or NGOs that have a specific social mission. There are approximately 2.3 million nonprofit organizations in the United States.[50] In 2010, the nonprofit sector represented 5.5 percent of the total GDP, or $804.8 billion and was the country's third largest employer.[51] In the first decade of this century, there was a 24 percent increase in the number of nonprofits registered with the IRS. Of course, some nonprofits, but certainly not all of them, are short-lived or remain very small.

So it's a surprisingly big sector that is getting even getting bigger. And this is not a purely U.S.-domestic phenomenon. At the beginning of this century, the *Economist* estimated that there were between 25,000 and 30,000 transnational nonprofits in the world—international NGOs with offices in more than one country—up from fewer than 5,000 in 1960. [52] In India in 2005, there were an estimated 1.5 million nonprofits (called Section 25s), with some 19 million volunteers and employees.[53] By 2014, the number of these nonprofits had climbed to more than 2.3 million.[54] Again, NGOs are a major employer with substantial resources, as well as a dominant societal influence, in both the developed and the developing world.

Clearly this is a large and growing sector that contains many good people interested in the role of business in alleviating social ills. Now let's go back to the question of diversity: Are all NGOs really the same? To explore this question, we look again at Oxfam and CARE. Both operate in many countries, are quite large, focus on addressing the same social issue (poverty in the developing world), and have formed a number of collaborations with for-profit players.

In 1942, Oxfam International was founded as a famine relief committee for World War II refugees. Its seventeen national affiliates (including Oxfam America) work together to serve local populations in more than 90 countries. It had an aggregated income of approximately 955 million euros in 2012–2013.[55] CARE currently operates in eighty-seven countries, has revenues of nearly half a billion dollars, and employs twelve thousand people in more than nine hundred poverty-fighting and emergency projects that reach more than 97 million people.[56]

Oxfam's corporate partnerships are mainly run on the national-affiliate level. For example, Oxfam America has partnered with—among others—Amazon and Visa.[57] CARE enjoys corporate partnerships with, among others, Vegpro, Procter & Gamble, and Pfizer.

Yet the differences between how these two highly visible NGOs approach corporate partnerships are also quite pronounced, and these differences—including level of interest, resources available, and history of advocacy—have implications for how the CED will need to introduce and manage these types of relationships.[58] Oxfam America's Chris Jochnick says about his organization:

> We perceive that our ability to do corporate partnerships rests on our reputation as a sort of trusted partner. You know, companies would look to Oxfam…a little bit warily, because most of our corporate work to date has involved high-profile corporate campaigning.
>
> That said, inside Oxfam, we're not really hurting for corporate partners. We feel like if we want to do a partnership with a company, we can proba-

bly do a partnership. Right now, we're approached by dozens of companies that would like to work with Oxfam, and we can't do it—either because we don't have the resources, or because we don't think the partnership is appropriate. So right now we are turning away a lot more than we can handle....

I would say that where we face challenges is more internal than external. We've got to bring more of Oxfam around to the business proposition, so to speak, of working with the private sector.[59]

Laté Lawson-Lartego, director of CARE's economic development unit, presents a somewhat different perspective:

We are putting a stronger emphasis on working with the private sector. We've been doing that, but we need to elevate it at a much larger scale. So we have to be very strategic in terms of how we set up those private-sector engagement roles.

And we have to learn how to work with this private sector, to speak their language and drive to win-win solutions, achieving their bottom line while reducing poverty. Given the enormous poverty problem this world is confronted with, especially when it comes to economic development, the private sector has to take the driver's seat in our strategy. Our role is to promote inclusive economic development, and from CARE's perspective, that has to be inclusive of women and young people. We also have a role to play in supporting and sharing knowledge together.

We want to look at the big picture, and see who are the key players in a given sector or sub sector, and see how we can maybe play more of a facilitation role to bring all the actors together, and how we can also support to remove some of the bottlenecks in the subsector.

And we also want to do more in terms of policy and advocacy, actually. Because oftentimes, we realize that the solution to a problem is not just in terms of intervention at the community level, but how can you look at the whole policy framework or business practices that really prevents most of the people to get access to a market and to make a decent living? That can be at a local level, regional level, or national level. And also at the global level....So more and more we are looking at those kinds of issues.[60]

Comparing these two quotes highlights important differences in how collaborations with these organizations might unfold. These potential partners are both focused on the same broad mission, but they have different perspectives and resource profiles. Both process and content matter: for example, one might appear easier to work with, but the other might have more appropriate resources. The CED must understand both how to facilitate different collaborations and what outcomes can emerge from a specific cross-sectoral partnership.

Comparing two nonprofits focused on environmental protection offers a complementary perspective of the risks of grouping NGOs into broad categories that conceal useful distinctions. Conservation International (CI), for whom I used to work, is an Arlington, Virginia-based nonprofit founded in 1987. Its mission is "building on a strong foundation of science, partnership, and field demonstration, CI empowers societies to responsibly and sustainably care for nature, our global biodiversity, for the well-being of humanity."[61] It operates in 44 countries, employing some 850 full-time staffers. It has annual revenues of around $100 million. CI enjoys corporate partnerships with companies like Starbucks, Bank of America, and Intel. Its revenue-generating arms include Verde Ventures Investment Fund (which makes microloans and grants), ecotourism, and agroforestry (including coffee and cocoa beans).

Although also having a strong focus on international conversation, Greenpeace International has a sharply different profile. "Greenpeace," according to its website, "is the leading independent campaigning organization that uses peaceful protest and creative communication to expose global environmental problems and to promote solutions that are essential to a green and peaceful future."[62] It is perhaps best known for its antiwhaling initiatives, which are variously depicted as courageous, noble, publicity oriented, misguided, or dangerously radical. And indeed, Greenpeace goes after many icons of American business, including (recently) Monsanto, ExxonMobil, and McDonald's. But at the same time, Greenpeace is an established, viable, and credible organization, with revenues of $32 million, a presence in thirty countries around the world, and some 2.8 million supporters.[63]

One question I would pose to any colleague who continues to hold on to the notion that all NGOs are the same is, "Which of these two environmental

NGOs would you prefer to have show up at your office unannounced, seeking a meeting with you?" I also like to cite Conservation International and Greenpeace in rapid succession, because to my eye, they illustrate another interesting fact about the nonprofit sector: These organizations, and others like them, are stakeholder conscious. The best of them are sophisticated users of various forms of media, including social media. They present themselves to the world in very particular ways and count on the fact that people will understand how they work and will support them.

And very important for the CED to understand, they compete against each other for attention, resources, and reputation. And while it's not exactly a zero-sum situation—people can and presumably do support both CI and Greenpeace—it's still a competitive sector, with many similarities in that regard to the for-profit sector. When I was at CI and seeking supporters, I wouldn't just focus on the challenges associated with environmental degradation; I would also highlight how CI's model was superior to its "competitors" like Greenpeace, the World Wildlife Fund or the Nature Conservancy.

In other words, just as in the case of for-profit businesses, NGOs identify their competition and present themselves as being different from and better than those competitors. Competition among NGOs can be quite ferocious—far fiercer than outsiders might think—and this is something the CED must account for. As Oxfam America's Chris Jochnick observes:

> NGO competition can be as ugly as or uglier than corporate competition. There are all kinds of political issues and jealousies and rivalries that happen in the NGO world that we don't like to…talk about—because of course NGOs are "pure"!—but in fact we can have as ugly a set of relationships and problems as any other sector. And navigating that can be quite tricky.[64]

So just as the people within these organizations are not all that different from their counterparts in business, some of their strategies and motivations can also track closely with each other. If someone in your organization says, "I don't think we can work with that sector; their cultures and values are just too different from ours," that bias represents their own lack of understanding of a complex and nuanced reality. In overcoming these biases, the CED must emphasize the similarities across sectors—underscoring that the players in the development sector are more familiar than one might think: "We can work across sectors." At the same time, he or she must also highlight the variety within the sector: "We can find appropriate partners." To establish collaborative interdependence, the CED has to be able to make the case internally that these partnerships are worth exploring and that inappropriate biases can influence our understanding of the opportunity.

RESPONDING TO CROSS-ORGANIZATIONAL TENSIONS

Now that we have a sense of the nonprofit reality and have developed some approaches for addressing and overcoming internal resistance, let's look at cross-organizational tensions and the strategies that the CED can use to address these potential barriers to successful collaborations with scaling facilitators.

The most substantial unaddressed problem in nonprofit-corporate alliances arises from one or both parties failing to understand how actual differences in culture and values can manifest themselves in implementing a cross-sectoral partnership. In other words, once you have overcome the myths about cross-sectoral partners and built sufficient internal support to engage in these partnerships, the CED must then be sure to keep a close eye on a set of cross-organizational tensions that can build up between the partners and damage or destroy the budding relationship.

My colleague Dennis Rondinelli and I conducted a cross-sectoral collaboration study for the Aspen Institute. Most of the participants in the study cited the ability to learn from each other as one of the largest potential benefits of collaborating.[65] But learning-motivated collaborations can be particularly difficult to manage. They require careful management of the level of transparency and knowledge sharing in the learning process between partners.

In relationships between organizations from the same sector, the partners often try to balance cooperation with competition. This can result, for example, in a learning race, with partners trying to learn more than they share to change the power dynamics in the relationship.[66] Cross-sectoral collaborations in which partners are not trying to create the same type of value may offer a more fertile ground for learning and sharing but also have their own unique challenges.[67]

Without sufficient transparency, cross-sectoral partnerships can spark tensions about the collaboration within both organizations. The nonprofit, for example, may wonder, "Why doesn't my for-profit partner share its operating plan?" or, "What influence will I have in the value-creation strategy?" The corporate partner too may be confused by too little transparency: "Is my nonprofit partner just waiting for us to make a mistake that they can then use against us in some sort of advocacy effort?"

I'm sure that these lack-of-transparency issues are familiar to those who have engaged in these types of collaboration. Paradoxically, the exact opposite—too much transparency—can also be a challenge. In many cases, both partners may hope and assume that they will serve as a teacher to the other. Corporations want nonprofit partners to learn about the value of strong financial performance; nonprofits want their corporate partners to learn about the importance of social performance. (Again, they may be holding on to outdated assumptions about the people and perspectives of the other sector.) While each wants its partner to better appreciate its own viewpoints and knowledge, conflict can arise when a partner becomes more interested in teaching than in learning and a "race to teach" occurs. Corporations interested only in extolling the virtues of private enterprise, just like nonprofits that are passionate only about preaching the social gospel, tend to make poor partners.

In the BoP context, the best collaborators recognize the value of respecting the perspectives and insights of their partners and the importance of balancing learning and teaching. To minimize tension and maximize the opportunity for co-creation, the CED should carefully research potential scaling facilitators and pursue the ones that seem to offer the best fit in terms of content (Are our resources complementary?) and process (Can we work together?). As I discussed in Chapter 2, business leaders may fall into the trap of forming partnerships of convenience—working with the organizations that approach them first or are well known—rather than using a tool like the PEF to build the most appropriate portfolio of scaling facilitators.

In considering potential partners, there are some questions a CED may want to consider:

- What is their track record of working with for profit partners? (They may already have extensive experience in this realm.)

- Are their skills complementary to ours?
- Who are their stakeholders, and how will they define success?
- What sort of commitment are they willing to make?
- Is their motivation to learn and co-create, or are they more interested in teaching-and-preaching?

While these types of questions are crucial at the early stage of partner development, CEDs should also keep them in mind throughout the duration of the collaboration because the quality and value of a relationship will vary over time. Indeed, having an exit strategy in place will allow both partners to continually assess the value of the collaboration. As we've seen, things change, and the value proposition of the collaboration for both partners is likely to evolve. Sometimes the value proposition will get stronger, calling for an even deeper and richer collaboration. At other times, a new scaling facilitator may emerge as being potentially more helpful than an existing one. It's often a good idea, therefore, to develop an exit strategy in advance, including specific language about the rules of disengagement if one or the other party feels it's time to wind things down.

The partners in a cross-sectoral collaboration may also have different perspectives on how to measure success, based on their respective experience bases. The CED should understand and work to align these differences with a focus on building greater interdependence among the partners. For example, a scaling facilitator may be most comfortable assessing success by resources invested and activities initiated. These measures, however, may offer only limited insights into the success of the enterprise. In cross-sector collaborations, the scaling facilitator should also value, and measure, the sustainability of business activities or the lessons learned with regard to developing a viable business model—types of metrics that are rarely embraced by the development community but are crucial for the ongoing success of the BoP impact enterprise.

The enterprise team, for its part, must value social performance, including poverty-alleviation impacts, a return highly prized by most scaling facilitators and crucial in building the enterprise's value proposition. Yet enterprise leaders may initially resist adopting these impact-oriented social metrics because they are hard to control. Again, the CED can help bridge this divide and create greater interdependence within a partnership by, for example, highlighting the link between poverty alleviation and value creation.

Similarly, thinking and talking explicitly about both the initial scope and the potential to scale up at an early stage can be helpful. In Oxfam America's collaboration with Swiss Re, while the initial commitment was for one year, the short-term relationship provided the opportunity to extend and enhance the partnership over time, which was what happened. The CED's goal is to manage the size and complexity of the relationship over time. Starting with a large and complicated partnership in the early stages of collaborative interdependence may be a bad idea—there may be too many chances for things to go off the rails as the partners get to know each other. Yet collaborations that are too small can get pushed aside if neither partner has much skin in the game. Both the development community and the for-profit sector want to see scale. The prescription here is to be realistic about the capacity to manage the collaboration in the earlier stages of the partnership, while also planning for impact, scale, and the possibility of a long-term relationship from the very beginning.

LOOKING FORWARD

Throughout this book, my goal has been to help make the BoP promise a reality. We have explored tools and frameworks for action, and my proposals in this chapter for creating the CED position and emphasizing a partnership model based on collaborative interdependence are very much in that spirit: putting in place an individual and an operating framework that can attend to a complex, critical, and demanding set of relationships, and thereby help build a strong and appropriate ecosystem of partners.

The final chapter reviews the major points of the journey taken in this book and underscores some of the key lessons that I hope will have helped answer these questions: How do we set ourselves up for success? How can we build BoP impact enterprises that are sustainable at scale? How can we create a strong value proposition that will have a net positive impact on the BoP? How can we effectively integrate development community support and investments into enterprise growth strategies?

I also raise and attempt to offer some initial insight into several other questions about the future development of BoP impact enterprise. How should we think about profits in a BoP impact enterprise? How do we respond to the potential negative environmental implications of a growing number of enterprises serving the BoP? What do other slices of the economic pyramid have to learn from the base? And finally, can we fulfill the BoP promise?

The answer to this last question is an emphatic yes.

7 MAKING THE PROMISE A REALITY

The key message and promise of this book is that we can build profitable, scalable enterprises in BoP markets—what I call BoP impact enterprises—that truly alleviate poverty. It can be done. Our challenge is to deliver on that potential.

Our efforts to build a strong and growing population of BoP impact enterprises that are sustainable at scale are at an inflection point. Yes, the promise is huge, but to succeed in the journey ahead, we need to establish tools, frameworks, capabilities, and mind-sets that can guide enterprise leaders and their partners in their business efforts.

In this book, I have tried to do just that. I have summarized the lessons that can be drawn from analyzing the experiences of individuals and enterprises that have gone before us. We must move beyond motivational stories, unrealistic representations of impact, and poorly structured partnership approaches. Using good data and good thinking, we must explore what works and what doesn't.

The tools and frameworks I offer are centered on three mutually reinforcing cornerstones, illustrated in Figure 7.1. BoP impact enterprises will flourish when their leaders have a set of guiding strategies based on creating value with the BoP—strategies that are integrated with support and investment from an ecosystem of partners from the development community and other sectors.

The BoP socioeconomic segment is increasingly seen as a potentially enormous and relatively untapped market. As markets in the developed world continue to mature, the global business community has a growing interest in finding new customers, producers, and partners. It's not only existing multinational businesses that are thinking about BoP impact enterprises. Interest also comes from multiple other actors: host country companies, social

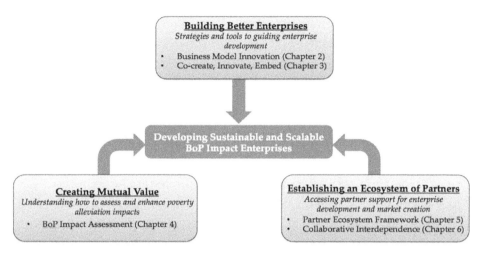

FIGURE 7.1 Three cornerstones for achieving sustainability at scale

entrepreneurs, socially minded investors, nonprofit organizations, development agencies, government officials responsible for alleviating poverty and improving well-being, and many others.[1]

More than ever before, business is seen as part of the solution to global poverty. The BoP domain has played an important role in catalyzing these efforts, even as it has made a substantial transformation from a BoP 1.0 model to a more robust BoP 2.0 perspective.[2] In particular, this change has meant moving beyond first-generation efforts that focused on introducing the BoP as a viable market opportunity to second-generation strategies that emphasize the need to co-create this market, with a particular emphasis on active engagement with the BoP in this process. BoP 2.0 is less about fortune finding and execution and more about fortune creating and innovation.

Each constituency has its own incentives, of course, but all see a huge socioeconomic sector, comprising some 4 billion of the 7 billion people on earth who lack access to a multitude of goods and services—and at the same time face constraints when trying to bring their own production to market. The challenge, and the opportunity, is to align these incentives and design businesses that can serve that segment well.

You may recall the story in the Preface to this book about the idealistic young Peace Corps volunteer who was driving his motorcycle down the road in the beautiful rolling hills of southern Malawi. Lost in thought and perhaps not paying enough attention to the potential obstacles ahead, I drove my bike right into a swarm of bees that was traveling the opposite direction along the same road. Thanks to a mix of skill, risk taking, and luck, I managed to swerve and—standing high up on my pegs—shake the mass of stunned bees off my seat, recover, and take off down the road.

Which thoughts was I lost in? I was thinking about how much I had learned about enterprise development during my time in Africa. I was thinking how much more effective I would have been if I had had access to a "user's manual"— a guide to working with the very resourceful Malawian people whom I had come to know and admire in the previous two years. I was thinking of the people who would come after me, who would learn many of the same lessons I had learned and might even find themselves reaching exactly the same conclusion that I was as I encountered those bees: It would be great to read the manual ahead of time. It would be great to have a field guide to help fulfill the promise.

I didn't write the book back then, and I'm glad I didn't. Back in 1991, I knew something about working with what later came to be called the "base of the pyramid," but nowhere near enough.[3] Throughout the ensuing quarter-century, I kept thinking about that field guide. In Chapter 1, I told a story about an experienced and successful entrepreneur who was visiting my office at the University of Michigan not long ago. He had become engaged in BoP impact enterprise development in India several years earlier, and I hadn't heard from him in a while. He had always struck me as a confident person, verging on cocky. Now, I noticed, he seemed far more humble.

"We thought we knew what we were doing," he said, in a forlorn voice, "but we have made all the mistakes in the book." He believed that his years as an extraordinarily successful entrepreneur in the United States—launching several businesses from scratch, creating jobs, bolstering the local economy wherever he set up shop—would translate smoothly into the BoP domain. But for a number of pretty predictable reasons, it didn't work out that way.

As he told me what had gone wrong, I found myself thinking: *I should write that book*. And now I have.

That's where the motivation for this book came from. It draws on my experiences as both a business practitioner and an academic, running a

BoP impact enterprise, working with local businesses and community members in BoP markets, being a director in a nonprofit organization, and collaborating with a wide variety of entrepreneurs and enterprise leaders. This work is certainly a personal manifesto of sorts. It relies on more than a decade and a half of research as an academic, mixed with nearly as much experience in practice across Africa, Asia, and the Americas. But it also offers prescriptions and strategies that I believe must be embraced if we are to be truly successful in building BoP impact enterprises that are sustainable at scale.

Despite the unconventional nature of some of my prescriptions (I'm thinking, for example, of the chief ecosystem director for which I advocated in Chapter 6), I hope that I have stayed in the realm of the practical and the doable. In developing this book, I have adopted the point of view of the business leader working to create a successful, scalable BoP impact enterprise and have drawn my examples mainly from the BoP business community—a base that is already large and growing by the day. Of course I strongly believe that development agencies, policymakers, and leaders in the NGO community will find this book useful and interesting—that would be a bonus from an author's perspective—but what I really hope is that business leaders will find my arguments compelling and my prescriptions useful.

Developing this book and the associated frameworks also reinforced in my mind the importance of humility—beginning with attempting to write a book like this. I believe that I have laid out some valuable and useful tools that can contribute to the development of BoP impact enterprises. At the same time, I recognize that they don't cover all the topics that an enterprise leader might wish to address. For example, there is much more to be discussed and debated along functional lines, such as marketing, financing, and operations. We could also benefit from delving more deeply into topics such as leadership teams, operating systems, and governance structures.[4]

The good news is that a growing number of bright and thoughtful people are contributing to this conversation.[5] As a result, there is also no reason for this book to be lonely on your bookshelf. One of the most gratifying developments in the past decade is the profusion of truly good books and articles about one aspect or another of operating enterprises in BoP markets, with more on the way. While I have tried to cite these resources at the appropriate opportunity, I am sure I have missed some good work.

Again, though, I think this book asks—and attempts to answer—some critical questions: How do we set ourselves up for success? What value can we create working with the BoP? What pilot can we launch to test that value proposition? How can we focus on scale from the outset? How can we create and measure, in real time, our value proposition? As we scale up, how can we maximize the good impacts and minimize the bad ones to enhance mutual value creation? If we can't do it alone—and I argue that most of us can't—how do we identify key collaborators from across the development community and other sectors and build a partnership ecosystem that supports both enterprise development and market creation? What's the value proposition behind these partnerships, and how do we build and maintain them? And can we make money at this?

This last question requires a little more comment. As I noted in Chapter 1, a BoP impact enterprise seeks financial sustainability and plans for scalability beyond the local market. Implicitly, this means that the enterprise must generate sufficient financial returns to expand and be profitable. How much profit to seek, and what is to be done with that profit, are decisions that the enterprise leadership and its key stakeholders must make. Also, investments by the development community can strongly influence the profit opportunity, as well as the prospects for sustainability at scale. But whatever term might be used—*profit, excess revenue, operating surplus*, something else—the enterprise's revenues must exceed its costs.

We all must get over our biases against mixing profits with poverty alleviation. We don't seem to have any substantial issue with this mix in the developed world, as illustrated by the example of Walmart and SNAP in Chapter 6. Yet when it comes to the developing world, and especially BoP markets, this seems to give us pause and sometimes even prompt a heated debate. Are businesses good or bad for the BoP? Again, this is the wrong question to ask. Businesses are serving, and will continue to serve, the BoP. Some will be "good" and some will be "bad." Think, for example, of the extractive local money lenders that the microcredit industry sought to displace. To move forward productively, we need to ask a more powerful and actionable question:

"How can we make business work better for the BoP?" We use the power of business to address poverty in the developed world; we need to adopt this same mind-set in our efforts to serve the BoP.

Here is one thing that I'd like to see more of: enterprise leaders not only making honest presentations about their social impact—and avoiding those biased anecdotes—but also more openly discussing their financial performance. In the developed world, business leaders are embarrassed by financial failure; in the BoP domain, they are often reluctant to discuss financial returns. They fear a backlash about profiting off the poor. But we need to become more comfortable sharing economic success.[6] As we've seen, BoP impact enterprises that are not sustainable and scalable won't have much impact on poverty alleviation. Let's celebrate the ones that can have that impact.

A crucial component of this argument is mutual value creation. Financial and social performance should not be considered separate goals. We can create shared value.[7] Making life better for the people you're trying to serve is not only the right (morally correct) thing for the BoP entrepreneur to focus on; it's the smart thing. This means that it's all about collaboration and co-creation. Successful venture building is not done "to," "in," or "at" the BoP; it's done *with* the BoP. The BoP population faces constraints in value creation and value capture. Enterprises that create and share value with the BoP are the ones most likely to develop value propositions that reflect the on-the-ground realities.[8] In short, mutual value creation is not only possible; it is absolutely critical to enterprise success.

This also applies to building an ecosystem of development community partners. The opportunity for partnership is premised on mutual value creation. The development community is not looking to make a profit; its members are looking for social impact. If their due diligence indicates that a given business partner isn't generating sufficient social impact, they may withdraw their support. This threat of withdrawal—and the associated impacts on an enterprise's performance that come with it—offers some ongoing assurances about the type and amount of value generated and shared by the enterprise.

How does the enterprise—and its development community partners—understand local value creation? I would say that it's by investing in assessing and enhancing poverty alleviation impacts. Alleviating poverty is more than just tracking output measures—how many mosquito nets we distributed last year, how many gallons of water we purified, and so on. These are laudable goals. But any assessment of the value being generated from these outputs needs to be based on input from the BoP. Poverty alleviation, moreover, is not just a hurdle that must be cleared in order to recruit development community partners. Rather, it's a key performance indicator that reflects the enterprise's viability because alleviating poverty is in many cases the most crucial aspect of the enterprise's value proposition. And of course, the more value that a business creates for the BoP, the more value it can potentially capture for itself.

To do all, this we don't need heroes. We need leaders who have a vision for impact and scale. Heroes in the BoP domain (at least from my perspective) tend to see themselves as saviors, have big egos that need to be satisfied, and suffer from a lack of humility. Going from pilot to scale is daunting and requires pushing well beyond the comfort zone of a small and controllable venture. Innovation and learning are crucial. This means committing to a long journey that tends to be characterized by mistakes, distractions, frustrations, and dead ends—but also the occasional victory and continued progress. A hero can satisfy his or her ego after having helped one person, or ten, or a hundred as long as the intervention is dramatic and personal. There is nothing wrong with this, but it's not sufficient in the BoP context. A leader dreams of affecting millions through the long journey of co-creating, innovating, and embedding. The good leader understands mutual value creation and the opportunities and challenges it presents. The best leader acknowledges this journey and celebrates the partners that help make it possible.

But to be effective, these leaders also must go in the right direction as they set off on that journey. To reiterate, these BoP impact enterprise leaders must understand how to effectively build ventures in a very distinctive context. They must understand how their business strategy affects poverty (which has many faces) as they seek to build a viable value proposition. Finally, they must establish an ecosystem of partners to sustain the venture.

It's that simple—and that difficult.

Looking forward, new challenges appear. For one, it is becoming increasingly clear that from an environmental sustainability perspective, the world can't sustain BoP models of production and consumption that mirror those of the top of the pyramid.[9] As they scale, BoP impact enterprises must develop models that recognize and respond to that challenge. And some of these enterprises can—and indeed some have to—demonstrate the potential for disruptive innovation. This means that these models, once developed and scaled in BoP markets, can move up the pyramid.[10] This in turn has substantial implications for the overall size of the business opportunity for BoP impact enterprises. At what point in the entrepreneurial process does the business leader need to consider this scenario, and how does he or she best understand its full potential?

How do we deal with the fact that every BoP intervention has both an upside and a downside? I've cited several cautionary tales in previous chapters. Giving people access to credit, for example, also gives them access to debt. Empowering women can also engender tension and violence within the family. The question is not, Are there downsides? It is, What are we going to do about them?

Other questions arise as well. This book has presented some overarching BoP impact enterprise strategies and frameworks. How can we take these and develop more finely tuned recommendations and best practices that more fully account for differences in stages of enterprise development, business models, industry sectors, and market environments, to name a few? Furthermore, the BoP is an aggregation of many different kinds of individuals and groups who represent potential markets for goods and services. These differences include level of income, educational attainment, geographic location (including rural versus urban), market institutions, and the public policy environment, to name just a few. How should we segment the BoP to better understand opportunities for successful enterprise development? While we have better tools to assess poverty alleviation impacts, how can we better understand the link between social impact and enterprise strategy and performance? Which enterprise strategies are likely to generate which types of alleviation impacts?[11]

This book presents frameworks for building an ecosystem of partnerships. But what gaps in support for enterprise development and market creation are still not being filled, and what can be done about that? Given that BoP impact enterprises often transcend industry boundaries—many health initiatives, for example, also need reliable sources of energy—how do we ensure that our partnership model extends beyond the traditional definition of an industry?[12] And how do we ensure that the latest ideas and information are shared across the domain in ways that most effectively enhance the capacity within BoP impact enterprises to build sustainable, scalable ventures?[13]

I hope my colleagues—whether researchers based at academic institutions, business leaders seeking the latest thinking for their own BoP impact enterprises, or development professionals looking for more effective poverty-alleviation approaches—will push forward on these fronts.[14] In many ways, this is the most exciting frontier in business. I know *I* intend to be there.

And this brings us to the final point in this book: Why should we care? For many, taking this journey and trying to deliver on the BoP promise is about a desire for a career that has impact.[15] As an academic who seeks to blend research and practice, I aspire not only to contribute to the development of BoP impact enterprises, but also to help shape the domain into an even more powerful approach for using the power of business to address social issues. I am not a hero—in the sense of the word introduced earlier in this chapter— but I hope to be a leader. If mistakes, distractions, frustrations, and dead ends mark the progress of a leader, I may well be on the right track.

Even if this type of impact is not a personal motivating factor, there is another good—and pragmatic—reason for being interested in the proliferation of successful BoP impact enterprises. Today our world is far more crowded and closely interconnected through cell phones, the Internet, and other communications networks than it has ever been before. The broad gaps that still remain between the haves and the have-nots are becoming more apparent to everyone. Those on the outside looking in increasingly perceive these inequities and increasingly resent them. Simply stated, things are not *fair*. By luck of birth, some are born into the top of the pyramid and others to the BoP. Being at the top or part of the base isn't about merit; it's almost entirely about where you start. The vast majority of the world—4 billion now, and likely growing to 5 or 6 billion—is part of the BoP, and they see the gulf that exists between them and those at the top of the pyramid.[16] They understand how poverty affects their lives, and they are increasingly expecting a better deal. If we don't deliver, what will the world look like in ten or twenty years? We have even more reason to look out for each other—preferably out of sense of shared humanity but at least out of self-interest.

Today most informed observers agree that a better deal—the alleviation of poverty along its many dimensions—can be crafted better when we let enterprises be part of the solution. They are not the only solution; donation-based efforts will remain an important component in efforts to alleviate poverty, the development community will continue its good work, and governments will certainly play an important role. But the business sector has to play a substantial role. We have to fulfill the promise of building BoP impact enterprises that are sustainable at scale.

The good news is that we have come a long way over the past decade or so. The bad news is that we have to do more, and we have to do better. And that can't happen unless, and until, business leaders and their partners better understand the journey they need to take.

That's what this book is about. You have in your hands the field guide that I first contemplated on that road from Mulanje to Blantyre all those years ago. (I am thankful that my encounter with those angry bees did not end my journey of exploration then and there.) This book is imperfect and incomplete, and new ideas will continue to emerge. But I hope and believe that it offers a set of the tools, frameworks, and techniques that BoP impact enterprises can use to build sustainable and scalable businesses in a unique and opportunity-rich market context.

I'll end where I started. By designing and developing BoP impact enterprises, it is possible to create mutual value with the base of the pyramid. We can fulfill the base of the pyramid promise.

NOTES

INTRODUCTION

1. C. K. Prahalad and S. L. Hart, "The Fortune at the Bottom of the Pyramid," *Strategy + Business* 26 (First Quarter 2002): 2–14.

2. With the notable exception of the beginning of this Preface—featuring motorcycles and bees—most of this book is not about me, but about things I have learned. For more about me, see my websites at the William Davidson Institute: http://wdi.umich.edu/about/people/staff-bios/ted-london and the Ross School of Business at the University of Michigan: http://www.bus.umich.edu/FacultyBios/FacultyBio.asp?id=000704346.

3. Michael Porter's five forces model (and similar strategy-oriented models) applies generically across a wide range of enterprises. My effort here is to lay out similarly generic tools and frameworks that have relevance across the diversity of BoP impact enterprise and allow for customization as appropriate. See, for example, Porter's *Competitive Strategy* (New York: Free Press, 1980).

4. Fortunately, we seem to be past the stage of speculating as to whether the fortune at the base of the pyramid is a mirage. But to explore that point of view, see A. Karnani, "Misfortune at the Bottom of the Pyramid," *Greener Management International* 51 (2007): 99–110. See also A. K. Jaiswal, "The Fortune at the Bottom or the Middle of the Pyramid?" *Innovations* 3 (2008): 85–100.

5. See, for example, T. London and S. G. Kennedy, "Movirtu's Cloud Phone Service: Funding a Base-of-the-Pyramid Venture," case 1–429–162 (Ann Arbor: GlobaLens Case Publishing, William Davidson Institute at the University of Michigan, 2012). *Harvard Business Review* (October 2012) ran an interesting retrospective article by Celtel founder Mo Ibrahim: "Celtel's Founder on Building a Business on the World's Poorest Continent," 41–44, summarized at http://hbr.org/2012/10/celtels-founder-on-building-a-business-on-the-worlds-poorest-continent/ar/1.

6. See, for example, Commission on the Private Sector and Development, *Unleashing Entrepreneurship: Making Business Work for the Poor* (New York: United Nations Development Programme, 2004). See also Growing Inclusive Markets Initiative, *Creating Value for All: Strategies for Doing Business with the Poor* (New York: United Nations Development Programme, 2008). And finally, see World Business Council for Sustainable Development, *Doing Business with the Poor: A Field Guide* (Geneva, Switzerland: WBCSD, 2004).

CHAPTER 1

1. After some initial disagreement, the definition of the base of the pyramid is widely seen as the socioeconomic segment with annual income less than $3,000 in purchasing power parity (PPP), when adjusted to 2005 U.S. dollars. This definition was well articulated in *The Next Four Billion*, published by the World Resources Institute and the International Finance Corporation online: http://www.wri.org/publication/next-4-billion. It was further developed in Stuart Hart's and my book, *Next Generation Business Strategies for the Base of the Pyramid* (Upper Saddle River, NJ: FT Press, 2011). Simply stated, PPP provides a standardization of real income across different countries by equating the price of an identical basket of traded goods and services across different currencies. See the OECD's definition at http://www.oecd.org/std/purchasingpowerparities-frequentlyaskedquestionsfaqs.htm.

2. Respectively, C. K. Prahalad, *The Fortune at the Bottom of the Pyramid: Eradicating Poverty Through Profits* (Upper Saddle River, NJ: Wharton School Publishing, 2005); V. K. Rangan, P. Polak, and M. Warwick, *The Business Solution to Poverty* (San Francisco: Berrett-Koehler, 2013); J. A. Quelch, G. Herrero, and B. Barton, *Business Solutions for the Global Poor: Creating Social and Economic Value* (San Francisco: Jossey-Bass, 2007); and S. Hart, *Capitalism at the Crossroads: The Unlimited Business Opportunities in Serving the World's Most Difficult Problems* (Upper Saddle River, NJ: Wharton School Publishing, 2005).

3. Prahalad, although writing about his own work, posed these questions in the dedication to him in Hart's and my book, *Next Generation Business Strategies.*.

4. See, for example, the annual reports by the Aspen Network of Development Entrepreneurs: http://www.aspeninstitute.org/policy-work/aspen-network-development-entrepreneurs.

5. There is a burgeoning literature from the development community on these topics. Interested readers should start with the 2004 report of the Commission on the Private Sector and Development, *Unleashing Entrepreneurship: Making Business Work for the Poor* (New York: United Nations Development Programme, 2004). Also informative is the Growing Inclusive Markets Initiative's 2008 report, *Creating Value for All: Strategies for Doing Business with the Poor* (New York: United Nations Development Programme, 2008).

6. The October 2012 issue of *Harvard Business Review* ran an interesting retrospective article by Centel founder Mo Ibrahim, "Celtel's Founder on Building a Business on the World's Poorest Continent," 41–44, summarized at http://hbr.org/2012/10/celtels-founder-on-building-a-business-on-the-worlds-poorest-continent/ar/1. For more on the BoP market size for information and communication technology, see *The Next Four Billion*.

7. See *The Next Four Billion*. Also see the IFC's global consumption database at http://www.ifc.org/wps/wcm/connect/ASEXT_Content/What+We+Do/Inclusive+Business/Market+Insights_Consumption+Data/GlobalConsumptionDatabase/.

8. For more on the how this number was calculated, see H. de Soto, *The Mystery of Capital: Why Capitalism Triumphs in the West and Fails Everywhere Else* (New York: Basic Books, 2000).

9. See, for example, J. R. Immelt, V. Govindarajan, and C. Trimble, "How GE Is Disrupting Itself," *Harvard Business Review* 88 (October 2009): 56–65.

10. See S. Hart and C. Christensen, "The Great Leap: Driving Innovation from the Base of the Pyramid," *Sloan Management Review* 44, no. 1 (2002): 51–56.

11. Note that the income line that is incorporated in the definition of the BoP is purchasing power parity (PPP), when adjusted to 2005 U.S. dollars. For more, see the IFC's global consumption database: http://www.ifc.org/wps/wcm/connect/ASEXT_Content/What+We+Do/Inclusive+Business/Market+Insights_Consumption+Data/GlobalConsumptionDatabase/. Also see how the international community reclassified extreme poverty from $1.00 to $1.25 per day (in 2005 prices).

12. As in many other things, my friend and colleague Stuart Hart came up with this perspective and influenced my own thinking.

13. See, for example, www.tetrapak.com/se/documents/Dairyindex_5.pdf.

14. See, for example, W. Easterly, *The White Man's Burden: Why the West's Efforts to Aid the Rest Have Done So Much Ill and So Little Good* (New York: Penguin Press, 2006); and R. C. Riddell, *Does Foreign Aid Really Work?* (Oxford: Oxford University Press, 2007).

15. See de Soto, *The Mystery of Capital.* For a definition of informal markets, see T. London, Heather Esper, Andrew Grogan-Baylor, and Geoffrey M. Kistruck, "Connecting Poverty to Purchase in Informal Markets," *Strategic Entrepreneurship Journal* 8, no. 1 (2014): 37–55.

16. See, for example, the Commission on the Private Sector and Development, *Unleashing Entrepreneurship.*

17. For more on the growth of impact investing, see Antony Bugg-Levine and J. Emerson, *Impact Investing: Transforming How We Make Money While Making a Difference* (San Francisco: Jossey-Bass, 2011).

18. T. London, R. Kennedy, and S. Sheth, *Impact Enterprise* (Ann Arbor: GlobaLens Case Publishing, William Davidson Institute at the University of Michigan, 2012).

19. For more on disruptive innovation from BoP markets, see S. Hart and C. Christensen, "The Great Leap: Driving Innovation from the Base of the Pyramid," *Sloan Management Review* 44(1):51–56; and Immelt, Govindarajan, and Trimble, "How GE Is Disrupting Itself."

20. Prahalad and Hart, "The Fortune at the Bottom of the Pyramid." Note the transition, over the past decade or so, from *bottom* to *base.* President Franklin D. Roosevelt may have coined the original concept in his April 7, 1932, radio address, "The Forgotten Man," in which he said, "These unhappy times call for the building of plans that rest upon the forgotten, the unorganized but the indispensable units of economic power... that build from the bottom up and not from the top down, that put their faith once more in the forgotten man at the bottom of the economic pyramid."

21. C. K. Prahalad and A. Hammond, "Serving the World's Poor, Profitably," *Harvard Business Review* 80, no. 9 (2002): 48–57. T. London and S. L. Hart, "Reinventing Strategies for Emerging Markets: Beyond the Transnational Model," *Journal of International Business Studies* 35 (2004): 350–370.

22. Prahalad, *The Fortune at the Bottom of the Pyramid.*

23. London and Hart, *Next Generation Business Strategies.*

24. For more on the difference between finding and creating, see S. A. Alvarez and J. B. Barney, "Discovery and Creation: Alternative Theories of Entrepreneurial Action," *Strategic Entrepreneurship Journal* 1, no. 1 (2008): 11–26. My friend and colleague Stuart Hart recognized how this approach to viewing entrepreneurship had close connections to BoP impact enterprise development. His perspective on this influenced my own thinking on the topic and on the presentation and content of Table 1.1.

25. For more on this topic, see T. London, R. Anupindi, and S. Sheth, "Creating Mutual Value: Lessons from Ventures Serving Base of the Pyramid Producers," *Journal of Business Research* 63 (2010): 582–94.

26. Our colleague Al Hammond first made this point in his chapter in London and Hart, *Next Generation Business Strategies.*

27. World Bank, *World Development Report 2000/2001: Attacking Poverty* (Oxford: Oxford University Press, 2001).

28. Amartya Sen, writing on this topic, emphasizes the importance of well-being, especially the ability of individuals to shape their own future. See his *Development as Freedom* (New York: Anchor Books, 1999).

29. As we will see, the CED function can also reside in the development community partner; here, for simplicity, I locate it within the enterprise.

CHAPTER 2

1. See, for example, Alexander Osterwalder and Yves Pigneur, *Business Model Generation* (Hoboken, NJ: Wiley, 2010).

2. For more on fast experimentation, including how to manage the process, see Eric Ries, *The Lean Startup* (New York: Crown Business, 2011). For more on a real options for developing a business case, see M. Amram and N. Kulatilaka, *Real Options: Managing Strategic Investment in an Uncertain World* (Boston: Harvard Business School Press, 1999).

3. Development agencies too have begun to embrace the notion of a tiered-funding model, which essentially stages investments in a way that rewards ventures that succeed at each stage. See, for example, USAID's Development Innovation Ventures at http://www.usaid.gov/div/about.

4. This is a substantially abridged version of a case I wrote with Heather McDonald and under the supervision of Stuart Hart: "Expanding the Playing Field: Nike's World Shoe Project," case 1–428–673 (Ann Arbor: GlobaLens Case Publishing, William Davidson Institute at the University of Michigan, January 2002).

5. Tom Hartge shared these insights on a videotaped interview in 2002 when he was discussing his reactions to "Expanding the Playing Field: Nike's World Shoe Project," a teaching case.

6. For a more sustained and in-depth treatment of business model development and related design variables, see my paper, "Business Model Development for Base-of-the-Pyramid Market Entry," in *Proceedings of the Seventieth Annual Meeting of the Academy of Management,* edited by L. A. Toombs (2010).

7. I thank my colleague, Vijay Sharma, for his insights here. Vijay has led BoP initiatives with GlaxoSmithKline and Hindustan Unilever, among others, and is one of the most experienced BoP managers in the field.

8. The Rockefeller Foundation has been a noted supporter of this approach. See also the Global Impact Investing Network's support of impact investing aimed at both social/environmental impacts and financial returns, at http://www.thegiin.org/cgi-bin/iowa/home/index.html.

9. Enterprise leaders should be awareness of the issue of self-dealing, which restricts the type of support a company's foundation can provide.

10. Allen Hammond, "BoP Venture Formation for Scale," in *Next Generation Business Strategies for the Base of the Pyramid*, edited by T. London and S. Hart (Upper Saddle River, NJ: FT Press, 2011), describes a somewhat different and interesting approach to a hybrid. In this perspective, a new hybrid venture is designed and created jointly by a for-profit enterprise and a development sector organization.

11. I am indebted to my colleague, Deborah Burand, at the Law School at the University of Michigan, for reviewing and enhancing this section on legal entities.

12. In 2008, Burand founded the International Transactions Clinic at the University of Michigan. The clinic brings the legal perspective to bear on many of the issues addressed in this book.

13. This idea is captured in the work on ambidextrous organizations. See, for example, Charles A. O'Reilly III and Michael L. Tushman, "The Ambidextrous Organization," *Harvard Business Review* 82 (April 2004): 74–81.

14. I discuss the idea of internal white space in more detail in my doctoral dissertation: "How Are Capabilities Created? A Process Study of New Market Entry" (University of North Carolina, 2005). See also Allen Hammond, "BoP Venture Formation for Scale."

15. This colleague asked me not to attribute this quote to him.

16. London, "Business Model Development for Base-of-the-Pyramid Market Entry." See also London, "How Are Capabilities Created?"

17. I thank Jim Koch, senior founding fellow with the Center for Science, Technology, and Society at the Leavey School of Business, Santa Clara University, for his insights throughout this chapter on the unique challenges that start-up ventures face in developing business models for BoP markets.

18. This is a substantially abridged version of Ted London and Magdalena M. Kote, "CEMEX's Patrimonio Hoy: At the Tipping Point?" case 1–429–202 (Ann Arbor: University of Michigan, Ross School of Business, 2006). See also Ted London, John L. Parke, and Jenn Korona, "Constructing a Base-of-the-Pyramid Business in a Multinational Corporation: CEMEX's Patrimonio Hoy Looks to Grow," Globalens case 1–429–202 (Ann Arbor: GlobaLens Case Publishing, William Davidson Institute at the University of Michigan, 2012).

19. From CEMEX, *Annual Report* (2013).

20. I thank Henning Alts Schoutz, who has been a key member of the Patrimonio Hoy team for many years, for his review and feedback on this summary of the Patrimonio Hoy initiative.

21. Inter-American Development Bank "ME-0137 Housing Finance Program," Board of Directors program description for loan to Banobras (December 14, 2000).

22. Hector Ureta shared these insights during a videotaped class session in 2004 in which he was discussing the development of CEMEX's Patrimonio Hoy initiative: "CEMEX's Patrimonio Hoy: At the Tipping Point?" Globalens video 1–429–205 (Ann Arbor: GlobaLens Case Publishing, William Davidson Institute at the University of Michigan, 2011). This video is also available on YouTube at: https://www.youtube.com/watch?v=nScU4sFAPIw.

23. The main focus of Patrimonio Hoy remains in Mexico. These other countries have seen only limited coverage.

24. See the recent case study on Patrimonio Hoy and CEMEX at www.BusinessCall-toAction.org.

25. My confidentiality agreement with this company gave me full access to its decision-making process in return for a guarantee of anonymity. A high-ranking company official read a draft of this chapter and made helpful suggestions for improving its balance and accuracy.

26. The senior manager who provided this quote reviewed my summary of the Mondophysic initiative.

CHAPTER 3

1. See T. London, Steen Sheth, and Stuart Hart, "Re-Energizing the Base-of-the-Pyramid Domain: Creating a Roadmap for the Next Decade" (Ann Arbor: GlobaLens Case Publishing, William Davidson Institute at the University of Michigan, 2014), we make the point that the lessons learned in the early stages of BoP piloting are rarely recorded, assessed, or applied to scaling.

2. In his *The Business Solution to Poverty* (San Francisco: Berrett-Koehler, 2013), Paul Polak argues that a business that wants to achieve true scale should "pick a problem that challenges the lives of a billion people."

3. For estimates of BoP markets, see World Resources Institute, "The Next 4 Billion" (2007), http://www.wri.org/publication/next-4-billion. More recently, the International Finance Corporation launched the Global Consumption Database (http://datatopics.worldbank.org/consumption), which provides a valuable lens for deeper exploration of the spending patterns of poor people around the world. This database shows 4.5 billion people in the base of the economic pyramid with a market estimated at about $5 trillion annually.

4. For a compelling example from the agricultural sector, bringing together both the business and academic perspectives, see Ravi Anupindi and Surampudi Sivakumar, "Supply Chain Reengineering in Agri-Business: A Case Study of ITC's e-Choupal," in *Supply Chain Issues in Emerging Economies*, edited by H. L. Lee and C.-Y. Lee, 265–307 (New York: Springer, 2006). Also see Chapter 1 for a discussion of the phenomenal growth of cell phones in BoP markets.

5. See, for example, Ted London and Stuart L. Hart, eds., *Next Generation Business Strategies for the Base of the Pyramid* (Upper Saddle River, NJ: FT Press, 2011) , chap. 1.

6. Two good resources on this topic are C. K. Prahalad and Venkat Ramaswamy, *The Future of Competition* (Boston: Harvard Business Review Press, 2004), and Venkat Ramaswamy and Francis Gouillart, *The Power of Co-Creation* (New York: Free Press, 2010).

7. This proverb was spotted on a wall at the Johannesburg Oliver R. Tambo Airport. My thanks to my colleague, Robert Harris, who sent me a photo.

8. See E. von Hippel, "Innovation by User Communities: Learning from Open-Source Software," *Sloan Management Review* 42:4 (2001): 82–86. Also useful here is E. S. Raymond, *The Cathedral and the Bazaar: Musing on Linux and Open Source by an Accidental Revolutionary*, rev. ed. (Sebastopol, CA: O'Reilly, 1999).

9. See, for example, Erik Simanis and Stuart Hart, "Innovation from the Inside Out," *MIT Sloan Management Review* (summer 2009), http://sloanreview.mit.edu/article/innovation-from-the-inside-out/. Their premise is that "you get the best answers by burying yourself in the questions."

10. Hector Ureta was the first director of the Patrimonio Hoy initiative within CEMEX. He is also a friend and colleague and has shared his experiences in developing the Patrimonio Hoy initiative with my students on several occasions.

11. These guidelines are introduced in London and Hart, *Next Generation Business Strategies.*

12. The critical importance of understanding the relationship between buyers and sellers in BoP markets is highlighted in the work on subsistence marketplaces by Madhu Viswanathan and his colleagues. This work also offers valuable insights into factors that influence buyer-seller exchanges. See, for example, M. Viswanathan, "A Microlevel Approach to Understanding BoP Marketplaces," in London and Hart, *Next Generation Business Strategies,* and M. Viswanathan, S. Sridharan, and R. Ritchie, "Understanding Consumption and Entrepreneurship in Subsistence Marketplaces," *Journal of Business Research* 63 (2010): 570–81.

13. See De Soto's insightful book, *The Mystery of Capital* (New York: Basic Books, 2000).

14. See T. London and Stuart Hart "Reinventing Strategies for Emerging Markets: Beyond the Transnational Model," *Journal of International Business Studies* 35 (2004): 350–70.

15. This is a substantially abridged version of Sachin Rao and Ted London, "Global Seeds to Village Farmers," case 1–428–612 (Ann Arbor: GlobaLens Case Publishing, William Davidson Institute at the University of Michigan, 2008), written with help from Moses Lee.

16. On this sad tradition, see Ellen Berry, "After Farmers Commit Suicide, Debts Fall on Families in India," *New York Time,* February 22, 2014, http://www.nytimes.com/2014/02/23/world/asia/after-farmers-commit-suicide-debts-fall-on-families-in-india.html?_r=0.

17. See the CARE mission and vision statement at http://www.care.org/about/mission-vision.

18. See the PEACE website: http://www.peaceap.org/.

19. See G. Ahuja and C. M. Lampert, "Entrepreneurship in the Large Corporation: A Longitudinal Study of How Established Firms Create Breakthrough Inventions," *Strategic Management Journal* 22 (2001): 521–43. Ahuja and Lampert provide a good discussion of invention and how it differs from innovation. While their research focuses on technological invention, they also note that invention can occur from a user/market perspective. Innovation is then the commercialization of the invention.

20. See, for example, Eric Ries, *The Lean Startup* (New York: Crown Business, 2011), which offers some great insights into rapid experimentation.

21. I first introduced this concept in my chapter in London and Hart, *Next Generation Business Strategies.*

22. This idea of taking ownership of risk runs counter to the traditional approach for writing business plans to access investment capital, whereby efforts are made to "derisk" an enterprise. Given that many of the potential investors are also interested in social performance, they may be more understanding of the enterprise owning these kinds of risks. In fact, it may be something they should require.

23. This is derived from J. Doh, T. London, and V. Kilibarda, "Building and Scaling a Cross-Sector Partnership: Oxfam America and Swiss Re Empower Farmers in Ethiopia,"

GlobaLens case GL1–429–185D (Ann Arbor: William Davidson Institute, Ross School of Business, 2010). I return to this story at greater length in Chapter 5.

24. In 2011, P&G sold the Pur name to Helen of Troy, but carried on its philanthropic water treatment business under the P&G brand. See Jack Neff, "Procter & Gamble Divests Pur But Retains Philanthropic Program," *Advertising Age*, December 6, 2011, http://adage.com/article/news/procter-gamble-divests-pur-retains-philanthropic-program/231407/. For more on the Children's Safe Drinking Water program, see http://www.csdw.org/csdw/.

25. This section is also uses some ideas introduced in the chapter I contributed to London and Hart, *Next Generation Business Strategies*, 19–44.

26. See, for example, S. A. Alvarez and J. B. Barney, "Discovery and Creation: Alternative Theories of Entrepreneurial Action," *Strategic Entrepreneurship Journal* 1, no. 1 (2008): 11–26.

27. These ideas are presented in greater detail in E. Simanis, S. Hart, and D. Duke, "The Base of the Pyramid Protocol: Beyond 'Basic Needs' Business Strategies," *Innovations*, 3, no. 1 (2008): 57–84; and in Simanis's chapter in London and Hart, *Next Generation Business Strategies*.

28. See Ted London, Ravi Anupindi, and Sateen Sheth, "Creating Mutual Value: Lessons Learned from Ventures Serving Base of the Pyramid Producers," *Journal of Business Research* 63 (2010): 582–94, for more information on the constraints that BoP producers face and the strategies that enterprises can use to overcome them.

29. Given that purchases are made on a daily basis, it has been noted that BoP consumers are often willing to try new brands. For more, see the work by Madhu Viswanathan and his colleagues on subsistence marketplaces: M. Viswanathan, "A Microlevel Approach to Understanding BoP Marketplaces," in London and Hart, *Next Generation Business Strategies,* and M. Viswanathan, S. Sridharan, and R. Ritchie, "Understanding Consumption and Entrepreneurship in Subsistence Marketplaces," *Journal of Business Research* 63 (2010): 570–81.]

30. The fact that these investments result in the creation of a common good can be an attraction for the development community, which is generally more interested in generating positive social change than in supporting the gains of a particular enterprise.

31. For the Honey Care story, I also draw on an article by Stuart Hart and Ted London, "Developing Native Capability: What Multinational Corporations Can Learn from the Base of the pyramid," *Stanford Social Innovation Review* 3 (summer 2005): 28–33.

32. For all you need to know about bee management using Langstroth hives, see L. L. Langstroth, *Langstroth's Hive and the Honey Bee*(1878; reprint ed., New York: Dover, 2004).

33. For some of the details of this story, I am indebted to Movirtu's founder and former CEO, Nigel Waller.

34. A subscriber identity module or subscriber identification module (SIM) card holds the account holder's personal data, such as phone numbers, address book, phone and text messages, and other information. A user can remove and insert the card across different handsets, with varying degrees of difficulty.

35. This is derived from T. London and S. G. Kennedy, "Movirtu's Cloud Phone Service: Funding a Base-of-the-Pyramid Venture," case 1–429–162 (Ann Arbor: GlobaLens Case Publishing, William Davidson Institute at the University of Michigan, 2012).

36. My understanding of these aspects of Movirtu's activities was enriched by conversations with Nigel Waller and our field work in Madagascar with the company.

37. BlackBerry's goals in purchasing Movirtu seem to emphasize the need for new product technology to retain and attract affluent individuals and companies in hopes of turning around its declining business. For more, see Euan Rocha and Alina Selyukh, "BlackBerry Buys UK Mobile Technology Start-Up Movirtu," Reuters, September 11, 2014, http://www.reuters.com/article/2014/09/11/us-blackberry-m-a-idUSK-BN0H61GC20140911.

38. The term *embeddedness* was introduced by Karl Polanyi. Mark Granovetter provides background on the concept of embeddedness as it applies to economic activities in developed markets in his classic article, "Economic Action and Social Structure: The Problem of Embeddedness," *American Journal of Sociology* 91(1985): 481–510.

39. For more on the influence of social norms of market transactions in informal markets, see T. London, H. Esper, A. Grogan-Kaylor, and G. Kistruck, "Connecting Poverty to Purchase in Informal Markets," *Strategic Entrepreneurship Journal* 8, no. 1 (2014): 37–55, and Viswanathan, "A Microlevel Approach."

40. Hernando De Soto provides valuable insights and examples into how the social norms influence transactions for local entrepreneurs in informal markets. See his *Mystery of Capital*. Also see A. V. Banerjee and E. Duflo, "The Economic Lives of the Poor," *Journal of Economic Perspectives* 21 (2007): 141–67.

41. M. E. Porter, *Competitive Advantage: Creating and Sustaining Superior Performance* (New York: Free Press, 1985). At the most basic level, competitive advantage occurs through offering a more compelling value proposition based on functionality, price, or a combination of both.

42. See, for example, Abhijit V. Banerjee and Esther Duflo, *The Economic Lives of the Poor* (Cambridge, MA: MIT Press, 2006). As reported in their study of people living on less than two dollars a day in thirteen countries, the median business had no paid staff. Nearly all local businesses that operate in these markets remain small.

43. The following articles offer good insight into the definition of capabilities and how they are different from resources: R. Amit and P.J.H. Schoemaker, "Strategic Assets and Organizational Rent," *Strategic Management Journal* 14, no. 1 (1993): 33–46; D. J. Teece, G. Pisano, and A. Shuen, "Dynamic Capabilities and Strategic Management," *Strategic Management Journal* 18 (1997): 509–33; and R. Makadok, "Toward a Synthesis of the Resource-Based and Dynamic-Capability Views of Rent Creation," *Strategic Management Journal* 22 (2001): 387–401.

44. See Ted London and Stuart Hart, "Reinventing Strategies for Emerging Markets: Beyond the Transnational Model," *Journal of International Business Studies* 35 (2004): 350–70, for an empirical assessment of the need for social embeddedness to complement existing capabilities when multinational corporations enter BoP markets. See also my chapter in London and Hart, *Next Generation Business Strategies*.

45. This section is derived in part from the chapter I contributed to London and Hart, *Next Generation Business Strategies*. I have also drawn on Ravi Anupindi and S. Sivakumar (CEO of ITC's International Business Division). "ITC's e-Choupal: A Platform Strategy for Rural Transformation," in , in *Business Solutions for the Global Poor: Creating Social and Economic Value*, ed. V. K. Rangan, J. A. Quelch, G. Herrero, and B. Barton (San Francisco: Jossey-Bass, 2007). Finally, I have included material from Katha-

rine Egan, Annie Kneedler, Pradeep Sagi, and Harveen Sethi, "ITC e-Choupal 3.0," case 1–428–915 (Ann Arbor: GlobaLens Case Publishing, William Davidson Institute at the University of Michigan, 2011).

46. I have been fortunate to have had the opportunity to engage with ITC, often with student teams, as they explore these new market opportunities.

47. It should be noted that not all of ITC's efforts to build on its eChoupal initiative have been successful. For more on this, see my article with Ravi Anupindi: "Using Base-of-the-Pyramid Perspective to Catalyze Interdependence-Based Collaborations," *Proceedings of the National Academy of Sciences*109 (2012):. 31, 12338–43, http://www.pnas.org/content/109/31/12338.abstract).

48. ITC, "Embedding Sustainability in Business," http://www.itcportal.com/sustainability/embedding-sustainability-in-business.aspx, September 24, 2014.

49. Filippo Veglio. "ITC's Farmer Empowerment Program in India—Building a More Efficient Supply Chain Leveraging the Internet," *Inclusive Business*, May 6, 2012, http://www.inclusive-business.org/2012/05/itc-e-choupal-india.html.

50. Writankar Mukherjee, "ITC's e-Choupal Boosting Company's FMCG Business," *Economic Times,* July 25, 2012, http://articles.economictimes.indiatimes.com/2012–07–25/news/32848625_1_fmcg-business-e-choupal-network-fiama-di-wills.

51. "ITC Steps Up Pace from Mandi to Market," *Economic Times*, July 25, 2012, http://www.itcportal.com/media-centre/press-reports-content.aspx?id=1232&type=C&news=ITC-Steps-up-pace-from-Mandi-to-Market.

CHAPTER 4

1. Ravi Anupindi and I explore this issue in T. London, R. Anupindi, and S. Sheth, "Creating Mutual Value: Lessons from Ventures Serving Base of the Pyramid Producers," *Journal of Business Research* 63 (2010): 582–94.

2. See Heather Esper, Andrew Grogan-Kaylor, Geoffrey M. Kistruck, and Ted London, "Connecting Poverty to Purchase in Informal Markets," *Strategic Entrepreneurship Journal* 8 (2014): 37–55. See also Ted London and Heather Esper, "Assessing Poverty-Alleviation Outcomes of an Enterprise-Led Approach to Sanitation," *Annals of the New York Academy of Sciences* 1331 (2014): 90–105.

3. Shared value powerfully argues that enterprises can create more value by seeing societal needs as business opportunities. For more on sharing value, see Michael Porter and Mark Kramer, "Creating Shared Value," *Harvard Business Review* 89, nos. 1–2 (2011): 62–77. Impact investing focuses on investments that specifically seek to generate social impact alongside a financial return. For more on impact investing, see Antony Bugg-Levine and Jed Emerson, *Impact Investing: Transforming How We Make Money While Making a Difference* (San Francisco: Jossey-Bass, 2011).

4. I have also seen other approaches to interpreting this difference. For example, poverty alleviation outcomes refer to results, for example, "50 percent of the target market has regular access to clean water." Poverty alleviation impacts are based on a comparison of what would have been without the intervention. If the enterprise had not been present, for instance, then only 20 percent of the target market would have regular access to clean water. Thus, the impact of the enterprise is to increase regular access by 30 percent.

5. For some concerns about the impact of microcredit, see A. Karnani, "Microfinance Misses Its Mark," *Stanford Social Innovation Review* 5, no. 3 (2007): 34–40

6. Robert Chambers and Amartya Sen have provided great insights into this perspective. For more background, see R. Chambers, *Whose Reality Counts? Putting the First Last* (London: ITDG Publishing, 1997), and A. Sen, *Development as Freedom* (New York: Anchor Books, 1999).

7. See London, Anupindi, and Sheth, "Creating Mutual Value," and London and Esper, "Assessing Poverty-Alleviation Outcomes."

8. United Nations Development Programme, *Human Development Report 1990* (New York: Oxford University Press, 1990). See also United Nations. *The Millennium Development Goals Report* (New York: United Nations Department of Economic and Social Affairs, 2010).

9. In Paul Godfrey's *More Than Money* (Stanford: Stanford University Press, 2014) identifies five types of capital important in alleviating poverty: physical, social, human, organizational, and institutional.

10. World Bank, *World Development Report 2000/2001: Attacking Poverty* (Oxford: Oxford University Press, 2001).

11. Amartya Sen has provided greater insight on the topic. He emphasizes the importance of well-being, especially the ability of individuals to shape their own future. See Sen, *Development as Freedom.*

12. Good sources include Chambers, *Whose Reality Counts?* D. Narayan, R. Patel, K. Schafft, A. Rademacher, and S. Koch-Schulte, *Voices of the Poor: Can Anyone Hear Us?* (Oxford: Oxford University Press, 2000).

13. I first presented this framework in "Making Better Investments at the Base of the Pyramid," *Harvard Business Review* 87, no. 5 (May 2009): 106–13.

14. IRIS is managed by the Global Impact Investing Network. For more on the work that does IRIS does, see https://iris.thegiin.org/.

15. The Social Progress Index is an initiative of the Social Progress Imperative. For background, see http://www.socialprogressimperative.org/.

16. This tool can also present a person's relative level of poverty. For more, see http://www.progressoutofpoverty.org/.

17. Jim Koch, senior founding fellow of the Center for Science, Technology, and Society, and Don C. Dodson, Distinguished Service Professor at the Leavey School of Business, Santa Clara University, provided particularly insightful comments in developing this comparison of different evaluation tools.

18. The IAF was recognized in *Measuring Socio-Economic Impact: A Guide for Business* (Conches-Geneva: World Business Council for Sustainable Development, 2013), http://www.wbcsd.org/impact.aspx, as particularly well suited to enabling enterprise managers to meet their socioeconomic impact measurement needs as well as facilitate aligning business action with social impact. But my main point here is that you need a proven tool—mine or someone else's—to assess and enhance your value proposition.

19. Readers who are interested in learning more about randomized control trials should visit, among other resources, the website of the Abdul Latif Jameel Poverty Action Lab (J-PAL), http://www.povertyactionlab.org.

20. An earlier version of the figure was presented in London, "Making Better Investments at the Base of the Pyramid."

21. For more on flourishing, see Chris Lazlo *Flourishing Enterprise: The New Spirit of Business* (Stanford: Stanford Business Books, 2014).

22. I own a strong debt of gratitude to Stuart Hart and Sanjay Sharma with regard to Figure 4.3. The idea for this was sparked by and adapted from their article "Engaging Fringe Stakeholders for Competitive Imagination," *Academy of Management Executive* 18:1 (2004): 7–18.

23. The work of Madhu Viswanathan and his colleagues in the area of subsistence marketplaces offers great insights into understanding the relationship between buyers and sellers in a BoP context. See, for example, M. Viswanathan, "A Microlevel Approach to Understanding BoP Marketplaces," in T. London and S. Hart, eds., *Next Generation Business Strategies for the Base of the Pyramid: New Approaches for Building Mutual Value* (Upper Saddle River, NJ: FT Press, 2011), and M. Viswanathan, S. Sridharan, and R. Ritchie, "Understanding Consumption and Entrepreneurship in Subsistence Market- places," *Journal of Business Research* 63(2010): 570–81.

24. Abdul Latif Jameel Poverty Action Lab (http://www.povertyactionlab.org/) and Innovations for Poverty Action (http://www.poverty-action.org/) are leaders in conduct- ing randomized control trials. Also see A. Banerjee and E. Duflo, *Poor Economics: A Rad- ical Rethinking of the Way to Fight Global Poverty* (New York: Public Affairs Press, 2011).

25. Much of the following discussion is derived from Molly Christiansen and Ted London, "VisionSpring: A Lens for Growth at the Base of the Pyramid," case 1–428–610 (Ann Arbor: GlobaLens Case Publishing, William Davidson Institute at the University of Michigan, 2008).

26. For more on Aravind Eye Hospital, see C. K. Prahalad, *Fortune at the Bottom of the Pyramid: Eradicating Poverty through Profits* (Upper Saddle River, NJ: Wharton School Publishing, 2004).

27. At the time of its launch, the enterprise was known as the Scojo Foundation.

28. For more information on presbyopia, see P. Nirmalan S, Krishnaiah, B. R. Sha- manna, G. N. Rao, and R. Thomas, "A Population-Based Assessment of Presbyopia in the State of Andhra Pradesh, South India: The Andhra Pradesh Eye Disease Study," *Inves- tigative Ophthalmology and Visual Science* 47 (2006): 2324–28; I. Patel , B. Munoz, A. G. Burke, A. Kayongoya, W. Mchiwa. A. W. Schwarzwalder, and S. K. West, "Impact of Presbyopia on Quality of Life in a Rural African Setting," *American Academy of Ophthal- mology* 113 (2006): 728–34; and A. Karnani, B. Garrette, J. Kassalow, and M. Lee, "Better Vision for the Poor," *Stanford Social Innovation Review* 9, no. 2 (2011): 66–71.

29. This is necessarily a much simplified summary of what to my knowledge was the first large-scale, quantitative evaluation of potential customers of a BoP impact enter- prise. For an in-depth explanation of our methods and baseline findings, see London et al., "Connecting Poverty to Purchase in Informal Markets."

30. For more information on these results, see ibid.

31. See A. V. Banerjee and E. Duflo, "The Economic Lives of the Poor," *Journal of Economic Perspectives* 21, no. 1 (2007): 141–67. D. Collins, J. Morduch, S. Rutherford, and O. Ruthven, *Portfolios of the Poor: How the World's Poor Live on $2 a Day* (Princeton, NJ: Princeton University Press, 2009).

32. For more on BRAC and its work in Bangladesh and elsewhere, see http://www. brac.net/

33. The Skoll Foundation has recognized VisionSpring and its founder, Jordan Kassalow, described at http://www.skollfoundation.org/entrepreneur/jordan-kassalow/.

34. To learn more about how VisionSpring understands and promotes its impacts, visit http://visionspring.org/.

35. This section is based on London and Esper, "Assessing Poverty-Alleviation Outcomes."

36. World Health Organization, http://www.who.int/topics/sanitation/en/.

37. World Health Organization, *Children's Health and Environment: A Review of Evidence* (Luxembourg: European Environment Agency and World Health Organization, Regional Office for Europe, 2002).

38. D. Spears and S. Lamba. "Effects of Early-Life Exposure to Rural Sanitation on Childhood Cognitive Skills: Evidence from India's Total Sanitation Campaign" Policy Research working paper. (New York: World Bank (2013), http://www-wds.worldbank.org/external/default/WDSContentServer/WDSP/IB/2013/10/16/000158349_20131016094658/Rendered/PDF/WPS6659.pdf.

39. See, for example, Lorna Fewtrell, Rachel B. Kaufmann, David Kay, Wayne Enanoria, Laurence Haller, and John M. Colford Jr., "Water, Sanitation, and Hygiene Interventions to Reduce Diarrhoea in Less Developed Countries: A Systematic Review and Meta-Analysis," *Lancet Infectious Diseases* 5 (2005): 42–52; World Health Organization, "Facts and Figures: Water, Sanitation and Hygiene Links to Health" (2004), http://www.who.int/water_sanitation_health/publications/factsfigures04/en.

40. E. Duflo, S. Galiani, and M. Mobarak, "Improving Access to Urban Services for the Poor: Open Issues and a Framework for a Future Research Agenda" (Cambridge, MA: Abdul Latif Jameel Poverty Action Lab, 2012). See also K. Kar, "Why Not Basics for All? Scopes and Challenges of Community-Led Total Sanitation," *IDS Bulletin* 43 (2012): 93–96.

41. These bottom-up initiatives often work better in rural areas, which tend to have the advantages of cultural cohesion and strong local leadership.

42. These are fast-moving numbers. See the Sanergy website for updates: http://saner.gy/.

43. I thank the Bernard van Leer Foundation and, in particular, Michael Feigelson for support for and guidance on this project. The foundation funds and shares knowledge and research on early childhood development. For more information, see its website at http://www.bernardvanleer.org.

44. For more details on our study, see London and Esper, "Assessing Poverty-Alleviation Outcomes." The data in Figure 4.6 summarize the finding presented in this paper, particularly the information presented in Table 1 on p. 98.

45. World Health Organization, "Early Child Development," fact sheet 332 (2009), http://www.who.int/mediacentre/factsheets/fs332/en/index.html

46. For details on our findings, see London and Esper, "Assessing Poverty-Alleviation Outcomes."

47. For example, Sanergy offers loans through Kiva (http://www.kiva.org/), which reduces the upfront financial burden to franchisees. Sanergy reported to us that entrepreneurs pay only 25 to 30 percent as a down payment and then get a loan at 0 percent interest.

48. For more on these tools, see http://www.socialprogressimperative.org/ and http://www.progressoutofpoverty.org/.

49. I thank Jim Koch and for his insightful comments on comparing evaluation tools.

CHAPTER 5

1. A good overview can be found in Harvey Koh, Nidhi Hegde, and Ashish Karamchandani, "Beyond the Pioneer: Getting Inclusive Industries to Scale" (April 2014), http://www.beyondthepioneer.org/; Ross Baird, Lily Bowles, and Saurabh Lal, "Bridging the 'Pioneer Gap': The Role of Accelerators in Launching High-Impact Enterprises" (June 2013), t http://www.aspeninstitute.org/publications/bridging-pioneer-gap-role-accelerators-launching-high-impact-enterprises; and Harvey Koh, Ashish Karamchandani, and Robert Katz, "From Blueprint to Scale: The Case for Philanthropy in Impact Investing" (April 2012), http://acumen.org/idea/from-blueprint-to-scale/. These reports introduce the concept of the pioneer gap, which describes a gap in funding and support available for inclusive start-up businesses, and examines the role of investors and other partners in addressing this and other gaps.

2. For insights on some of the challenges inherent in these bridge-spanning roles, see B. Shaffer and A. J. Hillman, "The Development of Business-Government Strategies by Diversified Firms," *Strategic Management Journal* 21 (2000): 175–90.

3. For more on the weaker business ecosystem in BoP markets, see Koh, Hegde, and Karamchandani, "Beyond the Pioneer."

4. With the support I received from the German development agency Deutsche Gesellschaft für Internationale Zusammenarbeit (GIZ) GmbH, we were able to test and refine the partnership ecosystem framework through field visits with variety of scaling facilitators and the enterprises they were working with in Kenya and Ethiopia.

5. See, for example, W. Easterly, *The White Man's Burden: Why the West's Efforts to Aid the Rest Have Done So Much Ill and So Little Good* (New York: Penguin, 2006); and R. C. Riddell, *Does Foreign Aid Really Work?* (Oxford: Oxford University Press, 2007).

6. Chris Jochnick, "Systems, Power, and Agency in Market-Based Approaches to Poverty," Oxfam America Research Backgrounder series (2012), www.oxfamamerica.org/market-based-approaches-to-poverty.

7. At that time, more effort was being made to highlight the potential of a greater role for the private sector in poverty alleviation. See, for example, Commission on the Private Sector and Development, *Unleashing Entrepreneurship: Making Business Work for the Poor* (New York: United Nations Development Programme, 2004).

8. This section is derived in part from Nick O'Donohoe, Christina Leijonhufvud, Yasemin Saltuk, Antony Bugg-Levine, and Margot Brandenburg, "Impact Investments: An Emerging Asset Class," *J. P. Morgan Global Research*, November 28, 2010, http://www.thegiin.org/cgi-bin/iowa/resources/research/151.html. It's helpful to have the investor's perspective front and center in this discussion.

9. While many impact investors expect to earn lower rates of return in exchange for the positive social impact of their investments, some assume that they can both "do good and do well"—i.e., earn fully competitive rates of return on their impact investments.

10. These data come from J. P. Morgan's report, "Spotlight on the Market: The Impact Investor Survey" (May 2014). The figure of $46 billion of assets under management deserves some clarification. It represents data from 125 members of the Global Impact

Investing Network (GIIN). Not all GIIN members responded to the survey, and there are impact investors who are not part of GIIN. It should also be noted that the respondents incorporate some microfinance institutions and that the geographies that these impact investors cover include developed world markets.

11. "Impact Investments."

12. This Acumen Fund summary is a condensed version of Moses Lee, "Acumen Fund: How to Make the Greatest Impact," case 1–428–592 (Ann Arbor: GlobaLens Case Publishing, William Davidson Institute at the University of Michigan, 2008). Lee was a research associate under my supervision.

13. For the latest information on Acumen's impact, see http://acumen.org/.

14. For more on Acumen's Fellows programs, see http://acumen.org/leaders/.

15. For more on Water Health International, see http://waterhealth.com/.

16. See Coca-Cola's press release on RAIN at http://www.coca-colacompany.com/press-center/image-library/rain, and a related video at http://www.coca-colacompany.com/videos/coca-cola-project-rain-yto4w-4acrsny.

17. The CARE story is derived from T. London and Moses Lee, "CARE: Making Markets Work for the Poor," case 1–428–645 (Ann Arbor: GlobaLens Case Publishing, William Davidson Institute at the University of Michigan, 2008), and the associated teaching note. The updated statistics are from the CARE website (www.care.org/work/where-we-work).

18. For more on Hindustan Unilever Limited and its efforts to scale into rural India, see M. Vakil and T. London, "Hindustan Lever at the Base of the Pyramid: Growth for the 21st Century," GlobaLens Case GL1–428–604D (Ann Arbor: GlobaLens Case Publishing, William Davidson Institute at the University of Michigan, 2006).

19. When the Shakti initiative was launched, it included a communication-led program, Shakti Vani (Sanskrit for speech). The Vani, designed as an advertising medium for both health challenges and company solutions, spread information and awareness on issues such as health, hygiene, sanitation, and personal care within the rural markets.

20. Colm Fay, a colleague at the William Davidson Institute at the University of Michigan, played an important role in helping me to refine and enhance this framework. His input and thoughtful questions were invaluable. I also thank Garrett Kirk, a research assistant while he was completing his MBA at the Ross School of Business at the university, who located useful examples of scaling facilitators providing various services identified in the partnership ecosystem framework.

21. For more on Living Goods, see http://livinggoods.org/.

22. See these websites to learn more: J-PAL: http://www.povertyactionlab.org/; William Davidson Institute: http://wdi.umich.edu/; and Grameen Foundation: http://www.grameenfoundation.org/; and IRIS: https://iris.thegiin.org/.

23. For a comparison of different tools, see the World Business Council for Sustainable Development's "Measuring Socio-Economic Impact: A Guide for Business" (February 2013), http://www.wbcsd.org/impact.aspx.

24. For a good summary of the need for sector-based support, see Matt Bannick and Paula Goldman, "Priming the Pump: The Case for a Sector Based Approach to Impact Investing" September 2012), https://www.omidyar.com/insights/priming-pump-case-sector-based-approach-impact-investing-0.

25. For more on the latter issue, see the Global Alliance for Clean Cookstoves: http://www.cleancookstoves.org/.

26. These have also been called push products, where consumer demand may not be readily available. For more on this perspective, see, for example, Koh, Hegde, and Karamchandani, "Beyond the Pioneer."

27. For more industry facilitation focused on value chain investments, see ibid.

28. This is a much-shortened version of J. Doh, T. London, and V. Kilibarda, "Building and Scaling a Cross-Sector Partnership: Oxfam America and Swiss Re Empower Farmers in Ethiopia," GlobaLens Case GL1–429–185D (Ann Arbor: GlobaLens Case Publishing, William Davidson Institute at the University of Michigan, 2012).

29. The initiative's lead in 2007 was Marjorie Victor Brans. Victor Brans was succeeded in that role in 2010 by David Satterthwaite, who left Oxfam America in 2014.

30. Elsewhere I have developed the logic for cross-sector partnerships but not presented a framework for managing the full ecosystem. See my articles with Dennis Rondinelli, including "How Corporations and Environmental Groups Cooperate: Assessing Cross-Sector Alliances and Collaborations," *Academy of Management Executive* 17 (2003): 61–76, and "Partnerships for Learning: Managing Tensions in Nonprofit Organizations' Alliances with Corporations," *Stanford Social Innovation Review* 1, no. 3 (2003): 28–35.

31. Oxfam America's financials are at http://www.oxfamamerica.org/explore/inside-oxfam-america/financial-information/.

32. See a reasonably recent write-up, see http://www.oxfamamerica.org/explore/research-publications/r4-rural-resilience-initiative-annual%20report%202013/.

33. See the company's website at http://www.swissre.com/about_us/our_business/.

34. Responsibility for these efforts rested with Mark Way, Swiss Re's director of sustainability and political risk management.

35. The Relief Society of Tigray played a key implementing role, including helping to bridge the gap between the companies and the local farmers.

36. This and subsequent quotes come from the 2011 video recordings of Chris Jochnik when he visited the Ross School of Business at the University Michigan, including excerpts from his presentation in my class and a subsequent interview with me. See http://wdi.umich.edu/publications/video/Jochnick_mov_MPEG4_512Kbit_DSL_streaming.mov/view.

37. See "Oxfam America Expands Rural Resilience Initiative to West Africa with support from the Rockefeller Foundation," May 2, 2012, http://www.oxfamamerica.org/press/oxfam-america-expands-rural-resilience-initiative-to-west-africa-with-support-from-the-rockefeller-foundation/. I infer that the initiative's new name reflected the fact that supporting resilience is a basic pillar of the Rockefeller Foundation's larger strategy.

38. See "Pilot Microinsurance Program Has a Successful Payout to over 1,800 Ethiopian Farmers after Drought," November 17, 2011, http://www.oxfamamerica.org/press/pilot-microinsurance-program-has-a-successful-payout-to-over-1800-ethiopian-farmers-after-drought/.

CHAPTER 6

1. Elsewhere I have referred to this role as "network orchestrator." Here, I use a more appropriate and colorful term that trades an IT metaphor (networks) for a more organic

metaphor, borrowed from biology: chief ecosystem director. See T. London and Ravi Anupindi, "Using Base-of-the-Pyramid Perspective to Catalyze Interdependence-Based Collaborations," *Proceedings of the National Academy of Sciences* 109 (2012): 12338–43, http://www.pnas.org/content/109/31/12338.abstract.

2. See ibid., in which Ravi Anupindi and I first introduce this term.

3. See, for example, T. London, and D. A. Rondinelli, "Partnerships for Learning: Managing Tensions in Nonprofit Organizations' Alliances with Corporations," *Stanford Social Innovation Review* 1, no. 3 (2003): 28–35; D. A. Rondinelli and T. London, "How Corporations and Environmental Groups Cooperate: Assessing Cross-Sector Alliances and Collaborations," *Academy of Management Executive* 17, no. 1 (2003): 61–76; T. London, D. A. Rondinelli, and H. M. O'Neill, "Strange Bedfellows: Alliances between Corporations and Non-Profits," in *Handbook of Strategic Alliances*, edited by O. Shenkar and J. J. Reuer, 353–66 (Thousand Oaks, CA: Sage, 2005); and D. A. Rondinelli. and T. London, "Partnering for Sustainability: Managing Nonprofit Organization-Corporate Environmental Alliances," working paper series (Washington, DC: Aspen Institute, 2001).

4. Marjorie Victor Brans served as—in my terminology—the CED for the initiative from 2007 to 2010. In 2010, David Satterthwaite assumed that role. Satterthwaite left Oxfam America in 2014.

5. Theoretically these ideas are linked to research on the value of social capital and the associated opportunity to bridge structural holes. For examples, see Ronald Burt's work in this area, including "The Contingent Value of Social Capital," *Administrative Science Quarterly* 42, no. 2 (1997): 339–65.

6. See http://wdi.umich.edu/publications/video/Jochnick_mov_MPEG4_512Kbit_DSL_streaming.mov/view.

7. This story is derived from T. London, J. Parker, and J. Korona, "Constructing a Base-of-the-Pyramid Business in a Multinational Corporation: CEMEX's Patrimonio Hoy Looks to Grow," case 1–429–202D (Ann Arbor: GlobaLens Case Publishing, William Davidson Institute at the University of Michigan, March 22, 2012).

8. See the video that is part of the following teaching case: T. London, J. Parker, and J. Korona, "Constructing a Base of the Pyramid Business in a Multinational Corporation: CEMEX's Patrimonio Hoy Looks to Grow," case GL1–429–202D (Ann Arbor: GlobaLens Case Publishing, William Davidson Institute at the University of Michigan, 2012).

9. Clients had to meet three criteria to qualify for a subsidy: (1) they had to use credit to pay for home construction. (2) they could not have previously received government subsidies for housing, and (3) they had to have a daily household income less than four minimum wages in Mexico, or $20. Since 2009, the Mexican government had disbursed $37 million in subsidies to Patrimonio Hoy's customers. By 2012, approximately 81,000 families had benefited from this partnership.

A family purchases $100 of building materials from Patrimonio Hoy and files for a federal housing credit under CONAVI's Esta Es Tu Casa subsidy program. Patrimonio Hoy helps submit the application to the government for review. If it is approved, the family is awarded a 70 percent subsidy, or $70, in addition to the $100 of materials the family initially purchased. In effect, Patrimonio Hoy provides $170 worth of materials, not cash, to the family, thereby limiting the customer's ability to spend the subsidy on something other than housing.

10. GTZ has been merged into GIZ (Gesellschaft für Internationale Zusammenar-beit). For more information, see https://www.devex.com/news/in-sweeping-aid-reform-merged-german-agency-becomes-operational-71908.

11. Again, see the video that is part of London, Parker, and Korona: "Constructing a Base of the Pyramid Business in a Multinational Corporation."

12. Quinceañera is the celebration of a girl's fifteenth birthday and marks the transi-tion from child to young woman.

13. While each offers some unique insights, all the approaches require a new way of thinking about collaborations, especially those involving cross-sector partners. For more on sustainable development, see Stuart Hart, "Beyond Greening: Strategies of a Sustain-able World," *Harvard Business Review* 75, no. 1 (1997): 66–76, and for more on shared value, see Michael Porter and Mark Kramer, "Creating Shared Value," *Harvard Business Review 89*, nos. 1–2 (2011): 62–77.

14. I thank Douglas Schuler, associate professor of business and public policy, Jones Graduate School of Business, Rice University for his suggestion to consider the difference roles of sector spanners in different contexts. Salespeople, who may be active within com-munities outside the company, can also play a sector spanning role.

15. This is not always the case. See the relevant research by that Dennis Rondinelli and I have conducted that focuses on collaborations between corporations and environmental nonprofits: D. A. Rondinell and T. London, "Stakeholder and Corporate Responsibilities in Cross-Sectoral Environmental Collaborations: Building Value, Legitimacy and Trust," in *Unfolding Stakeholder Thinking: Theory, Responsibility and Engagement,* edited by J. Andriof, S. Waddock, B. Husted, and S. Rahman, 201–15 (Sheffield, UK: Greenleaf Pub-lishing, 2002); D. A. Rondinelli and T. London, "How Corporations and Environmental Groups Cooperate: Assessing Cross-Sectoral Alliances and Collaborations," *Academy of Management Executive* 17, no. 1 (2003): 61–76; and T. London and D. A. Rondinelli, "Partnerships for Learning: Managing Tensions in Nonprofit Organizations' Alliances with Corporations," *Stanford Social Innovation Review* 1, no. 3 (2003): 28–35.

16. See work by Stuart Hart, Sanjay Sharma, and Mark Milstein, for example, for more on this approach to stakeholder management. These include: S. L. Hart and M. B. Milstein, "Creating Sustainable Value," *Academy of Management Executive* 17, no. 2 (2003): 56–67; S. L. Hart, *Capitalism at the Crossroads: The Unlimited Business Opportu-nities in Serving the World's Most Difficult Problems* (Upper Saddle River, NJ: Wharton School Publishing, 2005); and S. L. Hart and S. Sharma, "Engaging Fringe Stakeholders for Competitive Imagination," *Academy of Management Executive* 18, no. 1 (2004): 7–18.

17. For more on the need for closer coordination in BoP markets, see J. Brugman and C. K. Prahalad, "Cocreating Business's New Social Compact," *Harvard Business Review* 85, no. 2 (2007): 80–90.

18. An earlier version of this figure appeared in T. London and R. Anupindi,. "Using the Base-of-the-Pyramid Perspective to Catalyze Interdependence-Based Collabora-tions," *Proceedings of the National Academy of Sciences* 109 (2012): 12294–301.

19. For more on collaborative interdependence as a source of cross-sector innovation, see L. Dubé, S. Jha, A. Faber, J. Struben, T. London, A. Mohapatra, N. Drager, C. Lannon, P. K. Joshi, and J. McDermott, "Convergent Innovation for Sustainable Economic Growth and Affordable Universal Health Care: Innovating the Way We Innovate," *Annals of the New York Academy of Sciences* 1331 (2014): 119–41.

20. "Subsidy," *Economist*, November 14, 2008, www.economist.com/research/Economics/searchActionTerms.cfm?query=subsidy.

21. For their part, development community representatives also may be leery about putting their resources into enterprises that make (or aim to make) a profit. They work for mission-driven organizations, which are supposed to put their resources to work advancing their chosen cause, not help capitalists make money. Governments in the developing world may have the same kinds of concerns. Aren't they supposed to put their limited resources to work in ways that create direct, near-term, and concrete benefits for their citizens? I discuss this issue in greater detail in the following chapter.

22. I am purposely avoiding the word *subsidy* in this discussion, in part because that word has a specific technical meaning that is too narrow for our purposes and in part because it tends to generate more heat than light.

23. From "The World Trade Report 2006: Exploring Links between Subsidies, Trade and the WTO" (World Trade Organization, 2006), 45. This is included in T. London and Moses Lee, "Note on the Role of Subsidies in a Market Economy," note 1–428–648 (Ann Arbor: Michigan Ross School of Business, William Davidson Institute, February 1, 2009). Much of the subsequent discussion of subsidized support is drawn from this note.

24. Since the focus here is on domestic U.S. subsidies, I omit Europe's multibillion-euro support for Airbus.

25. A. R., "Uncle Sam, Venture Capitalist," *Economist*, March 18, 2013, http://www.economist.com/blogs/freeexchange/2013/03/innovation.

26. William Galston, "Government Is a Good Venture Capitalist," *Wall Street Journal Online*, August 27, 2013, http://www.wsj.com/articles/SB10001424127887323906804579036813022177326.

27. National Science Foundation. "On the Origins of Google," August 17, 2004, http://www.nsf.gov/discoveries/disc_summ.jsp?cntn_id=100660.

28. Although SNAP is federally funded, it is administered by the states, usually at the county level. States vary slightly in their eligibility requirements, as well as additional benefits programs.

29. Food and Nutrition Services. "Supplemental Nutrition Assistance Program," *Program Data*, July 7, 2014, http://www.fns.usda.gov/pd/supplemental-nutrition-assistance-program-snap.

30. SNAP benefits can be redeemed at qualified retailers for food products. The program covers a variety of food products, including baby food and infant formula, breads, cereals, fruits, vegetables, meats/fish/poultry, and dairy and bottled beverages (excluding alcohol). It cannot be used to buy nonfood household items. Eligibility is determined by income, resources, age, employment, household members, and similar categories. Income requirements are based on 100 percent of the current poverty level as set by the federal government. The federal government is required to provide benefits for all who qualify.

31. Peter Schweizer, "JP Morgan's Food Stamp Empire," *Daily Beast*, October 1, 2012, http://www.thedailybeast.com/articles/2012/10/01/jp-morgan-s-food-stamp-empire.html.

32. Food and Nutrition Services, "Supplemental Nutrition Assistance ProgramLondonNotes.docx.

33. The end of this increase in funding will cause roughly a 5.4 percent drop in benefits. The decline will vary based on benefits received. Those receiving the minimum amount of benefits will see a decrease of only $1, while those receiving maximum ben-

efits will see cuts up to $36 per month per household. Shelly Banjo and Annie Gasparro, "Retailers Brace for Reduction in Food Stamps." *Wall Street Journal*, November 4, 2013, http://online.wsj.com/news/articles/SB10001424052702303843104579168011245171266.

34. The cuts include eliminating so-called heat-and-eat programs. According to regulations in many states, households that spend a large portion of their income on housing and utilities are eligible for increased benefit levels. Under these programs, in sixteen states and the District of Columbia, households that qualify for heating assistance are assumed to automatically qualify for increased benefit levels for SNAP, so that even $1 of energy subsides from the government could qualify a household for increased levels of SNAP and other benefits. The cuts from the February bill would eliminate these types of programs. Randy Allison Aussenberg and Libby Perl, "The Next Farm Bill: Changing the Treatment of LIHEAP Receipt in the Calculation of SNAP Benefits," *Congressional Research Services*, September 17, 2013, http://nationalaglawcenter.org/wp-content/uploads/assets/crs/R42591.pdf.

35. Walmart Stores, "Walmart Stores Inc. Annual Report on Form 10-K for the Fiscal Year Ended January 31, 2014," Securities and Exchange Commission, March 21, 2014, <http://www.sec.gov/Archives/edgar/data/104169/000010416914000019/wmtform10-kx13114.htm.

36. Banjo and Gasparro, "Retailers Brace for Reduction in Food Stamps."

37. Phil Wahba, "Walmart Forecast Disappoints as Grocery Business Struggles," Reuters, February 20, 2014, http://reuters.com/article/idUSBREA1J0WX20140220?irpc=932.

38. Walmart, "Walmart Updates FY 14 Underlying EPS Guidance for Fourth Quarter and Full Year," January 31, 2014, http://cdn.corporate.walmart.com/b2/79/60d3a07145a998c6062b1cc4a87e/walmart-updates-fy-14-underlying-eps-guidance-for-fourth-quarter-and-full-year.pdf.

39. Bill Saporito, "Cutting Food Stamp Payments to the Poor Hurts the Rich," *Time*, February 24, 2014, http://business.time.com/2014/02/24/cutting-food-stamp-payments-to-the-poor-hurts-the-rich.

40. Wahba, "Walmart Forecast DisappointsLondonNotes.docx."

41. Besides the decrease in share values, the cuts in SNAP also have implications for Walmart. Many Walmart workers are on SNAP, Medicaid, or other public assistance themselves. If Walmart suffers increased losses and cuts hours or wages for employees, this could mean more people reaching out for public assistance. In essence, taxpayers are subsidizing Walmart's operational costs as well as sales. Because Walmart is one of the largest private sector employers in the United States, this has significant implications for the economy.

42. Bill Saporito, "Cutting Food Stamp Payments to the Poor Hurts the Rich," *Time*, February 24, 2014, http://business.time.com/2014/02/24/cutting-food-stamp-payments-to-the-poor-hurts-the-rich/.

43. Microfinance organizations have benefited from subsidized support over the years. A controversial example is Compartamos Banco. For more background on the microfinance industry, see M. Yunus, *Banker to the Poor: Micro-Lending and the Battle against World Poverty* (New York: Public Affairs Press, 1999). Similarly, the development of M-Pesa, the mobile phone–based money transfer platform in Kenya, was catalyzed through support from the Financial Deepening Challenge Fund, a fund-matching program of the U.K.'s Department for International Development.

44. Subsidized support used for nonbusiness purposes can also have serious (and negative) implications for local BoP markets. For example, well-intentioned efforts in the United States to provide free refurbished bicycles to the developing world had the unintended consequence of putting local bike shops, including all-important local and regional maintenance networks, out of business. The participating social service organizations soon shifted to a model of supporting local bike-riding populations by providing used bikes that their local stores could sell profitably and affordably. For more on this, see, the story of the collaboration between Re-Cycle and Bikes Not Bombs in Ghana, at http://www.re-cycle.org/bike-projects/partners/ability-bikes-cooperative-ghana.

45. I was the executive director of the Loudoun County Small Business Development Center from 1996 to 1999. While an independent organization, we were also part of the larger Virginia SBDC network. At that time, many, if not all, states had an SBDC network. That tradition continues.

46. DEMATT (Development of Malawian Traders Trust) was a program primarily funded by USAID. I worked for DEMATT from 1989 to 1991 while I was a Peace Corp volunteer in Malawi.

47. There was no illusion that charging these fees would allow DEMATT to become financially independent.

48. Our data collection indicated we were having a positive impact on enterprise revenues, profitability, and job creation.

49. *The New Nonprofit Almanac in Brief: Facts and Figures on the Independent Sector* (Washington, DC: Independent Sector, 2001).

50. See Kennard Wing, Katie Roeger, and Thomas Pollak, "The Nonprofit Sector in Brief" (Washington, DC: Urban Institute, 2010), http://www.urban.org/uploadedpdf/412209-nonprof-public-charities.pdf.

51. See Jaclyn Lambert, "Infographic: What Is Driving Nonprofit Sector Growth?" *Nonprofit Quarterly,* December 10, 2013, https://nonprofitquarterly.org/policysocial-context/23359-infographic-what-is-driving-nonprofit-sector-s-growth.html.

52. "The Non-Governmental Order," *Economist*, December 9, 1999, http://www.economist.com/node/266250.

53. See S. S. Srivastava and Rajesh Tandon, "How Large Is India's Non-Profit Sector?" *Economic and Political Weekly*, May 7–13, 2005, 1948–52.

54. See "Mind-Boggling Number of NGOs in India: CBI," *Times of India,* July 9, 2014, http://timesofindia.indiatimes.com/india/Mind-boggling-number-of-NGOs-in-India-CBI/articleshow/38033239.cms.

55. See the organization's 2012–2013 annual report: http://www.oxfam.org/en/annual-and-financial-reports.

56. See the CARE 2013 annual report: http://ar.care.org. The employment figure is from "Diversity at Care": http://care.org/careers/diversity.

57. See Oxfam America's description of how it partners with corporations: http://www.oxfamamerica.org/donate/corporate-engagement/.

58. I have worked with both organizations and have been impressed with the quality of the individuals and their work at each.

59. See http://wdi.umich.edu/publications/video/Jochnick_mov_MPEG4_512Kbit_DSL_streaming.mov/view.

60. *CARE Video: Interview with Laté Lawson,* GlobaLens Video GL1-428–839 (Ann Arbor, MI: William Davidson Institute/Ross School of Business, 2008). Lawson later edited his quote for clarity.

61. From CI's website at http://www.conservation.org/about/mission_strategy/pages/mission.aspx

62. http://www.greenpeace.org/usa/en/about/

63. See the Greenpeace website: http://www.greenpeace.org/usa/en/about/.

64. See http://wdi.umich.edu/publications/video/Jochnick_mov_MPEG4_512Kbit_DSL_streaming.mov/view.

65. Dennis Rondinelli and Ted London, "Partnering for Sustainability: Managing Nonprofit Organization-Corporate Environmental Alliances," working paper series (Washington, DC: Aspen Institute, 2001).

66. G. Hamel, "Competition for Competence and Inter-Partner Learning within International Strategic Alliances," *Strategic Management Journal* 12 (1991): 83–103.

67. See London and Rondinelli, "Partnerships for Learning."

CHAPTER 7

1. For more on how a BoP perspective can contribute to thinking about poverty alleviation, see Ted London, "The Base-of-the-Pyramid Perspective: A New Approach to Poverty Alleviation," in *Proceedings of the Academy of Management Meeting,* edited by G. T. Solomon (2008).

2. Stuart Hart and I explore this distinction in greater detail in the introduction to our *Next Generation Business Strategies for the Base of the Pyramid: New Approaches for Building Mutual Value* (Upper Saddle River, NJ: FT Press, 2011).

3. The term *base* (or *bottom*) *of the pyramid* first gained prominence as a business strategy in 2002, with publication of C. K. Prahalad and Stuart Hart's "The Fortune at the Bottom of the Pyramid," *Strategy + Business* 26 (First Quarter): 2–14.] The idea originated in 1999 and was circulated as a working paper before it was published. The term *BoP* reached a global audience with the 2005 publication of Prahalad's *The Fortune at the Bottom of the Pyramid* (Upper Saddle River, NJ: Wharton School Publishing, 2005).

4. I thank Jim Koch, senior founding fellow, Center for Science, Technology, and Society, and Don C. Dodson, Distinguished Service Professor at the Leavey School of Business, Santa Clara University, for always reminding me of the continued need for humility.

5. For example, Ans Kolk, Miguel Rivera-Santos, and Carlos Rufín, "Reviewing a Decade of Research on the 'Base/Bottom of the Pyramid' (BOP) Concept," Business and Society," 53, no. 7 (2014): 338–77, track the growth in articles published on the topic.

6. See Erik Simanis and Duncan Duke, "Profits at the Bottom of the Pyramid," *Harvard Business Review* 92, no. 10 (2014): 86–93, for more in this topic.

7. The concept of shared value, developed by Michael Porter and Mark Kramer, argues that enterprises can create value by seeing societal needs as business opportunities. For more background, see Michael Porter and Mark Kramer, "Creating Shared Value," *Harvard Business Review* 89 (2011): 62–77. Early work by Stuart Hart also highlights the opportunity for connecting business strategies with environment and social

challenges. See Hart, "Beyond Greening: Strategies of a Sustainable World," *Harvard Business Review* 75, no. 1 (1997): 66–76.

8. For more on success in mutual value creation and challenges of value capture in BoP markets, see/ for example, T. London, R. Anupindi, and S. Sheth, "Creating Mutual Value: Lessons from Ventures Serving Base of the Pyramid Producers," *Journal of Business Research* 63 (2010): 582–94.

9. See the work by Stuart Hart and Mark Milstein on how the challenges of global sustainability can be a catalyst for new entrepreneurial activity: "Global Sustainability and the Creative Destruction of Industries," *Sloan Management Review* 41:1 (1999): 23–33.

10. See, for example, S. L. Hart and C. M. Christensen, "The Great Leap: Driving Innovation from the Base of the Pyramid," *Sloan Management Review* 44, no. 1 (2002): 51–56.

11. For some early work on this, see T. London, H. Esper, and Y. Fatehi, "Exploring the link between Business Strategy and Social Impact: Comparing Poverty Impact Profiles," in *Proceedings of the Academy of Management Meeting*, edited by J. Humphreys (2014).

12. Some initial work along these lines was carried out at the BoP Summit that the William Davidson Institute hosted in Ann Arbor, Michigan, in late 2013. The outcomes of this gathering were captured in "Base of the Pyramid Summit: Shaping an Action Agenda," http://wdi.umich.edu. Stuart Hart, who was actively involved with me in the BoP Summit's development and implementation, has been a leading figure in pointing out the need to break out of the silos that a narrow focus on industry can create.

13. The efforts to aggregate some of the most important of these questions are contained in Ted London, Sateen Sheth, and Stuart Hart, "A Roadmap for the Base-of-the-Pyramid Domain: Re-energizing for the Next Decade" (Ann Arbor, MI: William Davidson Institute, 2014).

14. One model for such a collaboration was launched in 2013 by the William Davidson Institute, my academic home base, and Deutsche Gesellschaft für Internationale Zusammenarbeit (GIZ) GmbH. Our first joint project, focused on sub-Saharan Africa, involves an initial assessment of the successes and failures of different investment formats used by scaling facilitators, with the goal of developing a greater understanding of best practices.

15. See, for example, Ted London, "The Impact of a Scholar's Career: More Than Just the Usual Numbers for Jagdish Bhagwati," *Advances in International Management* 25 (2012): 15–22.

16. Hernando de Soto calls this "legal apartheid" to distinguish between those who can create capital and those who cannot. See de Soto, *The Mystery of Capital: Why Capitalism Triumphs in the West and Fails Everywhere Else* (New York: Basic Books, 2000).

INDEX

www.ingramcontent.com/pod-product-compliance
Ingram Content Group UK Ltd.
Pitfield, Milton Keynes, MK11 3LW, UK
UKHW042054240225
455503UK00003B/81/J